The War on Drugs and Anglo-American Relations

I0093551

Edinburgh Studies in Anglo-American Relations

Series Editors: Steve Marsh and Alan P. Dobson

Published and forthcoming titles

The Anglo-American Relationship
Steve Marsh and Alan P. Dobson

The Arsenal of Democracy: Aircraft Supply and the Anglo-American Alliance, 1938–1942
Gavin J. Bailey

Post-War Planning on the Periphery: Anglo-American Economic Diplomacy in South America, 1939–1945
Thomas C. Mills

Best Friends, Former Enemies: The Anglo-American Special Relationship and German Reunification
Luca Ratti

Reagan and Thatcher's Special Relationship: Latin America and Anglo-American Relations
Sally-Ann Treharne

Tacit Alliance: Franklin Roosevelt and the Anglo-American 'Special Relationship' before Churchill, 1933–1940
Tony McCulloch

The Politics of Diplomacy: U.S. Presidents and the Northern Ireland Conflict, 1967–1998
James Cooper

Jimmy Carter and the Anglo-American 'Special Relationship'
Thomas K. Robb

The Congo Crisis: Anglo-American Relations and the United Nations, 1960–1964
Alanna O'Malley

The War on Drugs and Anglo-American Relations: Lessons from Afghanistan, 2001–2011
Philip A. Berry

https://edinburghuniversitypress.com/series-edinburgh-studies-in-anglo-american-relations.html

The War on Drugs and Anglo-American Relations

Lessons from Afghanistan, 2001–2011

Philip A. Berry

EDINBURGH
University Press

To Sasha

Edinburgh University Press is one of the leading university presses in
the UK. We publish academic books and journals in our selected subject
areas across the humanities and social sciences, combining cutting-edge
scholarship with high editorial and production values to produce academic
works of lasting importance. For more information visit our website:
edinburghuniversitypress.com

Edinburgh University Press Ltd
The Tun – Holyrood Road, 12(2f) Jackson's Entry, Edinburgh EH8 8PJ

First published in hardback by Edinburgh University Press 2019

Typeset in 11/14 Sabon by
Servis Filmsetting Ltd, Stockport, Cheshire

A CIP record for this book is available from the British Library

ISBN 978 1 4744 2108 9 (hardback)
ISBN 978 1 4744 5847 4 (paperback)
ISBN 978 1 4744 2109 6 (webready PDF)
ISBN 978 1 4744 2110 2 (epub)

Contents

Acknowledgements   vii
List of Acronyms   viii
Maps and Chart   xi

1. Introduction   1

Part 1

2. Anglo-American Relations and 9/11   9
3. The Legacy of Drugs and a Weak State   25

Part 2

4. Taliban Drugs on British Streets, 2001–2002   43
5. Lead Nation on Counter-Narcotics, 2002   58
6. Counter-Narcotics on the Hoof, 2002–2004   68

Part 3

7. Plan Afghanistan, 2004–2005   83
8. Afghanistan's Poppy Capital, 2005–2006   101
9. The Lesser of Two Evils, 2006–2007   114
10. The Showdown over Aerial Eradication, 2007   125
11. Counter-Narcotics in Transition, 2008   141

Part 4

12. Obama and Shifting Anglo-American Relations,
    2009   155

13. A Poisoned Chalice, 2009–2011   168
14. Conclusion   185

Appendix   194
Notes   197
Bibliography   235
Index   255

Acknowledgements

I owe a debt of gratitude to all of the interviewees who participated in this research, several of whom kindly spoke to me on more than one occasion. Without their generosity, this research would not have been possible.

I would like to thank Professor Alan P. Dobson for his friendship, support and unending patience during both my PhD and writing of this book, especially as deadline after deadline came and went unmet. This study would not be what it is today without his valuable guidance and help.

I would like to thank my parents for their support throughout this research and the entirety of my academic career.

Most of all, I would like to thank my fiancé Sasha on whom I have placed the greatest burden whilst researching and writing this book. At times, I have not been easy to live with as each spare moment was spent trying to finish this book. But throughout, her unfaltering love, support, patience and, above all, encouragement has seen me through to the finish line.

Some sections of this book appeared in: Philip A. Berry, 'From London to Lashkar Gah: British Counter Narcotics Policies in Afghanistan 2001-03', *The International History Review*, Vol. 40, No. 4, 2018, 713–31, and also in Philip A. Berry, 'Allies at War in Afghanistan: Anglo-American Friction over Poppy Aerial Eradication 2004-08', *Diplomacy and Statecraft*, Vol. 29, No. 2, 2018, 274–97. Reprinted by permission of Taylor & Francis Ltd, http://www.tandfonline.com.

London
December 2018

Acronyms

ADIDU	Afghan Drugs Inter-Departmental Unit
AEF	Afghan Eradication Force
AIA	Afghan Interim Administration
AIOG	Afghanistan Interagency Operations Group
ANA	Afghan National Army
ANDCS	Afghan National Drug Control Strategy
ASNF	Afghan Special Narcotics Force
ATFC	Afghan Threat Finance Cell
ATT	Afghan Transit Trade Agreement
AVIPA-Plus	Afghanistan Voucher for Increased Production in Agriculture
BEDT	British Embassy Drugs Team
CIA	United States Central Intelligence Agency
CIDA	Concerted Inter-Agency Drugs Action Group
CJTF-180	Combined Joint Task Force 180
CND	Counter-Narcotics Directorate
CNPA	Counter-Narcotics Police of Afghanistan
CNTF	Counter-Narcotics Trust Fund
CPEF	Afghan Central Poppy Eradication Force
DEA	United States Drug Enforcement Administration
DFID	United Kingdom Department for International Development
DOD	United States Department of Defense
DOJ	United States Department of Justice
FAC	House of Commons Foreign Affairs Committee
FARC	Revolutionary Armed Forces Colombia
FCO	United Kingdom Foreign and Commonwealth Office
G8	Group of Eight

GBS	Ground-Based Spraying
GDP	Gross Domestic Product
GLE	Governor-Led Eradication
GNP	Gross National Product
GOIRA	Government of Islamic Republic of Afghanistan
Ha	Hectares
HFZ	Helmand Food Zone
HMCE	United Kingdom HM Customs & Excise
HMG	Her Majesty's Government
IMF	The International Monetary Fund
INL	United States Bureau of International Narcotics and Law Enforcement Affairs
ISAF	International Security Assistance Force
ISI	Pakistan Inter-Services Intelligence
JNAC	Joint Narcotics Analysis Centre
MCN	Afghanistan Ministry of Counter-Narcotics
MEPP	Middle East Peace Process
MOD	United Kingdom Ministry of Defence
MOI	Afghanistan Ministry of Interior
NA	Northern Alliance
NAC	North Atlantic Council
NATO	North Atlantic Treaty Organization
NSA	National Security Advisor
NSC	National Security Council
OPLAN	International Security Assistance Force Operations Plan
PDPA	People's Democratic Party of Afghanistan
PRT	Provincial Reconstruction Team
SACEUR	Supreme Allied Commander Europe (North Atlantic Treaty Organization)
SAS	United Kingdom Special Air Service
SIS	United Kingdom Secret Intelligence Service
SOCA	United Kingdom Serious Organised Crime Agency
SRAP	Special Representative for Afghanistan and Pakistan
SSR	Security Sector Reform
UN	United Nations
UNDCP	United Nations International Drug Control Programme
UNODC	United Nations Office on Drugs and Crime

US   United States of America
USAID   United States Agency for International
            Development

Maps and Chart

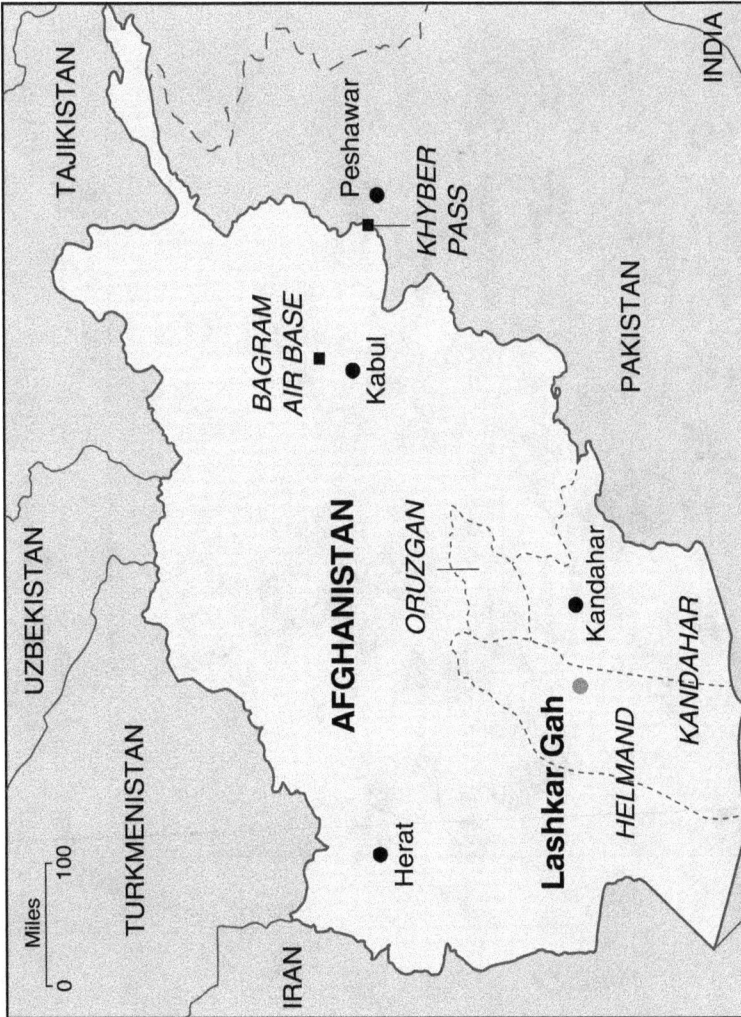

Map A   Regional View of Afghanistan.

Map B Afghanistan Opium Poppy Cultivation by Province, 2004.

Source: United Nations Office on Drugs and Crime (UNODC)/Government of Afghanistan Counter-Narcotics
Directorate, *Afghanistan Opium Survey 2004* (Kabul: UNODC/CND November 2004).

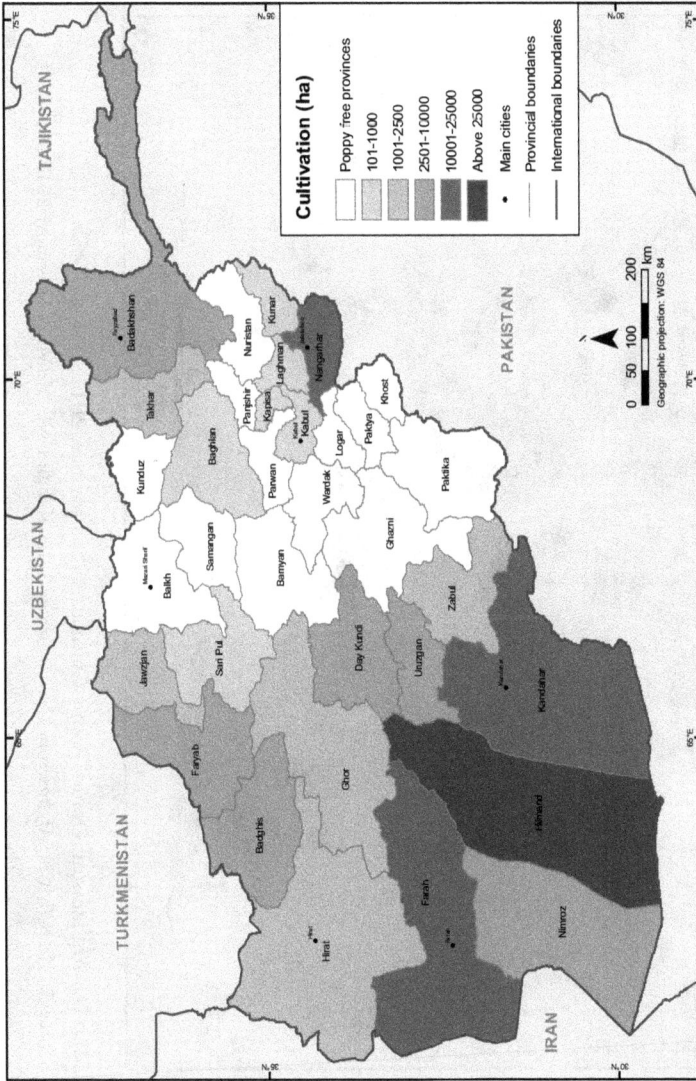

Map C Afghanistan Opium Poppy Cultivation by Province, 2007.

Source: UNODC/Government of Afghanistan Ministry of Counternarcotics (MCN), *Afghanistan Opium Survey 2007: Executive Summary* (Kabul: UNODC/MCN August 2007).

Cultivation (ha)

- Poppy free provinces
- 101-1000
- 1001-2500
- 2501-10000
- 10001-25000
- Above 25000
- Main cities
- Provincial boundaries
- International boundaries

Geographic projection: WGS 84

0 50 100 200 km

TAJIKISTAN

UZBEKISTAN

TURKMENISTAN

IRAN

PAKISTAN

Badakhshan
Takhar
Kunduz
Baghlan
Nuristan
Kunar
Laghman
Nangarhar
Panjshir
Kapisa
Kabul
Parwan
Wardak
Logar
Paktya
Khost
Paktika
Ghazni
Bamyan
Samangan
Balkh
Mazar-i Sharif
Jawzjan
Sar-i Pul
Day Kundi
Uruzgan
Zabul
Kandahar
Faryab
Badghis
Ghor
Herat
Farah
Helmand
Nimroz

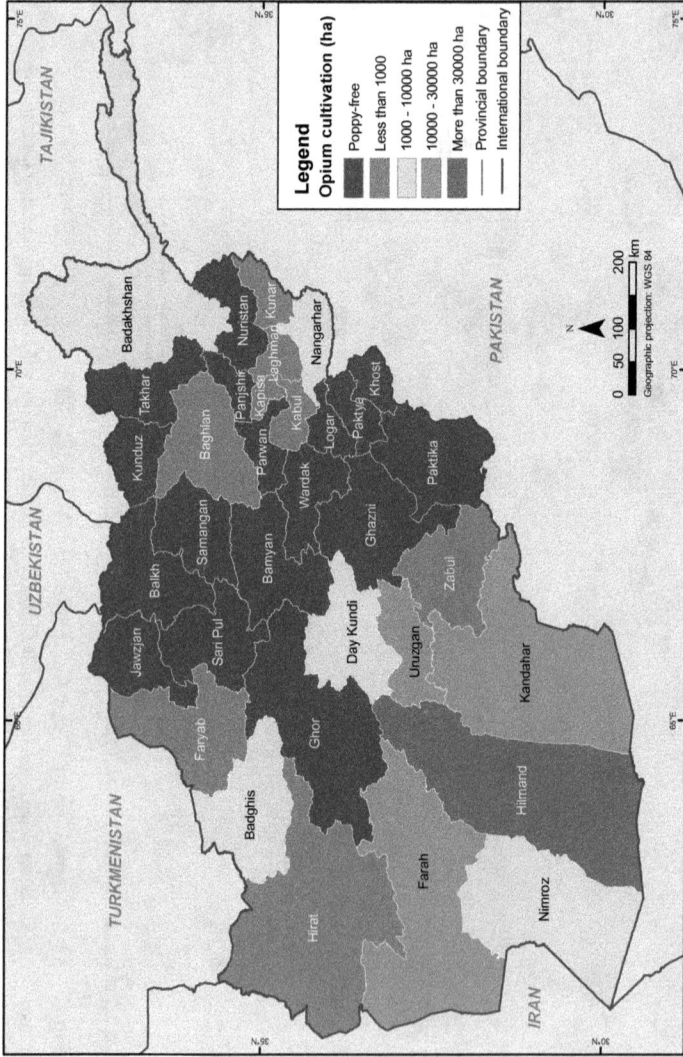

Map D Afghanistan Opium Poppy Cultivation by Province, 2011.

Source: UNODC/MCN, *Afghanistan Opium Survey 2011* (Kabul: UNODC/MCN December 2011).

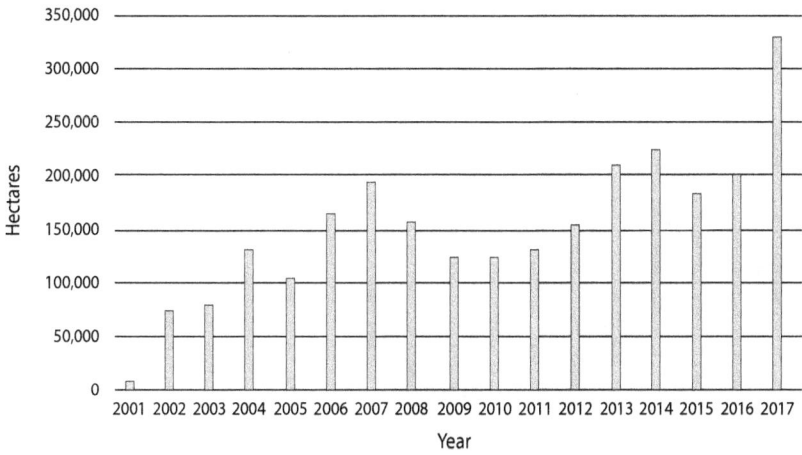

Chart A Opium Cultivation in Afghanistan 2001–2017.

1 Introduction

The conflict in Afghanistan has been one of the most important international crises of the twenty-first century. Among other things, it foregrounded the intractable problem of waging effective counter-narcotics strategies and troubled the well-established Anglo-American relationship. Whilst much has been written on Anglo-American relations and international counter-narcotics strategies in Afghanistan since 2001, important aspects have been neglected. This work addresses this by providing a detailed account of counter-narcotics policy formulation and implementation and the frictions that they occasioned within the context of the Anglo-American special relationship.

A sub-theme running through the narrative is a challenge to the conventional view that, in contrast to the fragmented nature of the American policy process, the British government was a unitary actor over counter-narcotics policy. A good example of this conventional wisdom, which several scholarly works have outlined, is Britain's compensated eradication scheme in the spring of 2002.[1] In fact, there has been a failure to detail the internal policy discussions that led to the scheme's implementation or execution which expose significant frictions within the British government. In short, there is a gap in the literature regarding how policies were arrived at and why they were adopted in Whitehall. The omission of the policymaking process from the literature on the British side is not exclusive to the discussion surrounding the compensated eradication scheme but is absent for much of the period in question – 2001–11. This oversight, which is particularly significant as Britain was Group of Eight (G8) lead nation on counter-narcotics, is corrected here by providing an examination of the formulation and implementation of British counter-narcotics policies within the broader Anglo-American framework. In doing so, it illustrates that British policymaking was not of a character often portrayed in other works.

Finally, there is also an important examination of what went wrong with the allies' counter-narcotics strategy. Despite the end of the North Atlantic Treaty Organization's (NATO) combat mission in 2014, Afghanistan still faces enormous challenges, not least in the sphere of narcotics control. Since 2002, the United States (US) and Britain have spent in excess of $9 billion[2] on a war against the narcotics industry, yet despite this, Afghanistan remains the world's premier producer of opium, with output now exceeding its pre-2001 level. In 2017, the United Nations Office on Drugs and Crime (UNODC) estimated[3] that 328,000 hectares (ha) of opium were cultivated, that equates to a 260 per cent increase in cultivation beyond the highest level recorded under Taliban rule – 91,000 ha.[4]

This then is a study of British and American counter-narcotics policies embedded in the larger strategic priorities of the conflict in Afghanistan, including the broad military, political and reconstruction landscape. The period under study, 2001–11, charts the trajectory of British counter-narcotics policies from conception to completion, that is to say, from the moment British Prime Minister Tony Blair outlined the objective of destroying the Afghan narcotics trade in October 2001 to when Britain transitioned its role as partner nation (lead nation was replaced by partner nation in 2006) on counter-narcotics to the UNODC in 2011. The changing fortunes of the counter-narcotics agenda was often used as an indicator of the success or failure of the broader state-building programme[5] and, that in turn, depended significantly on effective Anglo-American cooperation. Also, key lessons are drawn regarding the way in which policies succeeded or failed, and about how the partners cooperated, formulated policy and influenced each other during policymaking processes and their implementation.

In-depth interviews with policy practitioners from both sides of the Atlantic play a large part here in exposing both the complex and at times fraught relationships between British and American counter-narcotics policies and the problems afflicting the wider aims within the international objective to reconstruct Afghanistan. Charting policy formulation and implementation reveals the competitive cooperation[6] that characterised Anglo-American counter-narcotics strategies and enables assessments of both the degree of bilateral coordination achieved and the extent to which the partners synergised their counter-narcotics policies with the overall state-building project.

In explaining the key hinge points of policy formulation and implementation, a bureaucratic battleground of shifting alliances and conflicting priorities emerge within the Anglo-American alliance. Such shifting ground was not helped by the fact that counter-narcotics as a strategic priority in the campaign fluctuated up and down the policy agenda throughout the ten-year period this study covers. Periods of increased counter-narcotics activity and calls for reactive measures occurred when the aggregated statistics associated with opium cultivation reached record levels, for example in 2004 and 2007. During these periods, the existing counter-narcotics policies of Britain and the US came under sharp criticism, which influenced the policy debate in two important ways. First, the entire state-building project was called into question – as high levels of opium cultivation demonstrated (rightly or wrongly) a lack of state and international control over the levers of government.[7] Second, it bolstered the arguments of those advocating an aggressive approach to counter-narcotics and made reducing the overall level of opium cultivation an immediate political objective. Nevertheless, it is important to note that whilst counter-narcotics was an important strategic objective for both Britain and the US, it was subservient to the broader state-building mission and, one might add, to their overall strategic and political relationship.

In such shifting sands of bureaucratic policymaking it is often difficult to track developments, but scrutiny reveals that in fact the counter-narcotics campaign unfolded in three phases, throughout which the allies were often troubled either by the way they viewed the problem or by the means they advocated to tackle it.

Throughout the first phase of the intervention, 2001–3, both partners conceived their respective roles in Afghanistan through different prisms and this had implications for the successful implementation of policy. With the Pentagon largely shaping the debate in Washington, the US was determined not be drawn into state-building activities – let alone counter-narcotics work. Whereas Prime Minister Blair was convinced that combating the narcotics trade was not only an achievable task but in doing so Britain could increase its international prestige and fulfil its domestic ambition of reducing the flow of Afghan heroin to

British streets. As a result of Blair's enthusiasm, counter-narcotics became an important (but subsidiary) objective for Britain in Afghanistan.

As the second phase of the campaign progressed, 2004–8, friction in the Anglo-American alliance emerged as Afghanistan was engulfed by record levels of opium cultivation. As a result, the US was forced to commit itself more prominently to a counter-narcotics strategy; however, this proved to be controversial within both the Bush administration and in the wider Anglo-American alliance. The Department of State's Bureau of International Narcotics and Law Enforcement Affairs (INL) compounded that controversy by attempting to introduce a Colombian-style solution: aerial eradication. This not only antagonised the Pentagon, but also the British who agreed with the objective of eradicating opium but bitterly disagreed with aerial eradication as a means of doing so.[8] In short, the counter-narcotics policy-making process was dominated by multiple actors with competing objectives, intra-governmental and inter-governmental battles and a policy landscape that was shaped, particularly in the US, by individual agency decisions.[9] The conflict in the Anglo-American alliance over eradication policy proved to be a constant for the succeeding years, with the British, the Pentagon and the Afghans defending an embattled position against officials from the State Department, INL and White House. Despite cooperation on the main issues involved in the war, at times, conflict over the narcotics industry led to something approaching diplomatic warfare within the special relationship.

During the third phase of the campaign, 2009–11, as the Obama administration reviewed strategy and resources, relations between the allies shifted in several important ways, all of which impacted upon counter-narcotics policy. Whilst disagreement did not vanish completely from the Anglo-American counter-narcotics relationship, the bitter diplomatic exchanges experienced under the Bush administration dissipated. The period also saw a sustained reduction in the levels of opium cultivation, but it was not automatically apparent if this was the result of a successful counter-narcotics strategy, external factors or a combination of both. The British also undertook a review of their priorities and commitments to the conflict as the stabilisation of the much-troubled Helmand Province became Britain's foremost objective in Afghanistan.

In short, matters to do with counter-narcotics resonated out-wards, complicating not just counter-narcotics but wider allied policy issues in Afghanistan. In doing so they engulfed the Anglo-American relationship in difficulties and controversies that placed a strain on their well-established special relationship. Indeed, if the special relationship had not been so resilient, matters could have been far more damaging than they were. Given that this was the case, it is important first to examine the character of the special relationship before embarking on the closer focus on policies in Afghanistan in order to appreciate the existing Anglo-American relational context within which the experience of Afghanistan unfolded.

Part I

2 Anglo-American Relations and 9/11

The past always has a strong hold on the present: this is no more evident than in recent Anglo-American relations. Institutional heritage and well-established diplomatic mores between Britain and the US had an important impact on their respective experiences in Afghanistan. Ironically, the strength of their special relationship allowed disagreements, difficulties and controversy that would probably have fatally weakened relations between any other two countries. An appreciation of how these ties that bind the US and Britain so closely together developed is vital to any understanding of what happened in Afghanistan.

The special relationship, above all else, is rooted in the shared experience of fighting a common enemy in World War II and the Cold War. As such, the defence relationship has been the cornerstone on which the special relationship has been manufactured and maintained. Although the US acted contrary to neutrality with the 1940 destroyers for bases deal and the Lend-Lease agreement early the following year, it was not until the Arcadia Conference in late December 1941 that the defence relationship took some sort of formal shape.[1] That conference witnessed the foundations being laid of one of the most unique alliances in history. The allies agreed to merge their military operations establishing the Combined Chiefs of Staff, to coordinate the war.[2] Such institutional bonds, unprecedented consultation and cooperation during this period have survived in one form or another to the present day. But all this did not mean the relationship was without friction. In fact, friction – as much as cooperation – has always been a regular feature of the relationship and has often led to intense diplomatic exchanges. Early in World War II, friction emerged over strategy and the US's unease with Britain's concerns with saving its empire.[3] That said, the success of the wartime alliance was, in a large part, made possible by the close personal relations of politicians and military commanders, most notably between Prime Minister Winston Churchill and President Franklin Roosevelt. Churchill recalled in his memoirs that: 'My relations with the President gradually became so close that the chief business between our two countries was virtually conducted by these personal exchanges between him and me.'[4] Churchill deliberately tried to project this image and in doing so helped to establish a form of diplomatic modus operandi with US leaders. He had much success as prime ministerial and presidential summit meetings became a significant characteristic of Anglo-American relations. That combined with the institutional strength of the alliance covering defence, procurement, broad diplomatic cooperation and intelligence gathering formed a strong core for the special relationship.

Although Britain wielded considerable influence in the alliance during the first eighteen months of the conflict, it was soon to be confronted with a reality that would affect the relationship with the US ever after. By late 1943, it was clear that the US and Soviet Union – not Britain – would emerge from the war as the world's pre-eminent powers.[5] From its outset, the relationship was conditioned by asymmetry as Britain underwent relative decline at the same time that the US emerged as the world's foremost power.[6] Britain recognised that both its success during the war, and its position at the top table of global affairs after the war, were largely dependent on US support. The Foreign Office, by 1944 cognisant of Britain's declining power, opined:

> We . . . have the opportunity and the capacity to guide and influence
> . . . [the US] The transmission of their power into useful forms, and
> its direction into advantageous channels, is our concern . . . If we
> go about our business in the right way we can help steer this great
> unwieldy barge, the United States of America, into the right harbor.[7]

The British had variable success with this policy over the years, but it remained in the diplomatic tool chest and was occasionally evident in how they wanted to guide policy in Afghanistan.

In the immediate aftermath of the war, relations cooled as difficult realities hit home – the end of Lend-Lease and nuclear cooperation, harsh conditions for the US dollar loan and bitterness over Palestine and the emergence of the State of Israel.

The British would learn from these developments that American support could not be taken for granted and that work needed to be done to try to consolidate cooperative relations. Most notable once again so far as such matters were concerned was Churchill.

Now out of office, but nevertheless regarded as one of the, if not the, most notable of living human beings, Churchill was invited by President Harry Truman to address Westminster College in Fulton, Missouri, in 1946. In what became one of his most famous speeches, Churchill warned of the Soviet threat and talked of an 'iron curtain [that] has descended across the Continent'. To counter this, Churchill talked of the 'fraternal association of the English-speaking peoples. This means a special relationship between the British Commonwealth and Empire and the United States.'[8] As Reynolds suggests: 'Churchill's use of the term was prescriptive as much as descriptive. He was trying to will such a relationship into existence, or at least to build it on the foundations already laid in the wartime alliance.'[9]

The views espoused in the speech highlighted the cultural, linguistic and kinship ties between Britain and the US, and it was those ties that made the alliance different – indeed *special* – compared to other interstate relations. However, Marsh argues that while: 'myth, sentiment and kinship ... form intangible bonds holding Britain and America together in a special relationship'. In fact:

> Myth and tradition are merely important lubricants of the defence relationship. What has counted most are calculations of mutual utility, assiduous British cultivation of Washington, practices of military cooperation acquired over decades of experience and similar worldviews that enable unusually high political consensus on the use of force for foreign policy objectives.[10]

Dumbrell also contends that 'the "special relationship" was not a fact of nature. It was constructed at a particular historical period, the Second World War and continued, indeed thrived, in the conditions of the Cold War. It was certainly rooted in interests.'[11] Principally, these interests lay in containing Soviet expansion and it was this common threat that bound the partners together for the next four decades. The relationship was built on mutuality, with Britain playing a valuable role using its colonial bases and the Commonwealth in the Cold War.

During the 1950s, Britain was still in fact the world's third largest economy and rightly considered itself a world power; however, its close cooperation with the US in waging the Cold War disguised to some extent the continuing waning of its power.[12] To demonstrate its utility as a partner to the US, Britain joined the anti-communist war in Korea, which allowed Britain to be, in the words of Prime Minister Clement Attlee, 'lifted out of "the European queue" and we were treated as partners, unequal no doubt in power but still equal in counsel'.[13] However, as Foreign Secretary Anthony Eden later commented, the ability of Britain to influence the US was limited as they 'listen to what we have to say, but make . . . their own decisions. Till we can recover our financial and economic independence, this is bound to continue.'[14] In 1956, disregard for British views turned into open contempt as the Suez Crisis rocked the foundations of the relationship. After Egypt's leader Abdul Nasser nationalised the Suez Canal – which was owned jointly by the French and the British – Prime Minister Anthony Eden launched a joint Anglo-French invasion of the canal. The US profoundly disagreed with what they saw as old-world politics and placed substantial economic leverage on Britain, through sterling, to withdraw. Powerless in the face of American pressure, the British retreated. The episode underscored Britain's decline as a world power and its military and economic dependency on the US.[15] Although the incident generated considerable anti-American sentiment in Britain, and declarations of the end of the special relationship, the friction was relatively short-lived. As Dobson and Marsh conclude:

> far from marking the end of the special relationship, the rapid post-crisis healing of Anglo-American relations transformed Suez into part of the special relationship's mythology. The capacity to endure despite such a crisis came to symbolise the breadth and depth of the relationship.[16]

Nevertheless, Suez was something of a wake-up call and demonstrated British limitations, in particular that any major international operation was now probably unviable without US actual or tacit support. Eden's successor Harold MacMillan adjusted to this and thought as the junior partner there was scope for Britain to play Greece to America's Rome, using British experience and skill to influence and shape US policies for the better.[17] MacMillan's analogy tended to over-exaggerate Britain's influence over the US and pandered to the British sense of diplomatic superiority. Nevertheless, more than half a century later in Afghanistan, some British officials were still guided by this notion or, more accurately, were resigned to the fact that tempering US policies was the best they could hope for.

Even though Suez was deeply upsetting for the special relationship, its recalibration was far from being all negative. In 1957, MacMillan welcomed US Thor ballistic missiles into Britain to counter the danger of future Soviet blackmail, threatened during Suez. The following year, the repeal of the 1946 McMahon Act, enabled Britain to receive preferential treatment in nuclear cooperation with the US,[18] which later led President John F. Kennedy to sell Polaris missiles to Britain. Despite some within Kennedy's administration arguing that nuclear support to Britain should be cut, MacMillan was successful in extracting the purchase of the Polaris missiles on generous terms, in exchange for allowing the US to station more nuclear weapons on British soil. These agreements were made in parallel rather than being explicitly linked: the main British contribution was the site for the Holy Loch base.[19] In part, MacMillan's success in securing Polaris was not so much the actual procurement, but the ability to use them independently in Britain's national interest. Arguably if the two men had not been so close, the outcome might have been different.

So, by the start of the 1960s, the US and Britain enjoyed a relationship that involved a worldwide system of signals intelligence gathering, conventional defence and nuclear cooperation of a kind and quality not seen elsewhere in the world, generally close relations between prime ministers and presidents, and institutionalised diplomatic relations most publicly visible in summit meetings between prime ministers and presidents. Underlying much of this was also a complex web of economic, political, educational, cultural and individual – family and growing tourist – interactions that provided additional sinews for the ties that bound the two together. As the 1960s progressed, Britain's decline was more precipitous and more publicly obvious, and voices were raised in Washington concerning the imminent demise of the special relationship. In 1966, US Ambassador to the Court of St James David Bruce commented: 'The so-called Anglo-American special relationship is now little more than sentimental terminology, although the underground waters of it will flow with a deep current.'[20] Bruce was only partially correct. There were more than just currents left to the relationship even though Britain's financial and monetary problems and the Vietnam War both posed significant difficulties for the two allies once again. Britain's decline seemed encapsulated by the 1967 devaluation of sterling and its announced withdrawal of military forces from east of Suez. Then came Britain's turn to Europe and Prime Minister Edward Heath's successful application to join the European Community. This also had repercussions in the US as Heath sought to convince Europe that Britain was more European than Atlanticist.

The Wilson and Callaghan governments of the 1970s set about improving the special relationship that had deteriorated under Heath.[21] But it was not until the turn of the following decade that the special relationship was fully revitalised under Prime Minister Margaret Thatcher and President Ronald Reagan. The close relations between the two allowed for the creation of what Thatcher labelled as an 'extraordinary' and 'very, very, special' relationship.[22] The fact that Thatcher was able successfully to deploy the special relationship as a central and vital part of Britain's diplomacy was only possible because of the underlying strength of the relationship. It might have been buffeted in the late 1960s and throughout the 1970s, but it still had much life in it.

Thatcher quickly set about securing Britain's nuclear future and reached a very favourable deal with Reagan to purchase the upgraded Trident missiles in 1982. The deal again cemented the nuclear special relationship as Britain enjoyed unique and preferential access to US technology.[23] Shortly after, the rejuvenated alliance faced its first test as Argentina invaded the Falklands in April 1982. The US administration was initially cool to British requests for help, arguing that they had friendly relations with both countries, much to the dismay of Thatcher. Although Reagan eventually declared his support for Britain, the Pentagon had in fact assisted the British with ammunition, equipment and intelligence from their first request. The established institutional relationship that existed since World War II proved invaluable to Britain's ultimate success.[24] Demonstrating that Britain's military success, in a large part, depended heavily upon the support of their closest ally. The Thatcher–Reagan relationship was far from being without problems and difficulties, most notably occasioned by British indignation at the US invasion of Grenada, a Commonwealth country, without prior notice, but overall the relationship remained deeply special. Their mutual successors however, John Major and George H. W. Bush and Bill Clinton, got along though with cooler personal ties and with a much-changed international environment.

The existence of the special relationship was cast in doubt as the glue that held the partners together – the Soviet threat – dissipated with the end of the Cold War. As Britain turned to Europe, and was now fully embedded in the European Single Market, the US turned away, reducing its troops on the continent by two thirds between 1990 and 1995.[25] The presidency of Bill Clinton did little to dispel the fears that the special relationship would end in a transformed international environment. Relations between Major and Clinton were tested over several issues: Northern Ireland, Yugoslavia and Iraq, and were conducted on a 'grin-and-bear-it basis'.[26] However, even during this period with the relationship at a low ebb, it mostly remained intact.

Then in 1997, the special relationship was revived with the election of Tony Blair and New Labour. Blair and Clinton shared a generational identity[27] and enjoyed close personal relations. Like the relationship between Thatcher and Reagan, it was also bolstered by the fact that the men were ideological bedfellows, with New Labour drawing inspiration from Clinton's New Democrats.[28] Blair was also a committed Atlanticist, and in his 1997 Lord Mayor's banquet speech set forth his belief of the special relationship: 'When Britain and America work together on the international scene, there is little we can't achieve.'[29] Clinton, for his part, shared Blair's ambition for Britain to act as a bridge between Europe and the US.[30] In 1998, Blair endorsed US airstrikes in Afghanistan and Sudan and committed Britain to participate in airstrikes against Iraq.[31]

Although President George W. Bush was at the opposite end of the political spectrum to Blair, the latter was quick to forge a close personal relationship with the Texan. It was this close personal relationship, firm Atlanticism and confidence in his ability to shape events that resulted in Blair's firm support for the US after the 11 September (9/11) terrorist attacks. Dumbrell contends that Blair also subscribed to the '"Greeks and Romans" doctrine' and 'the view that London should seek intimate involvement with American decision-making, with a view actually to *improving* the quality of those decisions'.[32]

How successful Blair was in influencing and improving the US's policy choices will be considered below. Much has been written about the Anglo-American special relationship in terms of it amounting to good relations between prime ministers and presidents and the Bush–Blair relationship appears to provide compelling evidence of this, but as John Hemmings argues persuasively this is too simplistic. Given the constant changing of heads of state and the resilience of 'the "special relationship", it should not and cannot be understood as merely the relationship between a given president and prime minister'.[33] Institutionalised defence, nuclear, diplomatic and intelligence relationships, important economic interactions and high-level economic consultations, and cultural underpinnings, including similar political traditions, all weave together to provide not just the foundations but the superstructure of the special relationship within which personal relations of the leaders are conducted. Sometimes they are conducted negatively, but mainly they are conducted in a positive way. Either way they are only one aspect of what makes up the whole of the special relationship. Its constituent parts may fluctuate in importance and significance over time and, as we have seen, that is obvious in the public domain in which prime ministers and presidents operate. But relations at the top have so far neither made nor broken the special relationship as such. Its creation and sustenance is far more complex than just that and that became very evident in the study of Anglo-American relations and counter-narcotics policies in Afghanistan.

9/11 Terrorist attacks

On 11 September 2001, the US was devastated by a well-executed terrorist attack that struck at the symbols of its economic and military power, all in all killing 3,000 people.[34] The day after the attacks, US Central Intelligence Agency (CIA) Director George Tenet briefed Bush that all the available evidence indicated that Osama bin Laden – the Saudi extremist who was responsible for conducting terrorist attacks against US targets over the previous years – and al-Qaeda were responsible. Ominously, however, key members of the administration, including the president, Secretary of Defense Donald Rumsfeld and others, sought to link the attacks to Iraq and Saddam Hussein, viewing both as 'an existential threat to the United States'.[35]

It was clear from the start of the Bush administration that there were many ideological people in high places, but Bush himself came across as more moderate and pragmatic than many he had appointed. During the election campaign, he had presented a profile of caring conservatism and early in his administration he seemed little different from a conventional, albeit right of centre, pragmatist. However, the ideologically charged neo-conservatives and their fellow-travellers – Paul Wolfowitz, Donald Rumsfeld, Dick Cheney, John Bolton, Richard Perle, Stephen J. Hadley and Condoleezza Rice – had a clear agenda that they had either constructed over the past decade, or, as fellow-travellers, came to embrace after 9/11.[36] Thus, the response to 9/11 was not primarily against terrorists in Afghanistan, but against undemocratic rogue states such as Iraq that could develop weapons of mass destruction and use terrorist proxies to deliver them against the US and its allies. This was important as the view conditioned the upcoming intervention in Afghanistan.

Chief among these convictions was opposition to the US military being involved in state-building activities – a much-criticised trait of the Clinton administration[37] and an ideal Blair later promoted for Afghanistan. A memo written by Under Secretary of Defense for Policy Douglas J. Feith to Rumsfeld days after the US intervened in Afghanistan illustrates how this conviction shaped the early campaign, '[state] building is *not* our key strategic goal (emphasis in original)' in Afghanistan.[38] The forthcoming intervention in Afghanistan also presented Bush and Rumsfeld with an opportunity to test a new streamlined military force that could deploy with a minimum of manpower. This would enable a swift victory, and more importantly, an equally swift exit, thus allowing US forces to move onto phase two of the mission: Iraq.

The dominance of the Pentagon over the policymaking process – aside from the traditional lead that the Pentagon assumes during times of conflict – was down to the ability of the traditional Realist Rumsfeld to shape the landscape. Having already served as Defence Secretary in Gerald Ford's administration, Rumsfeld was a wily operator and was successful in sidelining competing views, in particular Secretary of State Colin Powell's. Unlike Vice President Dick Cheney and Rumsfeld who were able to act in concert to influence the president's decision-making, Powell was an 'outsider', often operating on the fringes of the administration.[39] Adding to this sense of isolation was Powell's hesitancy to interfere in military matters. Powell, a retired four-star general and former Chairman of the Joint Chiefs of Staff, had vast military experience but opted not to interfere with military matters that were now outside his remit as Secretary of State.[40]

Rumsfeld was also able to outmanoeuvre Bush, only obeying the president's wishes if they concurred with his own. Rumsfeld employed several tactics to manipulate the president and other White House officials, such continuously objecting to proposals not to his liking through an unrelenting succession of questions. If that failed to have the proposal rejected, Rumsfeld petitioned other administration members until his plans were adopted.[41] As will be explained shortly, the Pentagon's supremacy had great implications for US counter-narcotics policies, but overall the frictions within the US administration caused serious difficulties with their British allies.

Shoulder to shoulder

After the 9/11 terrorist attacks on the US, one ally stood above all others in the coming months and years: Britain. The historic bond was reinvigorated as the US and Britain were, once again, bound together against a common threat: radical Islamist terrorism. That said, it was more than happenstance that reinvigorated the special relationship. Blair deliberately used 9/11 to cultivate ties with America, which, he predicted, would result in increased British influence on the world stage. A Number 10 official remarked: 'what we wanted to do was influence American decisions, to be a player in Washington – as Churchill was with Roosevelt, or Macmillan with Kennedy, or Thatcher with Reagan'.[42] Blair was convinced of his ability to influence the president;[43] however, as will become evident later, his ability to do so was more limited than he had hoped. For his part, Bush also drew on the deep history of the special relationship knowing that British support would provide a counterbalance to unilateral action.

On 11 September, Blair was scheduled to deliver a speech to the Trades Union Congress; however, learning of the attacks, the prime minister abandoned his prepared speech and said a few impromptu words. Blair's words were laced with moralistic imagery as he indicated he had a very clear idea of the new threat to society and the response the international community should take, 'This mass terrorism is the new evil in our world today . . .

the democracies of this world, are going to have to come together to fight it together and eradicate this evil completely.'[44] The themes espoused by Blair in his short address alluded to the doctrine of international community, the focus of the prime minister's April 1999 Chicago speech. The Chicago speech highlighted the moral responsibility of western nations to intervene in countries to prevent acts of genocide as in Kosovo in 1999.[45]

Blair was the first foreign leader invited to the US after Bush's presidential victory as, in the words of the president, a 'tribute to the special relationship between the United States and Britain'.[46] Significantly, it was also Blair who was the first foreign leader the president called on 12 September.[47] During the call, Blair argued that if the Taliban refused to hand over bin Laden, the US would be within their rights to launch military action.[48] Bush recounted his view of the phone call: 'The conversation helped cement the closest friendship I would form with any foreign leader. As the years passed and the wartime decisions grew tougher, some of our allies wavered. Tony never did.'[49] The close leader relations, however, did little to smooth Blair's initial concerns that the US would launch a wide-ranging and disproportionate response, which could include targeting Iraq. In the days that followed, Blair was clear: the focus should remain, at least for the time being, on al-Qaeda and the Taliban – not Iraq.[50] He also advocated a multilateralist approach and urged coordination with Afghanistan's neighbours and the re-ignition of the Middle East peace process (MEPP).[51]

On 15 September, the Bush Cabinet convened for a two-day session at Camp David to discuss its response to the attacks. Notwithstanding the worthiness of an attack on Iraq featuring heavily in the discussions, the president decided that Afghanistan would be the first step in the war on terror. The best and only plan came from CIA Director George Tenet, who proposed that a CIA team deploy to Afghanistan to build ties with the anti-Taliban Northern Alliance (NA) and prepare the way for US Special Forces.[52] Six days after 9/11, the president authorised the invasion of Afghanistan.[53]

On 20 September, Bush addressed a Joint Session of Congress outlining the coming intervention. Bush also used the opportunity to strengthen ties with Blair, who was in attendance as the president's guest of honour. Before delivering the speech, Bush shared the key points with Blair, indicating to the prime minister he would be a chief ally in the coming war; however, it also indicated that the key decisions had already been made without Blair's input.[54] Crucially, the administration had decided the core policy decisions at Camp David, and Blair's influence on the forthcoming intervention was minimal. Blair's sway was felt, however, on what the US saw as the smaller issues, namely the need to restart the MEPP and to build a multilateral coalition force[55] – however, and significantly, the latter was rejected by Rumsfeld and Cheney because it could potentially constrain their actions.[56] In fact, multilateral action was largely a pretence and the MEPP was only ever pursued half-heartedly.

During his speech, Bush praised Blair: 'I'm so honoured the British prime minister has crossed the ocean to show his unity with America.'[57] Blair's show of unity was powerful and above all it cemented Britain as a valuable and trusted ally in the coming war(s). Bush also laid forth an ultimatum to the Taliban regime to hand over 'all the leaders of al-Qaeda . . . or share their fate' and that 'every nation . . . now has a decision to make: either you are with us or you are with the terrorists'.[58]

Less than two weeks later, on the other side of the Atlantic, Blair addressed the Labour Party Conference reaffirming his support for the US and publicly stating his case for the intervention in Afghanistan. He argued: 'we were with you at the first. We will stay with you to the last. We know those responsible . . . I say to the Taliban: surrender the terrorists; or surrender power. It's your choice.'[59] Blair's resolute support for the US was, in part, based upon his understanding of the long-standing ties of the special relationship. He knew what mattered most was British support for the US in 'bad times as well as good'.[60] In the traditions of previous British prime ministers, Blair was Bush's closest international confidant in his time of need. But even the especially close leader relations could not guarantee that all would go smoothly at lower operational levels. Nevertheless, in the coming months and years, Britain's role in Afghanistan was second only to the US.

Broader international support for the conflict was also forthcoming as the United Nations Security Council approved armed intervention and NATO, for the first time in its history, invoked Article 5: an attack on one member state is deemed an attack on all member states.[61] Although, perhaps ungraciously, the US rebuffed NATO's overtures[62] – a move designed to keep the US firmly in control of the upcoming mission.

Operation Enduring Freedom

The operation against al-Qaeda and the Taliban began in earnest when a CIA unit arrived in Afghanistan on 26 September. Armed with $3 million in cash, the unit set about distributing this largesse among NA commanders to form an anti-Taliban coalition.[63] It was during the months that followed that both American and British forces formed relationships with regional strong men who were involved in the narcotics trade; something that later came back to haunt the counter-narcotics campaign. On 7 October, the Anglo-American bombing assault began but took several weeks to make progress.[64] Like many previous Anglo-American ventures, the political commitment of the president and prime minister was not translated into a smooth military operation. From the outset, the presence of British Special Forces was more symbolic than vital to the success of the operation.[65] This was compounded by the US's focus on counter-terrorism and refusal to allow the British to deploy a large-scale military presence.[66] As was often the case in the early intervention period, Rumsfeld's insistence on hunting al-Qaeda complicated the special relationship.[67] This was no more evident than when the counter-narcotics campaign got underway and resources, and American support, was thin on the ground.

After Kabul fell, al-Qaeda was still operating in the eastern city of Jalalabad, but a poorly planned operation allowed bin Laden to escape across the border into Pakistan.[68] The early campaign was almost exclusively formulated and implemented by the US, with Britain playing a relatively minor role, which failed to reflect Blair's ambitions. The lack of involvement was so pronounced a Whitehall spokesman noted: 'at the end of September 2001 that, in terms of the "war on terror", "we don't have an exit strategy. And we don't have an entry strategy either"'.[69] Differences between the allies heightened as attention turned to what post-Taliban Afghanistan would look like.

As it became clear the Taliban were on the brink of collapse, plans for what came next were required. Somewhat inevitably, the Bush administration reaffirmed its opposition to state-building or retaining a large number of troops in Afghanistan after the conflict had ended.[70] This reluctance to stay in Afghanistan beyond killing bin Laden highlighted a fundamental difference within the Anglo-American alliance. Contrastingly, Blair believed that the international community should make a long-term commitment to Afghanistan by providing a peacekeeping force and a reconstruction plan.[71] A British minister noted a more fundamental difference between Britain and the US: 'state-building certainly under the Bush administrations ... was not been given the primacy that we would focus on as a country'.[72] There was not, however, clear direction from Blair in what form this commitment should take.

In December, the political roadmap for post-conflict Afghanistan was decided under the auspices of the United Nations (UN) in Bonn. Designed to circumvent ethnic unrest, the resultant Bonn Agreement specified for a multi-ethnic and representative administration – the Afghan Interim Administration (AIA)[73] – headed by a Pashtun leader.[74] The man chosen was US-backed Hamid Karzai who had links to the Soviet resistance and was a former member of the Rabbani government.[75] Whilst he was regarded as the most sanitised candidate able to bridge the gap between the country's main factions, he was without military patronage – something needed to be effective in Afghanistan.[76] Determined that the post-conflict settlement should reflect their efforts and ultimate victory over the Taliban, NA warlords demanded the lion's share of positions in the new administration.[77] This came to undermine the establishment of a democratic state.

The US, uninspired by the Bonn conference, afforded it minimal attention and, consequently, the US envoy to Afghanistan James Dobbins did not have any written instructions from Washington on the best way to proceed. In fact, Dobbins's very presence in Afghanistan was more for appearance and somewhat in response to Blair's appointment of a special representative for Afghanistan several weeks previously.[78] The agreement also requested that an international security force be deployed to Kabul with the option of it being later extended. This was something Blair was extremely keen to accommodate, but the Bush administration supported a 'light footprint' approach, advocated by the UN's envoy to Afghanistan Lakhdar Brahimi.[79] Even so, reluctantly, and with conditions, the US accepted Britain's proposal: the International Security Assistance Force (ISAF) was dispatched to Kabul in December 2001.[80] Concerned that an expanded force would generate popular resistance – as had been the case with the Soviet intervention – ISAF was limited to the capital, under the command of British forces.[81] Not only did the US distance itself from state-building, it also prevented others from doing it.[82]

The conflict was further complicated by the fact that there were two separate operations running concurrently. The first of which was the US-led Operation Enduring Freedom with the purpose of hunting Taliban and al-Qaeda operatives, but not to engage in soft missions such as reconstruction.[83] The second was the UN mandated ISAF which was involved in state-building and peacekeeping.

The special relationship allies were thus separated from the outset of the intervention. In contrast to the US's opposition to state-building, Blair demonstrated his commitment by visiting Afghanistan on 7 January 2002.[84] The prime minister stated:

> Afghanistan has been a failed state for too long and the whole world has paid the price – in the export of terror, the export of drugs and finally in the explosion of death and destruction on the streets of the US.[85]

Blair had committed to the reconstruction of Afghanistan, and he viewed the elimination of the narcotics industry as an essential component of that agenda: unfortunately, not all within the US administration agreed.

More broadly, Blair had only partially achieved his objectives by supporting the war on terror; he had helped to face down international terrorism in Afghanistan and, in the process, reinvigorated the special relationship. That said, while the relationship was, once again, strengthened as it fought shoulder to shoulder against a common enemy, Britain's military contribution to the effort was largely symbolic. More importantly, the US considered Afghanistan – apart from the capture of bin Laden – mission complete. Undoubtedly, Blair had secured Britain's role as the US's closest ally, but he had failed to persuade the Americans to stay the course in Afghanistan. This demonstrated that Britain's robust support for the US did not translate into significant influence in Washington, as Blair had hoped. The prime minister then made a fatal error by throwing his weight behind the US invasion of Iraq. This not only had disastrous consequences for the special relationship, but also the mission in Afghanistan, as attention and resources were diverted towards Iraq.

Inevitably, as Anglo-American attention swung westwards, the seeds of future instability were sown in Afghanistan. The situation was further complicated by the Bush administration's reading of Afghanistan's history. In a large part, the US had based intervention on a light-footprint approach in order to avoid the mistakes the Soviet Union committed – the most damning of which was being drawn into a long and costly war. However, as events unfolded it became necessary to engage more and more in Afghanistan in order to prevent catastrophic consequences. In turn, that created other dangers, some of which might still have been avoided if the Bush administration had read Afghanistan's history more carefully.[86] Unfortunately, they did not.

3 The Legacy of Drugs and a Weak State

Afghanistan's political history

The beginnings of modern day Afghanistan can be traced back to the emergence of the Durrani Empire, under Ahmad Shah, in the second half of the eighteenth century.[1] While the Durrani Empire collapsed soon after his death, Ahmad Shah's descendants remained in power for the next 200 years.[2] For much of the nineteenth century, Afghanistan became the frontline in a stand-off between the two competing imperialist powers of Britain in the east and Russia to the north. Christened the 'Great Game', both empires sought to maintain influence in Afghanistan, which culminated in the Anglo-Afghan wars of 1839–42 and 1878–80.[3]

Assuming power in 1880, Amir Abdur Rahman Khan launched a brutal modernising policy, which united Afghanistan and consolidated the authority of the royal family.[4] It was also during Rahman's tenure that the state was irrevocably destabilised by Britain's imperial interests. The second Anglo-Afghan war, launched after British envoy Sir Neville Chamberlain was refused entry to Afghanistan whilst Russia's Major General Nikolai Stoletov was admitted, resulted in 'British India gain[ing] practical control over Afghan fiscal, defence and foreign policies; and the demarcation of the "Durand Line"', which was established in 1893. The Durand Line, named after British Indian Foreign Secretary Sir Mortimer Durand, delineated the border between Afghanistan and British India[5] and acted as a buffer between the British and Russian empires.[6] The land running along eastern Afghanistan was not the 'result of local physical, ethnic and political realities',[7] but an artificial construction which divided Pashtun tribes and, to this day, is a source of tension between Afghanistan and Pakistan. The porous border has provided anti-government elements, since the Soviet intervention, access to sanctuary in Pakistan's Federally Administered Tribal Areas.[8]

The development of a unified Afghan state was also constrained by its ethnic diversity, which magnified its ungovernable complexion and led to the reoccurrence of domestic conflict, all in all complicating the state's efforts to establish control over the entire country.[9] To fully comprehend Afghanistan's 'political system' it is important to appreciate the delicate ethnic and tribal dimension that governs it. The political landscape is characterised by fluctuating alliances between ethnicities and tribes that can alter through the acquisition or loss of power. This multifaceted network of alliances has been present for centuries and still persists today. Ethnic groups which have been excluded from the formal power structures of Afghanistan's central or provincial governments are easily incorporated into anti-government elements. The ethnic and tribal composition of Afghanistan is complex, with groups being broken down at the national, provincial and village level. At the village level, interdependent alliances provide quid pro quo social services that the Afghan state has been unable to provide, and all this makes the formation of a modern state more difficult.[10]

Historically, the notion of statehood was not a concrete idea recognised by many in Afghanistan and, even today, many Afghans will place loyalty to their tribe or ethnicity – Pashtun, Tajik, Uzbek, Hazara – above that to the national government.[11] Afghanistan's most populated and powerful ethnic bloc is the Pashtuns – from which the Taliban and former President Hamid Karzai both hail (Karzai was appointed the head of Afghanistan's first post-Taliban Interim Administration in December 2001, then elected President of Afghanistan from 2004 to 2014). Afghanistan is fragmented into a collection of small autonomous fiefdoms under the command of local tribal elders, or more recently regional warlords, which, in turn, severely impedes the establishment of a strong central state. The only time Afghan factions have united under one banner has been to repel foreign invaders; however, even these efforts have subsequently disintegrated because of ethnic rivalries. It is not an exaggeration to say that Afghanistan presented the Anglo-American allies with one of the most complex and divided political systems in the world to navigate.

In addition to all these issues, the reign of King Zahir Shah marked a further significant shift that exacerbated the problems in Afghan politics. Between 1963 and 1973, Zahir attempted to initiate a diluted form of democracy in Afghanistan and introduced a constitution in 1964. This modernisation process enacted a series of reforms aimed at the 'democratisation of politics, liberalisation of social and economic life and rationalisation of foreign relations'.[12] The Afghan state, however, was critically weakened by its paltry tax intake – less than 2 per cent of domestic revenue – and dependence on foreign aid,[13] a legacy that confronted the international forces after 2001. As the competing powers in the Cold War vied for influence in Central and South Asia, Afghanistan capitalised on its non-aligned status by turning to both the US and Soviet Union for aid.[14]

King Zahir's 'experiment with democracy' proved unsuccessful and he was ousted from power, in a largely bloodless coup in 1973, by his cousin and former Prime Minister Sardar Mohammed Daoud Khan. Daoud proclaimed Afghanistan a republic and brought the state firmly under his control.[15] This period saw the augmentation of ideological extremism among the urban elite as young, educated Afghans gravitated towards the radical and opposed politics of communism and Islamism.[16] Many of the young Islamic students later formed the core of the anti-Soviet resistance and stood in opposition to the communists.

Daoud's new republic failed on several levels to convert the country to his 'vision of a nationalist, modern, secular, neutral Afghanistan'.[17] By employing repressive measures against its opponents, Daoud's regime alienated movements from the right and left. In an attempt to dilute Afghanistan's Soviet associations, Daoud distanced himself from the communist state and removed his leftist supporters from positions of power.[18] In 1978, Daoud's police murdered the influential member of the pro-Soviet People's Democratic Party of Afghanistan (PDPA), Mir Akbar Khyber. The PDPA's hierarchy feared it was only a matter of time before Daoud eliminated all of his communist opponents and launched a coup (the Saur Revolution) ousting Daoud from power and later murdering him. PDPA leaders Nur Mohammed Taraki and Babrak Karmal installed a Marxist government, which signalled the end of more than 200 years of almost uninterrupted rule by the family of Zahir Shah and Daoud Khan.[19] The PDPA, however, was weak and divided and relied upon help from Moscow to cement its power.[20]

The Soviet intervention (1979–1989) and warlord period (1992–1996)

The newly installed communist government set about extending its authority through a reign of terror. Resolute in their quest to be the first government to extend its authority throughout Afghanistan 'they launched a brief, but devastating campaign of land redistribution, resettlement, revised family law, and debt cancellation'.[21] The government faced armed opposition in twenty-four out of twenty-eight provinces along with the growing opposition from Islamic militants,[22] called the mujahideen.[23] As Afghanistan descended into chaos, the Soviet Union reluctantly intervened to stabilise the country. The intervention was characterised by a desire to protect Afghanistan from falling under America's influence and countering the radical Islamist threat posed to Soviet Central Asia. Above all, it was designed to be a short-term measure to help the new regime.[24]

In response to the intervention, Islamic militants and mutinous army leaders, among others, took up arms against the invaders. Identifying an opportunity to defeat the Soviet Union, President Jimmy Carter's national security advisor (NSA) Zbigniew Brzezinski convinced Carter to fund resistance groups in 1979.[25] However, it was not until the presidency of Ronald Reagan, that funding for the mujahideen grew exponentially and the CIA covertly armed the resistance.[26] American and most other foreign funding to the mujahideen was via the powerful Pakistan Inter-Services Intelligence (ISI), which, among other things, used it to conduct its own agenda in the region. Fearful of empowering any mujahideen group that might one day seek to readdress the Afghan–Pakistan border, the ISI favoured radical Islamist movements who were focused on religion and neglected moderate Pashtun nationalist factions.[27]

By 1986, the conflict had reached an impasse. The Soviet Union, despite deploying over 100,000 troops and significant airpower to Afghanistan, proved incapable of pacifying the mujahideen. Shortly after, General Secretary Mikhail Gorbachev ordered the slow drawdown of Soviet forces. Predictably, Afghanistan was left in a state of ruin with a shattered economy and agricultural sector, both of which significantly exacerbated its dependency on foreign aid.[28] The withdrawal of Soviet forces in 1989 did not conclude the fighting as the mujahideen fought against the communist-backed Najibullah regime. After three gruelling years of war, and the Soviet Union's collapse, President Mohammed Najibullah resigned.[29]

The victorious mujahideen declared Afghanistan an Islamic State. The mujahideen was not a single monolithic block but instead structured along tribal and religious affiliations. Consequently, a mosaic of factions emerged under the control of Pashtun Gulbuddin Hekmatyar, a coalition of Tajik forces under the control of Ahmed Shah Massood and Burhanuddin Rabbani, and forces under the Uzbek general Abdul Rashid Dostum. Unfortunately, history was to repeat itself as the warring mujahideen factions plunged Afghanistan into civil war. Kabul had seen relatively little fighting during the ten-year Soviet occupation, yet two years of civil war saw tens of thousands of dead, wounded or displaced.[30] Prior to the Taliban gaining power, there was no functioning state in Afghanistan. Instead, the competing mujahideen blocs 'laid claim to the seat of power but never exercised state authority in the most fundamental definition of the term: controlling the state's territory, or exercising basic state function in regard to the population'.[31] The new Taliban regime thus faced challenges, emanating largely from the divided nature of Afghan society.

One consequence of the covert funding operation to the mujahideen was a well-established logistical network between Pakistan and Afghanistan transporting a variety of legal and illegal goods. Connections between the 'trucking mafia' – responsible for bringing goods in from Pakistan – and regional strongmen in Afghanistan were made, which continue to this day. One of the most lucrative smuggling operations during the Soviet intervention was the transportation of heroin.[32] The Pakistani Army's National Logistical Cell would transport mujahideen-bound arms from Pakistan to Afghanistan and return with Afghan opium.[33] The smuggling networks were also boosted by the Afghan Transit Trade (ATT) agreement, which allowed land-locked Afghanistan to import duty free goods from Karachi. In 1997, it was estimated that the entire value of transported goods was $2.5 billion, proving a valuable source of revenue for the emerging Taliban.[34]

The Taliban (1994–2001)

Taliban is a Pashto word, derived from Arabic, meaning lower-level students of Islam. Most Talibs were enlisted from religious schools in Pakistan, where they were taught an ultra-orthodox version of Islam, whilst also gaining military experience fighting in the anti-Soviet and anti-Najibullah conflicts.[35] One of the most prominent of these was Mohammed Omar, a southern Pashtun Mullah, who formalised the Taliban as a movement in 1994.[36] His mission was to promote virtue and prevent vice in a country devastated by war and lawlessness.[37]

Backed by the ISI, the Taliban were groomed to maintain Pakistani influence in Afghanistan, and as such, received military and logistical support, which aided their rapid rise to power. Pakistan's support of the Taliban stemmed from long-held strategic objectives, motivated by their greatest of all fears: encirclement by India to their east and an Indian sympathiser to their west. They assumed that the Taliban's religious nature and initial focus on domestic affairs would negate any ambition to dispute the Durand Line. Moreover, Pakistan also endeavoured to protect its trade routes and truck drivers in Afghanistan from endless extortion. To enable safe passage, truck drivers had to pay several tolls per journey to regional strongmen.[38] This was also coupled to an ever-present threat of theft of their goods.

In October 1994, the Taliban's first major success came when, with Pakistani assistance, they captured an ammunition dump at Spin Boldak.[39] This was quickly followed by other successes across southern Afghanistan. Within a year of forming, the Taliban laid claim to twenty-seven out of Afghanistan's thirty-two provinces;[40] the following year, their meteoric rise to power was completed when they captured Kabul. Like many regimes that preceded them, the Taliban was unable to extend their authority throughout the entire country, with some north-eastern provinces under the control of the NA. This historical factor also pointed to the difficulty facing future regimes to unite the entire country. Even within the areas under their control, the Taliban's authority was not absolute, as it had to deploy a mixture of coercive measures and broker deals with local elites to maintain control.[41] Furthermore, the Taliban was not a unified structure but 'a loose coalition of factions' that were 'regionally based and pre-existed the Taliban'. This meant that the Taliban's grip on power was fragile and its policies 'differed from region to region'.[42] Although security was improved under the Taliban, they used draconian measures to cement their control over the population.[43] It was providing terrorists with safe haven, however, that defined the regime's relationship with the outside world, in particular the US.

Involved in the resistance against the Soviet Union, Osama bin Laden – after a spell in Sudan from 1992 to 1996 – returned to Afghanistan in May 1996. Bin Laden's presence in Afghanistan had repercussions for the regime as early as December 1996, when Secretary of State, Warren Christopher warned the Taliban that hosting bin Laden 'greatly hurt prospects for Afghanistan re-joining the world community'.[44] As will be considered shortly, the Taliban's desire to join the international community resulted in them launching, what some have characterised as, the most effec-tive narcotics suppression campaign in history.

The desire for the Taliban to eject bin Laden intensified after two US embassies in Africa were bombed in August 1998. The US responded by launching Operation Infinite Reach, a series of cruise missile attacks on bin Laden's camps in eastern Afghanistan.[45] The US made clear to the Taliban that they would be judged as co-conspirators for not agreeing to his extradition. Frustrated by Mullah Omar's response to extradition requests, the US imposed economic sanctions on Afghanistan. This was followed by UN sanctions in October 1999 and December 2000.[46]

Afghanistan's opium history

It is difficult to ascertain when opium was introduced to Afghanistan; some reports indicate that soldiers in Alexander the Great's armies may have brought it in.[47] However, by the eighteenth century, opium use – as a coping strategy for poverty and harsh conditions or as medicine – was still restricted to a small number of provinces.[48] Even as late as 1924, opium cul-tivation was only reported in three provinces.[49] In the first half of the twentieth century, under the control of the Afghan royal family, opium cultivation remained relatively modest. In 1932, Afghanistan produced seventy-five tons of opium; a decent quan-tity considering the small population and limited domestic use;[50] however, insignificant in comparison to the 6,000 tons produced by China.[51]

After aborting attempts to become a licit producer of opium, the Afghan government, under pressure from the US, banned opium production in 1945.[52] By 1956, production had decreased to twelve tons and the following year the government issued another ban.[53] For the next two decades, Afghanistan was over-shadowed by the opium producing Golden Triangle of Burma, Laos and Thailand. However, from the 1970s onwards, several external factors catapulted Afghanistan on its way to become the world's pre-eminent opium producer.[54] The combined events of the Iranian Revolution, the Southeast Asian drought, Pakistan's opium ban and the Afghan–Soviet war all coalesced to stimulate opium cultivation in Afghanistan. These factors were set against weak government rule that did not extend into areas where tribal communities dominated affairs 'isolated from the power centre both geographically and politically'.[55] The intertwined issue of narcotics cultivation and lack of government authority in the tribal areas proved equally as problematic for the government to address after 2001.

The Soviet intervention and opium industry

The Soviet intervention, more than any other event, was respon-sible for Afghanistan's rise to opium hegemon. To gain control of the countryside, Soviet forces adopted a 'scorched earth' policy, designed to obliterate the agricultural sector. A UNODC report catalogued the destruction:

> Between 1979 and 1989 . . . Between half and two thirds of all villages were bombed. The amount of live-stock fell by 70 per cent. Between a quarter and one third of the country's irrigation systems were destroyed. About one third of all farms were abandoned. The reduc-tion in fertilizer availability and affordability lowered crop yields further; in some areas fertilizer use declined by 90 per cent. Thus, by 1988 total food production had declined to around 45 per cent of the level prevailing before the Soviet invasion in 1979.[56]

As irrigation canals were destroyed, farmers had little alternative but to replace the traditional economy constructed on the export of dried fruit and nuts with opium cultivation, as it required far less irrigation, fertilizers or transportation.[57] The Soviet interven-tion, followed by two further decades of war, reduced Afghanistan to an importer country of grains, fruits and vegetables – in stark contrast to a country that was advancing towards self-sufficiency in the 1970s.[58]

Whilst the Soviet 'scorched earth' policy devastated the rural landscape resulting in the entrenchment of opium cultivation, several mujahideen commanders also became involved in the narcotics industry. Consequently, opium production increased from 350 tons in 1986 to 875 tons in 1987.[59] By 1989, it is alleged that the seven main mujahideen groups were responsible for producing 800 metric tons of opium.[60] Participation in the trade afforded several mujahideen commanders financial independence from other competing ISI funded mujahideen groups. A situation developed where the distributors of foreign aid, namely the ISI and Iran, favoured religious-based mujahideen groups at the expense of traditional elites. This was an incentive for those elites to circumvent that policy by exploiting the opium trade.

Opium cultivation continued to rise in the concluding years of the Soviet intervention as the Red Army withdrew from rural Afghanistan to urban centres. The rise was exacerbated further after the Soviet withdrawal – reaching 1,600 tons in 1990.[61] After replacing Myanmar in 1991 as the world's premier opium producing country,[62] Afghanistan began a process of setting and then breaking records for producing opium, first under the Taliban regime, then more latterly and conclusively after the 2001 intervention.

Entrenchment under the warlords' rule

After the Soviet Union's departure, foreign funding to resistance groups dwindled, therefore the mujahideen turned to the opium industry to fund their civil war.[63] With licit income streams severely weakened, opium was a reliable commodity that generated a healthy return. In a practise that survives to this day, opium became a trustworthy method of savings – as the government attempted to plug a financial hole by printing money.[64] A decade of war and economic contraction left the economy in ruins. The International Centre for Humanitarian Reporting concluded that the gross national product (GNP) per capita decreased by more than 25 per cent in seven years from $222 in 1984 to $164 in 1991. Only Mozambique and Ethiopia tabled below Afghanistan for GNP in that period. Overall, it is estimated that gross domestic product (GDP) declined by 60 per cent between 1981 and 1991.[65]

Afghanistan was, and still is, an agricultural country with approximately over 70 per cent of the population living in rural locations.[66] The opium industry, therefore, offers a secure source of income, especially under challenging economic conditions. Devastated by war and drought, Afghanistan's rugged terrain is inhospitable for the cultivation of many crops.[67] Opium, by contrast, is a drought resistant, durable, cash crop. It is important to note, however, that whilst opium can generate significant gross returns, when the costs of inputs are evaluated, opium is not always the most profitable crop.[68] It is too simplistic to view the decision to cultivate opium through the prism of profit maximisation. Other factors are important, such as 'access to land and water, household assets, number of able-bodied males in the household, access to urban markets for agricultural products and labor, transport linkages, price and availability of wheat (Afghanistan's main staple food)'.[69]

Nevertheless, the opium industry does play a vital role in rural Afghanistan. Given the labour-intensive nature of harvesting poppies, opium cultivation benefits the wider rural community by providing employment opportunities to landless peasants. Estimates indicate that 1 ha of opium needs 360 person days of work as opposed to thirty-one days for rainfed wheat and sixty-four days for irrigated wheat.[70] In 2017, the opium industry provided approximately 590,000 full-time-equivalent jobs and supported many more indirectly; whilst also increasing the wages of labourers.[71] Once harvested, opium is a robust crop that does not need refrigeration, so the lack of reliable roads and electricity is no obstruction. Counter-narcotics expert David Mansfield explains:

> Local traders . . . offer to purchase the crop before harvest as a form of loan, at harvest time, or later in the year. As this purchase would take place on the farm or within the village, farmers did not incur the transport and transaction costs, or incur the post-harvest losses associated with travelling on damaged and insecure roads that were controlled by armed factions looking to tax passing trade.[72]

Therefore, opium also serves as a vital source of finance to most of the rural population who have no access to modern banking systems to offer loans or other sources of credit. More broadly, it is hard to overstate the opium industry's economic value to Afghanistan; in 2004, the International Monetary Fund (IMF) estimated that narcotics represented as much as half of Afghanistan's GDP.[73]

The Taliban and the opium industry

Up until its 2000 ban, the Taliban did little to stem the rising tide of opium cultivation. The year before the ban, cultivation had expanded to 91,000 ha, up from 57,000 ha in 1996.[74] Furthermore, by 1999, cultivation had spread to provinces with no previous history of cultivation.[75] Three factors proved critical to this growth: first, Afghanistan was crippled by an economic crisis in the 1990s and opium cultivation offered farmers a viable economic avenue that was absent in the legal agricultural market. Second, landless farmers with opium cultivating experience, who were unable to buy land in traditional opium cultivating provinces, migrated to non-opium producing provinces where land opportunities were available. Finally, as overall security was improved, and checkpoints were removed along major highways, fewer obstacles confronted 'established' narcotics traffickers or 'new entrants to the trade'.[76]

Contrary to some reporting, the Taliban did not rule over a formalised narcotics industry through a centralised system. Mansfield states:

> some viewed this expansion of trade coinciding with the Taliban's territorial gains as evidence of the Taliban's control of the trade, the relationship was more complex. It reflected the local political settlements and bargains that were made when the Taliban movement extended its influence across a wider geographic area.[77]

The Taliban's policies towards the opium trade were not uniform but dependent upon the specific leadership in control of regions. Policies ranged from permitting the production and trade in some areas to active participation in other areas through taxation, production, processing and transport.[78]

Mirroring the regime's local and unequal involvement in the opium trade was the uneven profit that they derived from the industry. Critics of the Taliban claimed that the taxation of opium exports provided the regime's principle source of income and war economy.[79] Whilst the movement was operational in taxing the trade, tax was collected or donated in an ad hoc manner in the form of *ushr*: a tax raised on agricultural products, with a percentage going to the poor and the remainder going to local mullahs.[80] Taxation under the Taliban was not a unitary system applied nationally but a system that differed from location to location and was sensitive to the local environment. Nor was the rate of taxation uniform across the country, with some farmers paying only what they could afford – not a standard 10 per cent as reported – and others paying in cash or kind.[81] With this is mind, it is extremely difficult to ascertain the financial value of the narcotics industry to the Taliban. Moreover, the smuggling of legal goods also increased under Taliban rule and the ATT provided the regime with 'the largest source of official revenue'.[82]

It was not only financial benefit that the Taliban derived from tolerating the opium industry; it generated political support for the movement in rural Afghanistan.[83] Moreover, an examination of Taliban pronouncements can provide insight to the coadjutant relationship between the opium industry and the legitimacy it provided for the movement. As the head of the Taliban's counter-narcotics force in Kandahar, Abdul Rashid, stated: 'We let people cultivate poppies because farmers get good prices . . . There would be an uprising against the Taliban if we forced them to stop poppy cultivation.'[84] Another equally important reason why the Taliban failed to tackle the narcotics industry at this juncture was their lack of international recognition, which stymied the possibility of trading in legitimate agricultural commodities.[85] It was this desire to join the international community that led the Taliban to launch a comprehensive opium prohibition.

The Taliban's opium prohibition (2000)

Set against a backdrop of international isolation and economic weakness, the Taliban continually flirted with the idea of banning opium cultivation in exchange for international recognition. There was good reason for this as only Pakistan, Saudi Arabia and the United Arab Emirates recognised the regime,[86] and the Taliban was blocked from taking Afghanistan's seat at the UN.[87] The failure to gain international acceptance had grave consequences for Afghanistan's already shattered economy. Even compared to other underdeveloped countries, Afghanistan fell short, rarely experiencing running water, electricity, telephones, functioning roads or regular energy supplies.[88] The average monthly wage was approximately $1 to $3, and half of Kabul's 1.2 million residents were receiving western food aid.[89] Further complicating matters,

Afghanistan was subject to economic sanctions, which meant it was unable to receive development assistance from the World Bank or private sector.[90] Therefore, by banning opium production, the Taliban predicted it could gain international acceptance and much needed financial help.

Shortly after securing the capital, the Taliban made its first move to open dialogue with the international community over supressing the opium industry. Leading the international effort was the United Nations International Drug Control Programme (UNDCP – now part of the UNODC). The organisation had been active in Afghanistan since 1989, when it initiated an Alternative Development project – Drug Control and Rural Rehabilitation – that operated until 1996. However, like most counter-narcotics interventions during this period and after, the programme had limited impact on reducing opium cultivation.[91]

By September 1997, at the UNODC's insistence, the Taliban agreed to publicly prohibit the 'growing, using and trading in hashish and heroin'.[92] Soon after, the incoming Director of the UNODC Pino Arlacchi travelled to Afghanistan to discuss implementing a ban with the Taliban representative Mullah Mohammed Hassan.[93] The outcome of the dialogue with the Taliban was broad agreement that the regime would eliminate opium cultivation from its territory, in exchange for financial aid to the tune of $25 million over ten years.[94] However, there was little evidence to suggest that Arlacchi could fulfil his end of the bargain. The following year, the plan collapsed as cultivation increased in Taliban-controlled territories.

Throughout this period, the UNODC remained in dialogue with the Taliban organising a series of meetings to discuss narcotics control.[95] In 1999, another deal was proposed for the UNODC to fund a poppy reduction programme, with Mullah Omar issuing an edict for a one third reduction in opium cultivation in the upcoming growing season. By November 1999, again dismayed by the lack of international aid, the Taliban requested international recognition as a precursor for continued involvement in the project.[96] The UN observed that the Taliban's adherence to drug control 'remains questionable, as it continues to collect taxes on the opium crop that is harvested and the heroin that is manufactured'.[97] Whilst there were some reductions in the agreed target areas – mainly due to drought[98] – the Taliban failed to deliver a one third reduction in cultivation as promised.[99]

In July 2000, Mullah Omar issued a fatwa proscribing poppy cultivation under the pretence of upholding Islamic principles and adherence to international drug control. Like all previous attempts to ban opium cultivation, the motivation lay in the regime's desire for international recognition and financial aid,[100] the difference being that the Taliban was more successful in the implementing of this ban. Through a process of negotiation and bribes to local powerbrokers,[101] the Taliban initiated one of the most effective drug suppression campaigns in history,[102] a fact not lost on the international community, particularly in the light of subsequent record levels of opium cultivation under the western-backed Karzai administration.[103] Cultivation decreased from 82,172 ha in 2000 to 7,606 ha in 2001, representing a 91 per cent reduction.[104] The majority of the 7,606 ha cultivated were in areas controlled by the NA, where Taliban influence was negligible.[105] Nevertheless, the ban threw many rural households into poverty as certain regional economies collapsed while heightening the effects of a four-year drought.[106] Already suffering from a fall in domestic support, the ban resulted in support for the Taliban all but vanishing in certain areas and instances of large-scale resistance. This was a deliberate gamble as the Taliban hoped that the domestic distress would be transitory, as development aid would flow in from the international community. Mansfield sums up the Taliban's estimations of the situation:

> [There was] strong pressure on donors to respond with development assistance. The Taliban leadership likely calculated that the international political support gained by prohibiting opium outweighed the unpopularity the ban would engender among the rural population. This perception was reinforced in conversations between UNDCP and Taliban leaders. It was calculated that if the international community kept their part of the deal, the economic impact of the ban on the rural population would be short lived, while if the international actors failed to deliver, the ban could simply be rescinded.[107]

The motives behind the ban have been contested, with a UN report claiming if 'Taliban officials were sincere in stopping the production of opium and heroin, then one would expect them to order the destruction of all stocks existing in areas under their control'.[108] A UN official contended the stimulation to ban opium was, in part, driven by financial motives. As a result of over-production in the previous years, opium prices fell, thus a ban would dramatically increase the price of opium.[109] According to estimates the price for raw opium rose nine-fold between 2000 and 2001, from US $50/kg to US $430/kg.[110] The official did acknowledge other factors were at play:

> it was also used politically to deal with the UN and the west and say okay we have done something that you wanted what are you going to give us in return? [It was used to] push the other countries to get [international] recognition.[111]

Whilst it is credible that narcotics traffickers with ties to the Taliban benefited financially from the ban, this was of secondary consequence. The Taliban's desire for international recognition was the chief motivating factor.

Three months after the ban, the Taliban's envoy raised the issue of recognition for the regime at the UN.[112] The mission proved unsuccessful with the recognition failing to materialise. The Taliban believed they were unfairly treated, as a representative stated: 'we have done what needed to be done, putting our people and our farmers through immense difficulties. We expected to be rewarded for our actions, but instead we were punished with additional sanctions.'[113] The UN Security Council, led by the US, imposed further sanctions on the Taliban for the continued sanctuary of bin Laden. Conversely, the US delivered $43 million in humanitarian aid to the regime for successfully quashing opium cultivation. The delivery of aid in support of the opium ban should not detract from the US's attitude towards the regime nor the differences that set the two countries apart. Colin Powell stated: 'the ban on poppy cultivation, [is] a decision by the Taliban that we welcome'. However, he indicated that several issues remained outstanding: 'a number of fundamental issues . . . separate us: their support for terrorism; their violation of internationally recognised human rights standards, [and] especially the treatment of women and girls'.[114]

In February 2001, the Bush administration increased the pressure on the Taliban regime by expelling its representative from New York.[115] In June and July 2001, Bush issued executive orders continuing economic sanctions, then upheld the 'National

Emergency' with respect to the regime because it 'continues to allow territory under its control in Afghanistan to be used as a safe haven and base of operations for Usama bin Laden and the al-Qaida organisation'.[116] Ultimately the Taliban's quest for international recognition was a forlorn hope. If the regime continued to support and harbour bin Laden, a substantial reduction in opium cultivation would not be enough to gain the regime international recognition.

Domestically, the Taliban's power and legitimacy were irreversibly weakened by their prohibition of opium cultivation. The effect of the ban was compounded by an ebbing of support for the regime as they failed to improve the economy and faced armed rebellions in areas of traditional support.[117] As a result, the Taliban ended the ban in early September 2001.[118] As highlighted in subsequent chapters, the fall of the Taliban regime and the ushering in of a western-backed government in Afghanistan did very little to curb the level of opium cultivation. Given the nature of Afghan society and its historic experiences, and above all the recent failure of the Taliban, that is hardly surprising. However, there was also a serious mishandling of the Anglo-American response to the narcotics problem. Even when they learnt lessons from history, they went on to make new mistakes of their own. Their intervention not only guaranteed another period of instability and weak government but also the return of wide-scale opium cultivation, thus compromising much of what both Britain and the US wanted to do in Afghanistan.

Part 2

4 Taliban Drugs on British Streets, 2001–2002

The first phase of the counter-narcotics campaign was launched, almost exclusively, at Tony Blair's insistence. But few, including the prime minister, realised the insurmountable task that lay before them. Over the coming decade, countering the narcotics trade became an intrinsic part of Britain's mission in Afghanistan and, as such, had far-reaching consequences for its other objectives. Ignorant of the cold realities of operating in Afghanistan, the prime minister adopted lofty and unrealistic ambitions from the outset.[1] During a speech to the Labour Party Conference on 2 October 2001, Blair indicated that destroying the narcotics trade was a key objective for the British government:

> It is a regime founded on fear and funded on the drugs trade. The biggest drugs hoard in the world is in Afghanistan, controlled by the Taliban . . . The arms the Taliban are buying today are paid for with the lives of young British people buying their drugs on British streets . . . That is another part of their regime that we should seek to destroy.[2]

Four motives underpinned Blair's desire in linking destroying the narcotics trade to the intervention in Afghanistan. First, Blair's robust public statements to eliminate the Afghan narcotics trade did not take place in a vacuum but fed into a domestic policy debate that had been well established over several years. The origins of the debate can be traced to New Labour's policy priorities when they returned to government in 1997. The Blair administration had committed itself to tackle domestic drug use – enshrined in its 1998 national strategy, Tackling Drugs to Build a Better Britain – and aimed to reduce the availability of Class A drugs by 25 per cent by 2005 and by 50 per cent by

2008.[3] As 90 per cent of the heroin on Britain's streets originated from Afghanistan, discussions about how to combat the Afghan narcotics trade as a way of reducing domestic heroin consumption were a significant feature of the counter-narcotics agenda prior to 9/11. Stemming the flow of illegal drugs into Britain was of high importance to the intelligence agencies and this was reflected in the priorities of the Joint Intelligence Committee; the objective was a First Order of Priority for the Secret Intelligence Service (SIS) and Government Communications Headquarters. To put this into context, the objective ranked as highly as combating domestic and international terrorism.[4] In fact, Blair was reported to have appropriated resources from counter-terrorism to counter-narcotics work in 1999.[5]

That year, the Concerted Inter-Agency Drugs Action (CIDA) group was formed under the chairmanship of HM Customs & Excise (HMCE) to coordinate law enforcement activity designed to stop the flow of Class A drugs to Britain.[6] A central element of the debate and a top priority for CIDA was to determine to what extent was it worth applying pressure at source countries to cut off the supply of illegal narcotics to British streets. Upstream interdiction appealed to individual members of the intelligence community, CIDA, Foreign and Commonwealth Office (FCO), Cabinet Office and military but consensus was never reached across government about whether work on the ground was the correct strategy for Britain. Indeed, consensus on what form this engagement should take, development aid, law enforcement activity or military intervention, also proved elusive.[7] However, given that Britain and the Taliban did not have a diplomatic relationship, officials were limited to countering the trade of narcotics once they left Afghanistan.[8] According to an HMCE official: 'the strategy was a ring of steel around Afghanistan . . . sitting on the outside and waiting for drugs to come out . . . working downstream . . . [With countries] . . . around the region'.[9] Therefore, intervention in Afghanistan presented the government with, as one HMCE official testified to the House of Commons Home Affairs Committee, 'a golden opportunity'[10] – one that had been previously unavailable – to take supply side measures to fulfil its domestic ambitions. It was therefore incumbent on Britain to use this rare opportunity to attempt to cut off the supply at source.

In the days after 9/11, the argument to attack Britain's heroin problem at source gained some high-profile endorsements from senior intelligence and military officials. During a 17 September meeting at Number 10, the Chief of Defence Staff Admiral Sir Michael Boyce and Director General of the Security Service Sir Stephen Lander suggested that 'the heroin trail should also be hit' arguing 'more people had been killed by heroin' than by 9/11.[11] Whilst inconclusive, it appears that this meeting was the first time that officials suggested to Blair that the intervention in Afghanistan should also be used to destroy the Afghan narcotics trade at source.[12] Once suggested to the prime minister he was attracted to such a policy and this resonated with his notions of an ethical foreign policy and doctrine of nurturing the international community. However, there was also a more pressing concern – despite little evidence to substantiate the claim – that al-Qaeda was funded by the narcotics trade. If this was the case, officials feared narcotics money could fund more terrorist attacks.[13] Three days after the meeting, Blair mentioned tackling the narcotics trade in a note to Bush,[14] which is yet another indicator of its policy priority.

As will be explained shortly, during Blair's second administration, especially pre-Iraq War, foreign policy decision-making was largely withdrawn from the FCO and centralised in Number 10. Simultaneously, the contributions of the various intelligence chiefs were highly valued and became more determinative of policy. So much so, a British minister recounts: 'after 9/11, the spooks became very mainstream and were seen as very important . . . they became absolutely central to Blair's outlook'.[15] The prime minister consulted less and less with Whitehall departments before making foreign policy decisions; for example, both the FCO and Department for International Development (DFID) were not consulted before Blair decided to tackle the narcotics trade.[16]

Second, there was a belief, particularly in Number 10, that cutting off the supply of heroin to British streets at source was – *crucially* – an achievable task.[17] Blair espoused this belief during a parliamentary debate in November 2001:

> [It] will take some time, but as I was told when I was in Pakistan a few weeks ago, Pakistan used to have a very active drugs trade, but it closed it down with the help of measures taken with the international community. So, it is not impossible for a country that has been involved in drugs to shut down its drugs trade, and we must work to ensure that Afghanistan does that.[18]

While Blair's comments were cautious, there was a belief that with a concerted international effort – with Britain at the helm – and resources on the ground it was plausible that narcotics could be eliminated in Afghanistan.

Third, Blair's desire to combat the narcotics trade took place within the larger framework of rebuilding Afghanistan after years of Taliban misrule. Rebuilding the state and its main institutions was the most important objective set by the prime minister and occupied much of the time of Whitehall.[19] As such, Blair understood that for Afghanistan to transition to a stable, democratic state it had to be free from the pervasive ills generated by the narcotics industry.

Fourth, adding to the genuine sense of enthusiasm for upstream enforcement measures within Number 10, after 9/11 there was also a need to cater to domestic politics by identifying the destruction of the Afghan narcotics trade as yet another reason for intervention. Blair knew that by linking destroying the narcotics trade to direct benefits it would have for the British population, it would make the coming intervention more palatable for the domestic audience. Alastair Campbell noted in his diary: 'He [Tony Blair] also emphasised that we had continually to make the link to domestic policy – that this had implications for our fight against drugs and terrorism.'[20] A British minister was more critical of Blair's motives, concluding that:

> Blair was a very presentational politician . . . this repeated thing about most of the drugs that end up on British streets coming from Afghanistan was a way of popularising a policy that he supported for other reasons . . . it doesn't mean it [counter-narcotics] was a serious policy . . . I think it was presentational and not a seriously considered and developed policy.[21]

Whilst true that Blair deployed troops to Afghanistan with the aim of defeating international terrorism and strengthening the special relationship, tackling narcotics was an important objective in and of itself for the prime minister – one that had both domestic and international dimensions. Over the coming year, the prime minister maintained that destroying the narcotics trade was feasible with the help of the international community,[22] and indicated the wider benefits to British society. On one such occasion, he reminded the audience at the Labour Conference in 2002 of the connection between Afghan heroin and Britain, reiterating: 'Our young people . . . die from heroin imported from Afghanistan.'[23] The public statements by the British government over the issue demonstrated a degree of domestic and party politics, but tackling the narcotics trade to cut off the source of heroin to British streets would become a key strategic objective for the prime minister – however, even the savvy Blair did not appreciate the problems in Afghanistan created or exacerbated by the narcotics industry. Nor did the prime minister have any clear idea how he was going to deliver on his promises. The objective had been set and it was now the turn of policy mandarins to create a strategy to match Blair's ambitions.

The US's reluctance to confront the narcotics industry

The wider Anglo-American alliance did not reflect the importance on the issue placed by Blair. With the Pentagon dictating Afghan policy, it successfully prevented the US from being dragged into counter-narcotics work, arguing that destroying the opium trade was not part of the counter-terrorism mission. The refusal to consider counter-narcotics as a priority, let alone an objective, was prevalent throughout the Pentagon's high command – even when US counter-narcotics officials highlighted its strategic significance. Concerned by the Taliban's ability partially to sustain itself through narcotics funding, a Pentagon official formulated a policy proposal to target narcotics pipelines with the aim of disrupting the group's financial and logistical capabilities. The official sent the memo up the chain of command for consideration. During a November 2001 meeting, the official discovered the level of hostility to undertake counter-narcotics work when Under Secretary of Defense for Policy Douglas Feith threatened him with professional retribution for proposing the plan. The official stated: 'he told me he was not going to send that memo up because I would get fired for suggesting such a policy'. The official also encountered a similar response when he visited US Central Command (CENTCOM) the following month:

> I met with the Deputy Commander . . . I walked into the office but before I could even say hello he said, we don't do drugs. I said good General neither do I. I provide you the policy and resources to go

after narco-terrorists. He cocked his head, looked at me and said but we are killing all the terrorists. He fundamentally did not understand the battle space. That was the way the thinking was in US Central Command, and indeed within the Pentagon.[24]

When discussions took place at the wider administration level, the Pentagon remained firmly opposed to counter-narcotics work. In contrast, as early as October 2001, the State Department was 'concern[ed] regarding eradication of opium poppy cultivation'.[25] However, a State Department official recalled the difficulty in overcoming the Pentagon's opposition:

> The State Department ... believed that counter-narcotics was a very important piece of our policy in Afghanistan. But as in a number of things in this space ... our friends in the Defense Department, particularly Secretary Rumsfeld, did not think that there was any role for our military in counter-narcotics. And so there [was a] tremendous debate inside our government about what to do ... when it came to the narcotics question ... The arguments were pretty stern ... Secretary Rumsfeld was trying to focus on what he believed was a pure military mission and he did not think that ... burning warehouses full of drugs and dealing with narcotics ... was the business of the US military ... It was never really a resolved question.[26]

Several reasons underpinned the Defense Department's opposition. As outlined above, the Pentagon saw the intervention in Afghanistan as the first step in a global war against terror; therefore, the US's mission was framed in narrow counter-terrorism terms. To engage with counter-narcotics would constitute becoming bogged down in a state-building exercise – something that the Bush administration had consistently opposed. As far as the Pentagon was concerned, the military's primary and only purpose in Afghanistan was to kill terrorists.[27] Aside from theoretical concerns, there were also practical issues: the US did not have the troops or resources to become involved in, what they saw as, a law enforcement matter. Furthermore, unlike Britain, only 7 to 10 per cent of heroin entering the US originated in Afghanistan[28] – with the majority coming from Colombia and Mexico. With no direct threat to the US, the military argued that Afghan narcotics was a European not an American problem.

From the outset of the intervention, US forces had also allied themselves with warlords for immediate military reasons – many of whom had unsavoury backgrounds and were involved in the narcotics trade – to build a willing anti-Taliban coalition. Realpolitik and the exigencies of the war on terror were already overriding ethical considerations: if narcotics dealers could help find or kill bin Laden then so be it, but American hands were already tainted in a way that returned to damage their later strategies for Afghanistan. The US not only sought the support of these regional strongmen to utilise their services in direct military operations against al-Qaeda and the Taliban, but as a mechanism to gain local favour.[29] This strategy of ignoring its allies' backgrounds reached the highest levels of the Pentagon, but was deemed a prerequisite of victory. A Pentagon official stated:

> It was a case of sometimes you have to do business with someone you would rather not do business with. But let me be very clear: this is not a case of moral blindness or moral failing per se. This was a case of: we are in Afghanistan, and we know very little about the country and we know very few people. The likelihood that some of these people are going to be involved in activities that we would find repugnant is high. No doubt about it . . . There were some people that . . . we didn't know what we didn't know – that was the majority. There was a certain number we had suspicions about and there was a certain number that we knew were involved in certain activities. Absolutely.[30]

The lack of interest in pursuing narcotics traffickers can be illustrated by the reported release of the influential trafficker Haji Juma Khan from US custody in December 2001.[31] Although known to be involved in the narcotics industry and having ties to both the Taliban and al-Qaeda, US authorities released him after he falsely promised to help them in their counter-terrorism mission. This incident epitomised the US goal during the first few years of the intervention in Afghanistan: chasing down terrorists would override and marginalise all other activities.[32] From the start, US policy was geared around a quick military campaign and the avoidance of state-building; however, refusing to tackle narcotics traffickers had sinister implications, most importantly because they were inseparable from the wider problems of insecurity and the failing state that was Afghanistan.

The reconstruction agenda

Before any decisions were made on future counter-narcotics policies, British officials travelled to Bonn in December to discuss
the reconstruction of Afghanistan. While the resultant Bonn
Agreement pledged that the AIA would cooperate with the international community in the fight against narcotics,[33] there was
little recognition that this was a top priority for the AIA beyond
rhetoric to satisfy the international community. In fact, a US official commented:

> my guess is the provision was inserted by the UN and accepted by the
> Afghan representatives . . . I think most of the Afghan delegation rec-
> ognised drug trafficking was a source of corruption . . . but probably
> most of them had other concerns regarding security and other issues.[34]

The UN's enthusiasm to bind the new AIA to international
drug control laws was hardly surprising given that the UNODC
had been active in Afghanistan since 1989.[35] The Afghans were
already keenly aware that narcotics control was a condition of
international acceptance. Even the Taliban had recognised this:
imposing an opium ban in 2000 in an attempt to achieve international recognition.

The meeting in Bonn was followed by an international conference on reconstruction assistance to Afghanistan in Tokyo in
January.[36] During that conference, the president of the AIA Hamid
Karzai indicated that eliminating poppy cultivation was a priority for his administration. However, counter-narcotics policies
were not addressed in detail during the main plenary but during
a breakout session. At this session, the British 'stressed the need
for rapid institution building, early action against traffickers and
quick impact projects to address the problem of the current crop
while avoiding perverse incentives that could lead to further cultivation next season'.[37] At the conference a supplementary meeting
on Security Sector Reform (SSR) was held; the SSR would be spilt
into five main areas with a lead nation coordinating each sector. It
is important to note that in its original format, lead nations would
not be solely responsible for their sector[38] but instead would coordinate with the Afghan and international governments, 'act[ing]
as clearing houses; identify gaps; follow up on pledges and

disbursement; and ensure deconfliction'.[39] As such, whilst it was assumed that lead nations would be the dominant contributor it was hoped that other countries would share the burden of financing and resourcing.[40] At the meeting, it was provisionally agreed that the US would rebuild the Afghan army; Japan would lead on disarmament; and Germany would rebuild the Afghan police.[41] This left two sectors: counter-narcotics and judicial reform without lead nations. Notwithstanding Blair's rousing rhetoric about the importance of combating the opium trade, Britain had yet to commit to lead on any portfolio.[42] Despite this hesitancy, events were unfolding in London which indicated that Blair may well volunteer Britain as lead nation on counter-narcotics. Shortly after the meeting, the connection between Afghan heroin and Britain was again presented to the public. On 31 January, Blair and Karzai held a joint press conference at 10 Downing Street. During the presentation, the prime minister indicated his willingness to eradicate Afghanistan's second-best known export:

> One of the things that we were able to discuss was the huge importance of making sure that Afghanistan is not just no longer used as a basis for terrorism in the world but also not used either for the drugs trade . . . Afghanistan has . . . been the centre for round about 90 per cent of the drugs on British streets and so to be able to bring about a situation in which Afghan agriculture is focused on mainstream agriculture not the poppy trade is obviously of huge significance and importance.

In his response, Karzai highlighted that opium cultivation was of mutual concern to both Afghanistan and Britain:

> We discussed various issues of mutual concern here and we had agreement on almost all of them. The question of drugs, the question of terrorism, the eradication of drugs. Afghanistan is committed to eradicating poppy cultivation and the trafficking of drugs. And we will do our best to finish it on our absolute own, but we will also need the international community to come and help us.[43]

Compensated eradication: policy discussions

In early 2002, as discussions turned to how Britain would achieve the elimination of the Afghan narcotics trade, Blair and his closest confidants shaped the debate. The prime minister not only dominated the direction of British foreign policy but also the policymaking process as he abandoned the 'regularised institutions of decision making such as the Cabinet and the Foreign Office' in favour of an informal process consisting of consultation with his inner circle. In particular, this group included Chief of Staff Jonathan Powell, Foreign Policy Adviser David Manning and media strategist Alastair Campbell and would meet frequently, sometimes multiple times per day, in the prime minister's office.[44] The intelligence chiefs, Chairman of the Joint Intelligence Committee Sir John Scarlett, Head of the SIS Sir Richard Dearlove and Sir Stephen Lander, were also part of the prime minister's inner circle. Opting to conduct policy through the 'sofa' cabinet, formal Cabinet meetings were held infrequently. In the two weeks following 9/11, the Cabinet only met twice and were bereft of rigorous policy discussion.[45] Moreover, Blair was opposed to disagreement during Cabinet meetings so before each meeting he would speak privately with ministers to ensure they were clear with *his* direction of travel.[46] It was in this informal policymaking environment that those who commanded the prime minister's ear were able to influence British counter-narcotics policies that were widely argued against by the FCO – the chief foreign policymaking organ of the British government.

In the policy discussions that took place in January and February, SIS proposals came to the fore.[47] Whilst SIS had a history of counter-narcotics work and had also been active in Afghanistan since the invasion in late 2001, they were an operational not a policy formulating department. However, in the weeks and months that followed 9/11, the intelligence chiefs, particularly Dearlove, rose in prominence. The Cambridge University graduate and twenty-five-year intelligence operative travelled extensively with Blair, becoming highly influential in his policy circle.[48] Dearlove relished commanding the prime minister's ear and proposed that his agents on the ground utilise their existing network of contacts to reduce the opium crop.[49] The task, however, was complicated by the fact that some of the poppy had already been planted by the time of the policy discussions, which limited the options available.[50] Nevertheless, the discussions were underpinned by a political imperative to act: it was inconceivable that under western supervision Afghan farmers would be unhindered in producing a substantial opium crop, especially as the previous year a Taliban ban reduced opium output by 91 per cent.[51] The Taliban's success, unfortunately, provided a measure by which British efforts would be judged.[52] Thus, SIS first advocated purchasing the entire 2002 poppy harvest from farmers to the sum of $50–150 million; however, after FCO officials objected the proposal was dropped.[53] Reportedly, the proposal was discarded because it was feared it would actually encourage more farmers to plant poppy.[54] It was not only the FCO who considered the policy to be flawed. During a statement to the House of Commons in late January, International Development Secretary Clare Short highlighted her objection to proposals to buy the crop: 'that tends to be a disastrous strategy'.[55] A modified but not too dissimilar version of the rejected SIS proposal was considered in which SIS agents would distribute money to Afghan regional leaders to compensate farmers to self-destruct their opium fields.[56] The rate of compensation was set at a lower level than a farmer would achieve selling opium. Dearlove claimed that the plan would reduce the opium crop by as much as 50 per cent.[57] The scheme was designed as a one-off and would not be repeated in future seasons. It was reasoned that once the AIA consolidated its power it would be able to implement the rule of law and provide development aid to allow farmers to transition to legal alternatives. The British government, wishfully, contended 'this year's programme is designed to reinforce this strategy'.[58] Nevertheless, Blair was attracted to the plan.[59]

Enthusiasm gathered pace within Number 10 that such an intervention was not only achievable, but it could score a success for Britain both on the international stage and domestically by reducing the flow of heroin onto the British market. Officials close to the prime minister argued that eradicating the source of British heroin would create a shortage of heroin on British streets, which in turn would result in a significant rise in the number of heroin users seeking treatment. To cope with this projected outcome, Number 10 instructed the Department of Health to formulate a plan to deal with a sudden and exponential rise in drug users presenting themselves for rehabilitation. Contrary to the projections of Number 10, Department of Health officials contended that eliminating the Afghan opium trade would not be an instantaneous process but a complex and lengthy endeavour. Moreover, health officials highlighted, even if Britain did manage to halt Afghan opium production, the British market would respond by transitioning to another heroin source to counter the shortfall and/ or heroin users would transition to another drug as opposed to seeking treatment.[60] These arguments failed to move key players, including Blair, who were now committed to upstream intervention in Afghanistan.

Whitehall, however, was divided over involvement in such a complex task. Proponents of eradication included the prime minister, HMCE and SIS. Senior HMCE officials argued that any reduction in cultivation – sustainable or otherwise – would reduce the amount of heroin reaching British streets – a key objective in their counter-narcotics strategy. In the discussions that followed, HMCE acted 'like a pressure group' to implement eradication, dismissing possible negative repercussions for Afghanistan as not *their* problem.[61] Demonstrating the proposal's divisiveness, not all HMCE officials were convinced: some argued this was a 'fucking crazy idea'.[62] Other opponents of the plan included certain officials from DFID, the Cabinet Office and the FCO's Drugs and International Crime Department.[63] The unit was headed by Michael Ryder, a former Cambridge University academic and long-standing diplomat.[64] Intelligent and well-versed in counter-narcotics policy, Ryder and his officials cautioned against Dearlove's proposal, knowing it would create perverse incentives and consequently result in more opium being grown the following year. Poppy farmers take out loans at the beginning of the growing season with the majority borrowing against delivery of their future opium harvest.[65] Therefore, by eradicating the crop without sufficient compensation, farmers would be unable to repay their debts leaving them with little option but to grow more the following year. This was compounded by the fact that the Taliban's ban had increased opium's market value from $100 per kilogram in September 2000 to $500 in July 2001.[66] There would also be problems verifying the results of the programme; a precarious security environment meant that British officials could not deploy into the provinces to verify who had or had not destroyed their crop. Nor was there a mechanism to verify that those who had destroyed their crop received compensation. Additionally, the plan would incentivise farmers to grow more opium in future seasons, as they believed that they were guaranteed to receive a cash payment for their crop.[67] A Cabinet Office official also indicated the shortcomings of the measure: 'it was a message that I gave to people as well and it was one they listened to but weren't particular keen to hear'.[68]

Before the policy was formalised Blair held an ad hoc meeting on the issue. Prior to the meeting, FCO officials briefed the Foreign Secretary Jack Straw that compensated eradication was 'a bad idea' and he should object to its introduction.[69] Straw was convinced by the arguments of his staffers, but before the meeting Blair spoke with Straw privately – which was not itself unusual.[70] Although Straw was not an integral element of Blair's foreign policy operation,[71] he had a straightforward relationship with the prime minister. Whilst it is unclear what was said in the meeting, if Straw thought there was merit in making Blair aware of the downsides, he would have.[72] As outlined above, Blair did not tolerate dissention or rigorous debate in Cabinet meetings; when the wider discussion took place, Straw did not object and the policy was approved.[73] However, with Blair's firm grip on the policymaking process, even if Straw did object, his chances of affecting a shift in policy were limited.

As noted above, the plan was adopted despite Whitehall opposition. However, two reasons had won the policy debate: first, Blair abandoned the traditional foreign policymaking process in the wake of 9/11, opting instead to conduct policy with a small group of advisors. It was in this policy environment that Dearlove, the chief proponent of the proposal, convincingly 'sold' the plan to Blair as a deliverable project.[74] The control of Downing Street over the policy was noted by a British official: 'the plan was run from Number 10, independently, secretively if you like, and with relatively little information passed on to the rest of Whitehall. It was Mr Blair's project.'[75] A British minister reiterated the same view: 'Blair had a sideshow and got on with it and we [the Cabinet] were not significant players in it.'[76]

The second reason was that other actors, most notably the FCO, failed to offer an alternative plan of action.[77] As so often was the case in the coming years, those who suggested action commanded the policy debate, as any policy – good or bad – was considered a better alternative to no policy.[78] The prime minister, therefore, was guided by the overly optimistic assessments of key decision-makers in his office, and ignored the sober arguments coming out of the FCO. The direction of counter-narcotics policy over the coming years, on both sides of the Atlantic, was heavily influenced by the views of individuals operating without the full endorsement of all government agencies.[79] It is also important to recognise that much of the early

Afghan policy was decided by those who had little knowledge of Afghanistan or its history.[80]

With the issue settled domestically, an FCO delegation travelled to Afghanistan in March to discuss the plan with the AIA and the American military. The delegation held a series of meetings with Karzai and his finance minister Ashraf Ghani. A former World Bank official (and current president), Ghani saw the limitations of the plan and agreed reluctantly on the condition that ISAF, which was stationed in and restricted to Kabul, be rolled out across the country. Karzai, however, was encouraging and agreed to the plan without condition. The British also met with US military officials, who considered the plan of little consequence to their counter-terrorism operation, therefore had no objections. Rand Beers, Assistant Secretary for INL (the US agency responsible for international counter-narcotics policies), was also equally content with plan.[81]

Not all of Britain's international partners were as ambivalent towards the proposal as the Americans, as an FCO telegram stated that 'some of our international partners expressed doubts ... [about] the programme'.[82] Whilst the document does not explicitly state the identity of the partners, UNODC officials also shared their concerns with their British counterparts, both in Kabul and in the UNODC headquarters in Vienna.[83] Despite having assumed the position of de facto lead on counter-narcotics in early 2002,[84] the UNODC's institutional and financial weakness led Britain and the US to dismiss it as 'not a significant player'.[85] Moreover, with the policymaking process centralised in Number 10, the ability of the UNODC to influence policy was considerably more limited than those in Whitehall. That said, several reasons underpinned the UNODC's opposition; foremost among them was to do with legality. A UNODC official recalled the motivation not to, at least, endorse the scheme:

> From the beginning, we had to separate ourselves from this because of legal issues. Cultivating narcotics is illegal and you do not compensate people to not do an illegal thing ... We cannot pay a trafficker to ask him, please do not traffic in our neighbourhood. It is illegal; it is internationally prohibited. At the United Nations, at that time it was my conclusion that the UN had to abide by international law and we cannot do such a thing.[86]

At the time, the UNODC estimated that opium farmers accounted for approximately 7 per cent of the total Afghan population of 24 million and that opium poppy cultivation covered 1 per cent of total arable land and less than 3 per cent of irrigated arable land in Afghanistan.[87] It was therefore argued by another UNODC official that to reward farmers for doing something illegal would send the wrong message to the 93 per cent of law abiding farmers.[88] The logic of this, unfortunately, was set against a political imperative to act.

5 Lead Nation on Counter-Narcotics, 2002

In parallel to the discussions regarding compensated eradication, the lead nation approach suggested at the Tokyo conference began to formalise. The British government had yet to decide what assistance it would provide Afghanistan but FCO officials suggested that Britain could provide the German policing effort with specific support on narcotics interdiction work. An FCO official commented that the Germans lacked capacity in that area and 'we had a bigger, more skilled and experienced counter-narcotics enforcement capacity both through the intelligence agencies and HMCE'. Shortly thereafter, FCO officials travelled to Berlin to propose their plan to their counterparts, which the Germans accepted.[1] Despite advocating helping the Germans with specific interdiction work, FCO officials at this stage warned against volunteering to lead on counter-narcotics in its entirety. With great foresight – considering Anglo-American friction between 2004 and 2007, outlined below – FCO officials assumed any long-term commitment to reduce opium cultivation through eradication would bring them into direct conflict with their closest ally: the US and its INL.[2]

Whilst the US was not concerned with counter-narcotics work in Afghanistan in 2002, it was conceivable that their policy stance would shift and, in such circumstances, they may attempt to introduce aerial eradication. The Anglo-American allies had a long history of cooperation in international narcotics-control, mostly notably in Latin America and the Caribbean. In all these instances, Britain normally played a supporting role to the main US effort, especially in Colombia. Whilst the partners broadly agreed on policy in Colombia, they held divergent views on aerial eradication, with the US (most notably INL) strongly in favour and Britain opposed. However, owing to alliance politics – and its junior role in the relationship – Britain always avoided confrontation over the issue. An FCO official recalls, 'Britain never criticised [aerial eradication] publicly but we didn't believe it worked; on the contrary actually we believed it was counterproductive.' The official further noted that if Congress

> started to take an interest [in counter-narcotics in Afghanistan] then INL would press for aerial spraying and we would be on the other side of the argument and, inevitably then, publicly so. This was a position we had always managed to avoid before.[3]

If Britain assumed lead nation on counter-narcotics in Afghanistan, it would have no choice but to oppose INL's push for aerial eradication. The views expressed above reveal that even when the US was not an active participant in the policymaking process, a major consideration for FCO officials before deciding policy was: how will this affect alliance unity?[4] Above all, the maintenance of the special relationship was the core objective. But it was not only the prospect of direct confrontation with the US that persuaded FCO officials against taking on lead nation on counter-narcotics. Evidence from Thailand, Burma and Latin America indicated that it could take thirty years for counter-narcotics policies in developing nations to be successful.

The FCO position therefore had merit. If Britain took the G8 lead nation role it would either be confronted with Pentagon indifference to the narcotics brief or significant policy friction with INL over aerial eradication. Nevertheless, such a well-reasoned position could not stand if the occupier of 10 Downing Street threw his weight behind the idea of Britain taking the lead role on counter-narcotics. In fact, several reasons underpinned Britain's decision to volunteer for the position. First, the forthcoming compensated eradication scheme had inflated Number 10's belief that they could be successful in destroying the Afghan narcotics trade, and because of their role in the programme, Britain was somewhat thrust into the most obvious choice for lead nation.[5] Second, with Blair positioning Britain as the US's key partner in the global war on terror, it needed to take on a role that was commensurate with its international stature. Additionally, combating the narcotics trade was, as the prime minister stated on several occasions, directly beneficial to Britain. With the US assuming the lead for reforming the military, Germany for the police and Japan for disarmament, counter-narcotics was the best option left available. A British minister suspects:

> He [Blair] decided it would look good and sound good and he would do it. And of course, he intended to instruct officials to get on with it . . . There was never a Cabinet discussion on drugs . . . [nor was the decision to lead on drugs] thrashed out.[6]

Third, there was a perception within some sections of the British government that the Taliban's poppy ban a few years previously indicated that opium cultivation could be eliminated. Once again, despite the warnings of those within the FCO and other departments, Number 10 officials demonstrated a poor reading of the problem by volunteering to take on the role of G8 lead nation on counter-narcotics.

On 2 April, during a G8 donors' meeting at the Canadian Embassy in Geneva, Britain confirmed its intention to lead on counter-narcotics.[7] According to an FCO telegram sent back to London the following day, the Germans had indicated they were happy with the new arrangement: 'the Germans seemed content to hand over the counter-narcotics portfolio to Britain, saying to us that there was plenty of work to go around'. The telegram went on to comment: 'The British contribution to Afghanistan so far; our willingness to consider further SSR support; and our agreement to lead on counter-narcotics were much appreciated, in particular by the US, Brahimi and [Afghan Foreign Minister] Abdullah.'[8] The US, however, was less interested in what area Britain led on, as opposed to the fact that they made a substantial commitment.[9] Britain's involvement provided the US with a legitimising counterweight to unilateral action, demonstrating British fulfilment of a historic role in the relationship.

Compensated eradication: it's a success!

Meanwhile, Blair was so optimistic about the success of the forthcoming compensated eradication plan he was reported in the *Sunday Mirror*, saying the aim of the eradication plan 'is about persuading the local population with incentives to grow other things. With a relatively small commitment from us, we can hopefully curb the flow of hard drugs into Europe and on to our streets.'[10] Convinced by the arguments of Dearlove, the prime minister believed upstream interdiction would 'create a big win in terms of the British drug problem'.[11] This confidence and even more modest ambitions of later years were all to prove over-optimistic and unrealistic.

On 3 April 2002, after approval by the Cabinet, the AIA issued a decree that outlined the eradication programme designed by the British government. In a not so subtle nod to the motivations for supporting the project, Karzai stated 'drugs were not only poisoning the lives of young Afghan people, but also of the people in countries supporting Afghanistan. Continuation of drug cultivation and trafficking would endanger this support.'[12] Although eliminating opium cultivation was more of a western than an Afghan objective, the AIA judged that development aid might not be forthcoming if they did not take steps to curb the trade.

The eradication programme, under the British codename Operation Drown, commenced on 8 April 2002 in Helmand and Nangarhar provinces (it later rolled out to Badakhshan, Uruzgan, Kunar and Laghman provinces).[13] As part of the compensated eradication agenda, farmers were originally promised compensation of US $1,250 per ha destroyed, which would be paid in cash at the time of destruction. However, three days after the programme commenced, Karzai, for reasons unknown (but presumably to placate farmers or to convince regional authorities to sanction the scheme), raised the compensation to $1,750 per ha.[14] The eradication scheme was also accompanied by a one-off interdiction operation at an opium bazaar in Nangarhar Province.[15]

By May, a superficial reading of compensated eradication's effectiveness was positive, and this was reflected in the FCO's guardedly optimistic progress reports. Telegrams reported that the scheme had had a positive impact, with farmers realising opium cultivation was illegal and would not be accepted – all of which bode well for the future elimination of opium cultivation. The reports also repeatedly reinforced the link between domestic and foreign policy by translating the number of ha of opium destroyed in Afghanistan to the equivalent reduction of heroin on British streets.[16] This was important as several British newspaper articles had questioned the effectiveness of the programme. To counter these claims, an FCO report suggested that the best course of action would be to release the eradication figures stating: 'we now have an excellent story to tell' which illustrated how much heroin had been taken off British streets. This would 'play well across the . . . media'.[17] There was also the need to deliver a positive political statement to Parliament. Given FCO reservations about compensated eradication it was all rather ironic, but as Blair had sanctioned the scheme, FCO ministers now had little option but to sell it. Their job was helped by the fact that, taken at face value, the scheme was working. In May, FCO Minister Denis MacShane addressed the House of Commons:

> It is a key, if unsung, aspect of Foreign and Commonwealth Office work to cut off, disrupt and delay the flow of heroin . . . to the United Kingdom . . . I should like to inform the House that the Interim Administration in Kabul today announced the eradication of 16,[500] ha of opium poppies, which is about half the size of the New Forest, with a street value in Britain of approximately £5 billion. The United Kingdom has taken the lead with the Interim Administration in that task, and work to eradicate opium poppies continues as I speak. I congratulate the Interim Administration on the progress that they have made so far . . . The very good news about the opium poppy eradication programme shows that farmers are ready to turn away from opium poppy production and from drug barons and drug traffickers, to build new lives for themselves and their families, with the help of further investment.[18]

Buoyed by the apparent success of the compensated eradication plan, ministers declared that they had dealt a substantial blow to the Afghan narcotics trade. The operation had reportedly destroyed 16,500 ha of opium cultivation, which was equivalent to 25 to 30 per cent of the entire crop. FCO reports repeated the domestic link: 'this equates to 76 tons of heroin, or up to three times the annual heroin consumption in Britain, worth about £5 billion at current street prices . . . by any standards this is a dramatic intervention'.[19] The British government contributed approximately £21.25 million to the programme.[20] There was also a comparison drawn to illustrate that compensated eradication was value for money: for a cost of £21.5 million, £5 billion of heroin was taken off the streets. It was reasoned that this 'success' would spark a permanent shift away from opium cultivation until the entire opium trade in Afghanistan was eliminated.[21] Around the same time, HMCE dispatched its first Drug Liaison Officer to Kabul to prepare the groundwork for gathering intelligence against narcotics networks and building the capacity of Afghan law enforcement.[22]

Britain's ten-year counter-narcotics target

With Britain now coordinating the international counter-narcotics effort in Afghanistan, Number 10 had repeatedly requested that the FCO's Drugs and International Crime Department formulate targets for what they wanted to achieve in Afghanistan and a timeline to achieve them. Although compensated eradication appeared to be working, officials in the department were still concerned that any success in Afghanistan would be hard fought. As a result, they were reluctant to quantify their aims and, more importantly, any timelines. In particular, the lack of government capacity in Afghanistan and the difficulty in achieving any targets in a post-conflict zone convinced FCO officials that the likelihood in achieving their targets were non-existent – therefore, it would be prudent not to set any. Downing Street was aware of the FCO's reasoning not to do so.[23]

In June 2002, Blair planned to use a G8 summit in Kananaskis, Canada, to encourage the international coalition to support and, significantly, contribute funds to the counter-narcotics mission in Afghanistan. To do this, he needed a timeline to sell to the international community. Political expediency was about to compromise the reality of the task ahead. Shortly before the prime minister was scheduled to address the summit, his secretary contacted FCO officials and tasked them with formulating a timeline.[24] Representatives from across Whitehall had previously reported to Number 10 that any attempt to eliminate the narcotics trade could take up to a generation. This assessment did not have the political impact that Blair and his advisors wanted, therefore officials had no option but to amend their projection to a more politically advantageous timescale of reducing opium cultivation by 70 per cent in five years and the complete elimination of cultivation by 2013.[25] The targets were qualified and contained numerous caveats but were based on several assumptions: first, the fact that British assets were on the ground could potentially hasten progress; second, as the lead nation roles were originally conceived as collaborative efforts, it was assumed that the US and the rest of international community would contribute resources to the counter-narcotics effort which would further accelerate the timetable.[26]

In the event, Blair for reasons unknown, did not present his plan at the G8 summit, but it emerged anyway. Unaware that the prime minister had not discussed the issue, his press officer mistakenly informed the media that Britain had outlined a roadmap for the complete elimination of opium cultivation within ten years. With a Spending Review approaching, HM Treasury tasked the FCO with formulating a delivery plan to honour this commitment that was now in the public domain.[27] Thus, the British government had committed to eliminate opium cultivation in ten years, in a fashion that would have been at home in a satirical television programme. The targets failed to appreciate the complexities of the problem and the limited capacity of the AIA to implement an accelerated counter-narcotics strategy. Nevertheless, Britain now had this target to deliver, even though FCO officials believed it improbable. By publicly declaring such a goal, success or failure would be easy to judge, which, ultimately placed more pressure on the British government.

Reality sets in: compensated eradication

By mid-2002, it was evident that the optimism and self-congratulation of ministers was premature as the compensated eradication plan ran into several problems. It was, in fact, severely flawed on many levels. The most basic and fundamental problem with the scheme was that it proved ineffective: it did not lead to a 50 per cent reduction in the opium crop, as Dearlove had claimed.[28] Instead, the UNODC estimated that 74,000 ha of opium were cultivated – up from 8,000 ha the previous year – and had spread to twenty-four out of thirty-two provinces.[29] Moreover, MacShane's assertion that the policy had destroyed 16,500 ha was refuted by internal FCO reports, which claimed there had been fraud and over-reporting.[30] An HMCE official recalled:

> there was a dispute about how effective it had been. [There were] figures floating around Whitehall [claiming] that it was completely ineffective [but] other figures [claimed] that it seemed effective . . . Nobody really knew the percentages . . . There was no accepted truth.[31]

Although the true eradication figure is unknown, it certainly was less than the figure cited by MacShane. Nor did the policy discourage farmers from planting the following season. Instead, by August, FCO reports indicated that not only were farmers replanting opium in the expectation that they would be compensated, the programme also incentivised them to increase the amount planted.[32]

The programme was beset by mismanagement and chaotic implementation. Not unsurprisingly – given the historically weak nature of the Afghan state and the transitional process at government level – the AIA lacked the capacity to administer the programme. A UNODC official summed up the lack of functioning capability at AIA level: 'There was no Afghan government . . . there was nobody on the Afghan side, you only had Karzai . . . and then his national security advisor.'[33] Britain's ability to administer the programme was also constrained by a precarious security environment[34] and the institutional infancy of the British Embassy in Kabul: it only reopened in late November 2001.[35] Consequently, FCO officials' fears were realised: limited manpower and resources hindered Britain's operational capacity to oversee the programme. The British and AIA, therefore, resorted to local Afghan authorities to administer and supervise the programme.[36] With local non-governmental organisations in control of the programme and no independent adjudication in place, the scheme was marred by corruption and fraud, particularly in Helmand. In some instances, farmers claimed more compensation than they were due, and, in more extreme cases, some farmers claimed compensation after harvesting their crop.[37] Other farmers, however, were less fortunate and despite complying with the eradication programme did not receive compensation and were left with no crops and no money. FCO documents indicated that there were anecdotal reports that 3,000 farmers in Nangarhar did not receive any payment and had launched legal proceedings. Without being able to verify if the claims were true or not, the reports demonstrate that at least some farmers did not benefit from the scheme.[38] As with most eradication campaigns in Afghanistan, corruption was a significant influence on whether a field was eradicated, with the main determining factor being the ability to 'buy off' eradication teams. Consequently, it was poor farmers with no financial backing who suffered the most.

In southern and eastern regions, the scheme was also disrupted by violence as farmers staged protests resulting in the abandonment of some eradication efforts. The scenes of violence worsened in Helmand Province with police killing eight farmers and wounding several other protestors.[39] Also, landmines were used to destroy eradication tractors[40] as protestors fought to save their crops. The one-off interdiction of narcotics from Nangarhar Province was also marred in controversy. The narcotics seized during the operation were taken to Kabul and ceremonially burned in a display of triumph; however, British analysis of the narcotics revealed that they were in fact waste product from processing.[41] Not for the last time in the counter-narcotics campaign, the integrity of some Afghan law enforcement officers was brought into question after narcotics were seized.

Ultimately the programme was an unmitigated failure. After the scheme failed to deliver on its promises of compensation, farmers returned to poppy cultivation. Both the British and Afghan governments distanced themselves from the scheme, blaming each other. Back in Whitehall, officials refused to publicly accept full responsibility for the failure and indicated that while Britain funded the programme this was an Afghan-run programme. Internally, recriminations over the botched scheme took place as Straw confronted Dearlove over his failure to deliver the promised results. The two men engaged in a heated discussion and the latter downplayed the promised results of the scheme.[42] Reportedly, the Foreign Secretary would not have Operation Drown mentioned in front of him again.[43] Karzai, according to a British official, was more sanguine: 'Karzai did not complain about the failure of the compensated eradication scheme, he liked Blair and he thought that Blair was trying to help him. He was not critical.' That said, Karzai did not see compensated eradication as an end to narcotics control efforts, as the official further explains:

President Karzai from the second half of 2002 was concerned that the revival of the drugs economy would undermine him and the legitimacy of his government. He thought that something needed to be done, and like so many facing this problem, he thought enforcement measures and eradication was the way to do it. Karzai pressed the British government to stop this crop from being harvested and wanted to use British troops to do it.[44]

It is not entirely clear if Karzai genuinely believed in the importance of tackling the narcotics trade as a prerequisite for a stable
and democratic Afghanistan; or was concerned that a resurgent
narcotics trade would undermine his authority domestically and
internationally; or was simply playing to the western audience.
Whatever his motivation, Karzai continued to lobby British officials to use British soldiers to destroy the following year's poppy
crop.[45] Whilst Karzai attempted to generate support for his plan,
Britain and the UNODC set about laying the foundations of counter-narcotics institutions. They established the Counter-Narcotics
Directorate (CND) under the authority of the National Security
Council (NSC).[46] The CND was responsible for counter-narcotics
policy formulation and coordination, with the implementation of
policy the preserve of the various ministries.[47]

In the meantime, Britain was confronted with a more immediate
problem: how to accelerate its interdiction activities to deal with
the remnants of the 2002 opium crop. With, at least, two thirds of
the crop heading into the trafficking chain, British security agencies and Special Forces undertook action to interdict 'narcotics in
transit, [and in] processing facilities and stockpiles'. Along with
quick impact alternative livelihoods, interdiction was promoted
as Britain's most immediate counter-narcotics objective in the
latter half of 2002.[48] In addition to reducing the volume of narcotics available, British officials hoped to inflict a 'psychological
impact' on the narcotics trade by increasing both the 'perceived
and actual risks' associated with trafficking. Equally important
was the desire to demonstrate 'to farmers, in many ways the
victims of opium cultivation, that they were not the sole focus of
law enforcement'.[49] Nevertheless, during this period, interdiction
– like all counter-narcotics interventions – was reactive and ad
hoc. Consequently, narcotics seizures were small, totalling only
0.4 per cent of output.[50] It soon became clear to the British that
with few resources on the ground, added to the complexity of
operating in Afghanistan, countering narcotics was an indomita-
ble challenge. The British desperately needed US support to make
progress; however, its special relationship ally was unwilling to
veer from its counter-terrorism mission.

6 Counter-Narcotics on the Hoof, 2002–2004

Throughout 2002, Rumsfeld and the US military remained opposed to counter-narcotics work, but despite this, British officials and politicians gently petitioned their counterpart for help.[1] On one occasion, Defence Secretary Geoff Hoon raised the issue with the commanders of the Combined Joint Task Force 180 (CJTF-180) at Bagram Air Base, north of Kabul. Hoon's message was direct: the US military needed to do more to help Britain with counter-narcotics work. A US military officer recalls:

> We had an intense talk about counter-narcotics, and it was something of a dilemma to me because Rumsfeld had made it very clear, I was not to involve myself in counter-narcotics unless it had something directly to do with a tactical situation . . . Hoon was adamant that I had to do more . . . I said okay, I got it and I will keep that in mind, but I was not unmindful of what Rumsfeld had told me.[2]

While CJTF-180 did, occasionally, destroy narcotics facilities if it was to its tactical advantage, a US military officer noted that: 'if it [narcotics] was not directly in the way, I didn't typically do a lot with it'.[3] Therefore, the US military held to Rumsfeld's line, as they were duty bound to do, and Hoon's request was rejected. The issue, however, remained unresolved and was not long in coming to light again.

In October 2002,[4] an FCO delegation travelled to Afghanistan to assess British operations and on their return Parliamentary Under-Secretary Mike O'Brien suggested – a carbon copy of Karzai's plan – that Britain deploy soldiers to enforce the eradication of opium fields. Ministry of Defence (MOD) officials, concerned by the possible blowback to British forces, objected to this. They feared that they would alienate farmers and rural communities and, in doing so, push them into the hands of the Taliban. So, a revised plan emerged with the British military supporting an Afghan military unit to oversee eradication. The plan was unpromisingly like Britain's failed eradication scheme the previous spring; it relied on an Afghan military unit being combat ready, which it was not. The logic of that fact dictated that for the plan to be effective it would require the US to provide emergency extraction support in case the unit ran into difficulties, something the US military would be reluctant to do, and which could likely cause friction between Britain and the US. In effect, what the British were doing was drawing the US into counter-narcotics activity against the stated wishes of the Pentagon.

In November, the issue went before a Whitehall ministerial meeting chaired by Straw and attended by Short, and MOD and Cabinet Office representatives. The outcome of the meeting was agreement on the broad contours of the policy. To facilitate the US's acquiescence, Blair wrote to Bush outlining the proposal and asking for support. However, in the words of an FCO official, 'there was no reply for an extremely long time'.[5] British officials were then forced to contact their US counterparts to enquire over the long delay. This was followed by an FCO delegation travelling to the US to discuss the issue with INL, Department of Defense (DOD) and other Washington officials. Shortly afterwards, in January 2003, Blair finally received a letter from Bush indicating that crucially the US military in Afghanistan would provide the necessary support.[6]

So, after an unusual breakdown in communication between the heads of state, there was apparent consensus in the Anglo-American alliance to launch, what would be in effect, the first joint Anglo-American counter-narcotics operation in Afghanistan. FCO officials travelled to Kabul 'armed with the president's letter' to discuss the plan with the US military. British officials met with Lieutenant General McNeill and Major General Karl Eikenberry to discuss the plan, both of whom politely but blankly refused to help.[7] A US military commander repeated what he had told Hoon several months previously: 'my orders were not to involve myself in counter-narcotics operations'.[8] Without written instruction from Rumsfeld that the mission was to change, even the president was limited in his ability to shape policy in Afghanistan. An FCO official suspected that the US position was bolstered after they had persuaded the AIA not to authorise the plan:

The Americans said: it's a nice letter but we are not doing that – in only the way the US military can ignore their commanding officer. The Afghans who had clearly been worked on by the Americans in advance – and so had the British military – said we don't want you doing that, thank you very much. This is exactly the point in which Britain and the US were gearing up to invade Iraq. So that, far more than anything to do with Afghanistan, is what had the attention of ministers.[9]

The official also suspected that the British military, which were sceptical about the compatibility of counter-narcotics work and winning hearts and minds, had in fact supported the American military's refusal to grant the British government their wish. As detailed below, the British military, much like the US military, remained opposed to counter-narcotics work for most of their time in Afghanistan. There was also a division between civilian and military officials over objectives, outcomes and resources.

On their return to Britain, the delegation learned that the plan that had the prime minister's and president's approval was dead. The US military had prevented any joint counter-narcotics programmes even though the president had committed the US to counter-narcotics. An FCO official stated why there was no further debate or recourse over the proposal:

had it only been the Americans then we might have got Mr Blair to write to Mr Bush again saying surely there has been a misunderstanding here. But the Afghans [who had been pressured by the Americans] had also been very clear they did not want it; so, in those circumstances there was obviously no point.[10]

The episode reinforces two themes: first, that the direction of the campaign was dominated by the Pentagon and military command in Afghanistan. Second, that the US military paid little attention to the wishes of its special relationship ally – even when the plan received the approval of the prime minister and president – when it did not suit its aims and objectives.

With the failure to reach an agreement on a military-backed eradication force, civilian, governor-led eradication (GLE) was introduced. The scheme, in theory, incentivised provincial governors with financial reimbursement to eradicate poppy fields in their provinces. The policy was meant to act as a deterrent to prevent farmers from planting poppy and reward those governors who showed 'commitment' to tackle opium cultivation. However, like its predecessor, this policy was open to abuse and corruption. Farmers, if they could afford to, could prevent their fields being destroyed by bribing the governor. Likewise, there were allegations that those governors who were involved in the narcotics trade themselves directed action against their political opponents.[11]

Given the sensitive nature of eradication and hangover from Operation Drown, Straw commissioned a review to assess the effectiveness of eradication.[12] FCO officials concluded that eradication was a necessary tool – as a deterrent to cultivation – but one only to be utilised when there were clear alternative livelihoods to opium cultivation available. Crucially, considered counterproductive, were poorly targeted eradication schemes, which often led to increased opium cultivation in subsequent years to retrieve the financial loss of eradicated poppy fields. That in turn damaged coalition military objectives by turning the local population against the allies. Designed to provide a balance between incentive and disincentive, British policy held promise only when applied when local security and economic conditions were appropriate.[13] Moreover, British officials argued it was only acceptable to eradicate poppy fields during the infancy phase of growth, when farmers had invested minimum effort. They opposed eradication at the flowering pre-harvest stage, when farmers had invested considerable money, time and effort, which would increase the possibility of a hostile response from farmers. Additionally, farmers would not have the option of sowing and harvesting an alternative.[14]

With Geoff Hoon and Clare Short's support, this was adopted as Britain's official eradication policy.[15] While from a rational point of view, British policy might now seem cogent, it quickly led to a disagreement with its transatlantic partner. This time not so much with the Pentagon, but with those agencies in Washington that favoured aggressive eradication, namely INL. It favoured a policy that attacked poppy fields regardless of whether the local conditions were right or alternative livelihoods were in place. The scene was set early for serious problems to develop among the allies on counter-narcotics policy.

Limp on with alternative livelihoods and interdiction

As the British government grappled with the complexity of the opium problem, it abandoned one-dimensional policies, such as compensated eradication, and developed a broader counter-narcotics strategy. Although Britain moved towards developing longer-term policies, officials were still under pressure to deliver unachievable results. Cabinet Office officials explained to the prime minister the experience of reducing high-value, high-demand narcotics cultivation in other developing countries: it took a long time and correlated with wider economic development. Blair listened carefully but probably thought this another example of officials producing good analysis but lacking the dynamism to solve problems.[16] Nevertheless, in Whitehall, there was 'a constant doctrinal debate' regarding the best way to tackle the opium problem. A British official noted that the government half-heartedly 'limped on and resolved its differences around the idea that interdiction, alternative livelihoods and capacity building were the best policies for counter-narcotics'.[17]

One consequence of compensated eradication's failure was that the decision-making process – something that to that point had been centralised in Number 10 – was broadened to include other Whitehall departments and those who were not in Blair's inner circle. Cabinet Office officials had argued that to give the counter-narcotics strategy the best chance of succeeding, a strong cross-government effort, with the full engagement of all relevant spending departments, including DFID – which held expertise on alternative livelihoods – FCO, HMCE and intelligence agencies was required. Until the 2003 Iraq War, formal Cabinet foreign and defence subcommittees had been absent from governmental decision-making, but Blair now agreed to also start ministerial meetings for Afghanistan, enabling a more balanced and transparent policy debate on counter-narcotics.[18] Other than several ad hoc meetings – between either Blair or Straw or among other ministers – most of the policy meetings prior to this point were conducted by civil servants, with limited ministerial input.[19]

Although alternative livelihoods were promoted as a central pillar in Britain's strategy, disagreement ensued about where development aid should be directed and who should benefit from it. DFID never fully embraced the counter-narcotics mission, arguing that its core objective was poverty alleviation – the 2002 International Development Act required that the purpose of all aid spending was poverty reduction – not providing aid to poppy farmers, who already had an income. During the subsequent discussions, Short was determined not to launch an alternative livelihood programme in Helmand, Afghanistan's most prolific poppy producing province.[20] In the end, a middle ground was reached as DFID launched an alternative livelihoods programme in Badakhshan, which had the dubious honour of being one of Afghanistan's poorest and highest opium producing provinces.[21] Even in later years, however, DFID never fully resolved the tension surrounding how to combine poppy reduction with poverty reduction. Nevertheless, it remained a reluctant participant in the counter-narcotics process.

As a more formalised approach to counter-narcotics emerged, Britain drafted a 2003 Delivery Plan then transferred the key elements of it to the first Afghan National Drug Control Strategy (ANDCS). Coming into effect in May 2003, the ANDCS was centred on four key principles: improved drugs law enforcement; alternative livelihoods for poppy farmers; capacity building for Afghan anti-drugs institutions; and public awareness campaigns/ treatment programmes to help reduce demand.[22] The document demonstrated a degree of apt measure when assessing the correct prerequisites to address the narcotics problem and stipulated that alternative livelihoods were an essential condition of eradication.[23] Unfortunately, the ANDCS reaffirmed the overly ambitious and unhelpful target – which emanated from Blair's trip to the G8 summit the previous June – for total elimination of opium cultivation within ten years.[24]

In support of the new strategy, Britain established the British Embassy Drugs Team (BEDT) in Kabul,[25] to deliver its counter-narcotics strategy, devised by the FCO in London.[26] However, the investment in resources failed to match the scale of the problem, causing a British military officer later to note, 'the Embassy was very poorly manned, not a great influence [and] . . . did not have the horsepower to do the job'.[27] In both London and Kabul, staff were posted on short-term contracts, working anywhere between one and three years. As detailed later, this constrained the formation of an institutional memory about why and how policy positions had developed.[28] Additionally, the high turnover of staff meant there was never an entirely consistent approach to policy, as incoming officials often had different ideas about what the problem was and the best method to tackle it.[29]

More importantly, the counter-narcotics mission was grossly under-funded. Over the subsequent three-year period, Britain committed £70 million to tackle narcotics in Afghanistan – an undemocratic, low-income, highly corrupt society that had been devastated by decades of conflict, not to mention the fact that it was one of the largest narcotics producers in the world. To place this into context, the Labour government committed approximately four-and-a-half times more – £300 million from 2001 to 2004 – to fight narcotics use in Britain[30] – a democratic, high-income, rule of law society. The lack of resources, however, was symptomatic of the wider problem: counter-narcotics – because of its inherent complexity and Whitehall's lack of enthusiasm to deal with it – was separated out as strand of policy, divorced from the larger effort. Britain may have been lead nation on counter-narcotics, but as a British official observed, for most of the Government 'the drugs issue was in the too difficult tray'. Unfortunately, counter-narcotics remained siloed for most, if not all, of Britain's time as lead nation. The official further notes:

> Whitehall could not get their ducks in a row over this . . . [and were] . . . hamstrung . . . In this period, counter-narcotics was done on the hoof . . . activity was deployed in a piecemeal fashion with a number of small initiatives. I would counsel against thinking counter-narcotics policies were highly organised or coherent.[31]

With counter-narcotics being 'done on the hoof', Britain failed to make significant headway against the narcotics industry. During this phase of the counter-narcotics campaign, it is fair to say that Britain never got to grips with being lead nation or implementing any thoroughgoing or long-term policy to eliminate opium cultivation.[32] All of which demonstrated that it did not have the resources to run an independent strategy for dealing with narcotics; that complicated the relationship with the US. One of the fundamental problems was that the lead nation approach originally expected that each designated country coordinate the international effort, not to assume the effort in its entirety. With little international help, Britain was under-equipped and ill prepared to deal with rising levels of opium cultivation.[33]

There was also a broader international context to consider. In

2003, Britain was gearing up, as part of the US coalition, to invade Iraq; therefore, it was predictable that counter-narcotics – a small but important part of the conflict – was relegated from ministers' thoughts. A British minister recalled the panic in government: 'in the run-up to Iraq the whole of Whitehall was fraught and worried; they were mesmerised by Iraq'.[34] Paradoxically, as Afghanistan was downgraded in favour of Iraq, Rumsfeld accepted that the Afghan conflict – apart from the counter-terrorism mission against al-Qaeda – had progressed to a predominately state-building effort.[35] This came largely as a result of Marin Strmecki's work, who was the DOD's Afghanistan policy coordinator and former assistant to Richard Nixon.[36] Strmecki's efforts also coincided with the work of Zalmay Khalilzad, the president's special envoy to Afghanistan, who proposed what became known as Accelerating Success in Afghanistan. The plan was a blueprint to increase support in a range of political, economic and military areas and, once approved by Bush, was funded to the tune of $1.6 billion.[37] Rumsfeld's volte-face on state-building was not, as Farrell suggests, 'about America making a long-time commitment to Afghanistan but rather the reverse . . . [Rumsfeld thought] that pouring more aid into Afghanistan would actually enable the US military to pull out more quickly'.[38] With this in mind, and to allow the US to concentrate on Iraq, Rumsfeld passed the reconstruction agenda onto NATO, which was soon to be responsible for post-conflict Afghanistan.

As the US accepted a limited form of state-building, there was steadily growing pressure to include counter-narcotics in the reconstruction agenda. Over the course of 2003, small improvements were made at the US Embassy in Kabul. The Drug Enforcement Administration (DEA) reopened its Afghanistan office for the first time in twenty-four years[39] – although most of its staff were not permanent. This was followed by the deployment of a single INL official based at the embassy, who oversaw both the counter-narcotics and police programmes, funded by millions of dollars. This was not promising and, moreover, most staff posted to Afghanistan during this period were of junior rank and consequently inexperienced.[40]

In Washington, there was also some limited movement towards incorporating counter-narcotics into the broader mission. One of the most ardent proponents of this was Robert B. Charles, Rand Beers' successor as head of INL. An Oxford University and Columbia Law School graduate, Charles had practiced law before briefly serving in the George H. W. Bush administration. It was his time as chief staffer to the House Speaker's Task Force on Counter-Narcotics,[41] and exposure to US policy in Colombia, however, that most profoundly shaped his view of the Afghan narcotics problem.[42] Concerned that escalating opium cultivation would engulf the state-building project, Charles advocated that the US formulate a counter-narcotics strategy for Afghanistan, something which to that point had been absent.[43] Nevertheless, this strategy was some time in coming as most of the Bush Cabinet were still either ignorant of Afghanistan's narcotics problem or simply refused to dedicate any significant attention to it. A State Department official complained: 'I think the problem was, except for a few of us, nobody believed that the narcotics problem was really that important.'[44] With Iraq commanding the attention of the Cabinet, Charles struggled to raise the profile of the Afghan narcotics problem in Washington, with his message going unheeded by everyone at senior levels apart from his boss, Secretary of State Colin Powell.[45]

Law enforcement, interdiction and criminal justice

Another key pillar in Britain's strategy was building counter-narcotics law enforcement capacity. However, the challenge was complicated by the fact that Afghanistan lacked a functioning civilian police force, law enforcement institutions and judiciary.[46] Nevertheless, in October 2003, HMCE began training the Counter-Narcotics Police of Afghanistan (CNPA) to conduct mobile detection missions around Kabul's city gates.[47] Unsurprisingly, the CNPA – which was formed nine months previously as Afghanistan's premier counter-narcotics law enforcement agency – did not have basic law enforcement skills, let alone specialist counter-narcotics skills.[48] An HMCE official recalled the frustration: '[we] thought sod it; give us a bunch of individuals and we will work with them and turn them into something remotely useful'.[49] The situation, however, was far from encouraging. An illustration of the task facing HMCE was that the CNPA did not have the mechanisms or resources to pay informants so, instead, they let them keep 'a portion of the opiates [the CNPA] seized'.[50]

In December, the team deployed units around the city's five

gates to conduct stop and search missions.[51] It was a limited operation, but despite the odds, the project yielded modest results. However, an HMCE official put things in broader perspective by observing that:

> people said interdiction on that level is good, but it is not going to set the heaven on fire. About 2 to 3 metric tons of heroin comes into Britain each year and you have only seen 20 kilos of it? People wanted more than that.[52]

Again, the political pressure to achieve progress did not mesh with the realities of Afghanistan.

The period also saw the emergence of a limited but functional Anglo-American counter-narcotics partnership. A disillusioned DEA advance party had withdrawn from Afghanistan in 2002, but HMCE petitioned the DEA to come back, which they did in 2003.[53] Constrained by a lack of US support and Afghan law enforcement capacity,[54] the DEA agent worked in close collaboration with HMCE officials. Both partners forged a good working relationship but an HMCE official attributed that to the DEA mission being small:

> You get DEA [agents] in small numbers they work well, you get lots of cooperation, and understanding – they are not particularly selfish. Get them in large numbers and they are impossible to work with, because [they think] who are you? We don't need you. That's the Americans for you, you just have to live with that.[55]

By late 2003, Britain had established an elite level interdiction unit, the Afghan Special Narcotics Force (ASNF), or Task Force-333, under the guidance of British Special Forces. A military officer noted: 'they were . . . well trained, well equipped and well-motivated . . . they were very effective'.[56] Although the Special Air Service (SAS) had been active in small-scale targeting of narcotics targets since late 2001,[57] the creation of the ASNF formalised Afghanistan's interdiction capability. The officer noted why the British considered interdiction a fruitful course of action:

> dealing with the level of the farmer was always going to be fraught with difficulty. So [we wanted to] deal with the next tier up, the people who make money out of it, [those] it wasn't an essential part of their

livelihood, it was mere criminal activity. [That is why] interdiction was our favoured approach.[58]

The commando-style unit, which was held in high regard on both sides of the Atlantic, scored some tactical successes as interdiction increased in the succeeding years.[59]

Although interdiction efforts were moving in the right – albeit slowly – direction, there were still fundamental problems complicating their effectiveness, namely discriminatory implementation and corruption. Adam Pain argues that corrupt Afghan officials targeted low-level producers and traffickers for interdiction campaigns while major producers and traffickers, linked to the authorities, strengthened their positions through the elimination of their competition. Provincial authorities charged traffickers to protect their merchandise against impoundment from the government or theft from rival narcotics dealers. As with eradication campaigns, those most affected were small traders with little financial and tribal backing. Those who capitalised on this system had connections with insurgents, warlords or the provincial and central government.[60] It was not unusual for corrupt government officials to work with narcotics traffickers or insurgents.[61] The weakness of the new authority lay in the fact that, in an effort to temper the power of regional warlords, they were incorporated into the national administration.[62] Warlords who were heavily involved in the narcotics industry were given high-ranking government positions, in what David Bewley-Taylor described as 'the development of a criminal-political nexus'.[63] While in office many warlords increased their power whilst continuing in illegal activities.[64] Instead of strengthening the position of the government through the integration of local warlords, the new administration was prevented from developing a corruption-free and accountable government. This criminal–political nexus ran through the core of the state, affecting the police, judicial system, parliament and all levels of the national, provincial and district apparatus.[65]

Interdiction campaigns were also hindered by the lack of a functioning judicial and correctional system. Much like every other facet of the Afghan state, decades of conflict had eroded Afghanistan's legal structure and its ability to implement the rule of law. It was no surprise that in the post-2001 landscape, the judiciary was non-existent and was bereft of legal experts, prosecutors, judges and a corruption-free prison system.[66] Therefore, British and Afghan forces were unable to apprehend major narcotics traffickers due to institutional weakness, as a British minister commented: 'we knew where some of the ring-leaders were but if you captured them where do you take them?' The minister further elaborates the pitfalls of making high level arrests: 'if you couldn't follow through because of law enforcement [weakness] you almost make the situation worse'.[67] To combat this, several projects were initiated by Britain and the US to rebuild the criminal justice infrastructure, but they were a long time in developing.

Counter-narcotics moves into focus

By early 2004, counter-narcotics had gravitated up the US policy agenda. In part, this was a spill-over from the increased focus on state-building, and Khalilzad's appointment as US Ambassador to Afghanistan the previous November.[68] Born in Mazar-e-Sharif, Khalilzad gained a PhD from the University of Chicago then served in numerous government departments, including Defense, where he worked for both Cheney and then Rumsfeld.[69] During his two years in Kabul, Khalilzad exercised unrivalled influence over US policy, earning the nickname the 'American Viceroy'. Not only was he well connected to the influential neo-conservatives in Washington, Khalilzad also developed an extremely close relationship with Karzai – with both men dining together each evening.[70] As counter-narcotics became a live issue, Khalilzad appointed veteran DEA agent Doug Wankel as director of the Kabul Counter-Narcotics Task Force to coordinate US counter-narcotics efforts.[71] This was a major step up in US counter-narcotics capabilities.

There was also a second more pressing reason why counter-narcotics rose in prominence. By spring, reports had surfaced that Afghanistan was on course to produce a record amount of opium.[72] This dramatic rise in cultivation led to consternation in the State Department and Kabul Embassy and fuelled a belief that the lead nation approach – the international burden-sharing effort – had failed. A State Department official recalled the frustration: 'the idea that [the] various international players – Britain, Germany, Italy [and Japan] . . . were going to solve certain problems on behalf of the international community [in the end proved] not to be a very good strategy.'[73]

In fact, Britain had not only failed to control cultivation, but were on course to preside over a situation that was far worse than when the Taliban were in power.[74] But Britain was confronted with an intractable problem: how to balance the fact that any sustainable counter-narcotics policy would take decades to produce results and the fact that every spring there was a highly visible and quantifiable illustration of criminal activity. In statements to the House of Commons, various FCO ministers attempted to manage expectations by conceding that experience from other narcotics-producing countries has shown cultivation tends to increase before decreasing.[75] Nevertheless, a record level of opium cultivation was a difficult 'sell' – especially to Washington. Even Khalilzad, who was not as hard-line on counter-narcotics policy as some in the administration, considered British policies as 'underpowered, under-resourced, and conceptually misguided'.[76] In Washington, pressure grew for Britain to do more.[77]

Criticism was not only directed at the British, congressional ire also focused on the US military's opposition to engage the narcotics industry. Despite Capitol Hill providing legislative approval and funding for the military to support counter-narcotics law enforcement missions, many in the DOD still refused to consider counter-narcotics as part of *their* mission.[78] Henry J. Hyde, chairman of the House Committee of International Relations, alarmed by the potential links between narcotics and terrorism, wrote to Rumsfeld expressing his growing concerns about the future of Afghanistan. During a February 2004 committee hearing, Hyde concluded that if action was not taken against the narcotics industry, Afghanistan was in danger of becoming a narco-state undermined by instability, terrorism and violence.[79] The growing chorus of noise forced the US to confront the narcotics problem, but it was some time in coming because of abiding opposition to it in Washington, particularly and most strongly from the Pentagon and the intelligence community.[80] But when that was gradually eroded it created even more scope for Anglo-American friction as the two allies differed dramatically over how best to tackle the problem.

Part 3

7 Plan Afghanistan, 2004–2005

By 2004, the second, and most contentious, phase of the counter-narcotics campaign was well underway. In short, it was dominated by the development of a US counter-narcotics strategy for Afghanistan and the friction that generated within the Bush administration and wider Anglo-American alliance. Central to both was Robert B. Charles's proposed Plan Afghanistan.[1] This, however, was not a new policy, but had its roots in the US's counter-narcotics strategy for Colombia: Plan Colombia.[2] The most controversial aspect of the proposal was the introduction of coercive eradication through aerial spraying, promoted as the *key* element in the strategy. Aerial eradication was considered – by the State Department and INL – the most effective method of eliminating opium fields, as an official commented: 'the best way . . . to get a large percentage of crop eradicated was from the air because that works very well in Colombia'.[3]

Underpinning policy was the opinion that ultimately opium cultivation was not a consequence of economic necessity but an illegal activity and required dealing with as such. Therefore, while INL advocated the need to create alternative livelihoods, crucially, the argument existed for strong action first against criminal activity. There could be no exceptions; rule of law required adherence in Afghanistan in the same way it had to be adhered to by poor Americans mixing methamphetamines in their trailers.[4] As a State Department official commented: 'nowhere in the world does alternative development work by itself. You have to be able to create a criminality associated with the behaviour you are trying to stop.'[5] Instead of gradually transitioning farmers away from opium cultivation by increasing alternative livelihoods, access to markets and improved security, the State Department wanted to signal that opium cultivation would not be tolerated and immediately set about formulating effective deterrents.[6] This line of argument was difficult to reconcile in practice with the objective of creating alternative livelihoods.

Charles also advocated a more forceful interdiction policy against narcotics traffickers; however, the Pentagon remained thoroughly against involving US forces in counter-narcotics work.[7] INL warned that the Afghan insurgency might morph into a Revolutionary Armed Forces Colombia (FARC) style organisation with their operations funded by the narcotics trade. This group of US actors believed that widespread eradication had cut off the flow of finance between the narcotics trade and FARC in Colombia and could similarly defeat insurgent groups in Afghanistan. Over the coming years, the appetite to implement a 'Colombian solution' to Afghanistan intensified as prominent State Department and INL officials were transferred from the Colombian to Afghanistan brief. Unfortunately, their enthusiasm to transplant policies from the former to the latter belied the vast differences between the two countries.[8] Colombia was a more prosperous and stable country than Afghanistan, with the latter being one of the poorest countries in the world. Colombia had established political institutions and law enforcement capacity, with a president fully committed to the counter-narcotics mission. In contrast, Afghanistan's government was barely functional, with its political institutions shattered by decades of war; Karzai's commitment to counter-narcotics was also in question. Moreover, the coca industry comprised a smaller proportion of Colombia's GDP compared to opium in Afghanistan. In Colombia, the US military, State Department and DEA worked in tandem, whereas in Afghanistan each department was at loggerheads. Furthermore, in Colombia the US was the dominant actor, whereas in Afghanistan, Britain was lead nation on counter-narcotics,[9] and that was about to generate significant friction.

Anglo-American discord over eradication

The relationship between Anglo-American counter-narcotics officials mirrored the relationship between the allies over the war in general: close cooperation, agreement on the larger issues, but differences of opinions on some approaches. There was a large degree of institutionalised coordination, with both partners funding and cooperating in many initiatives.[10] In London and Washington both parties were in regular communication over strategy; similarly, in Afghanistan, British Embassy officials were in daily contact with their US counterparts.[11] In short, relations over counter-narcotics policies followed the well-established norms of institutionalised cooperation between the special relationship allies. Also important was the relationship between Blair and Bush. A State Department official notes:

> The president and prime minister were each other's closest friend on the Afghan project. What Britain cared about was given much more than a fair hearing, it was carefully considered – no matter what the question. [On] counter-narcotics, the views of the British were always looked at carefully.[12]

However, the official further observed that the long-standing relationship was not without friction: 'it is a mature relationship, so if we don't agree, we don't paper things over. We have a candid exchange about where each party stands.'[13] It was not long before INL's quest for robust action against the narcotics trade led to a 'candid exchange' in the alliance. The most inflammatory issue in discussions was the strategy of eradication: specifically, what method to use, where to implement it and how extensively.[14] Tension was present at formal counter-narcotics meetings to discuss policy formulation. A British minister commented: 'they wanted to go down the route of aerial spraying. My dialogue . . . whenever I was in Washington with State and others was: look we hear what you are saying but this is not something we want to do' because of alienating the local populations.[15] The British were concerned that, given its indiscriminate application from the sky, aerial eradication would damage water supplies, livestock and other crops. Buttressing this was the fact that most farmers inter-cropped, meaning that if fields were sprayed from the air it would be very difficult not to contaminate food supplies. Concerns were also raised about potential negative health consequences if farmers were exposed to the spray. At diplomatic and ministerial level, with the issue constantly pushed, Britain 'held the line'.[16] State Department officials were left in no doubt regarding Britain's view on the issue, as one official recalled: 'they opposed it – flat out!'[17] Although British reluctance on the issue was well known, it did not stop State Department and INL officials from continually pressing it.[18] All this meant that alliance relations were beginning to move from candid to rather fraught.

The dispute erupted into something close to diplomatic warfare when Charles criticised Britain's eradication approach in congressional testimony in spring 2004. The title of the hearing, 'Afghanistan: Are the British Counternarcotics Efforts Going Wobbly', was a pointed reference to Margaret Thatcher's warning to George Bush Senior 'not to go wobbly' before the first Gulf War.[19] The hearing was convened to examine rapidly expanding cultivation and assess whether the 'the British-led effort on eradication of opium poppy [had] stalled'.[20] US officials showed dismay at the progress of British efforts as Representative Mark Souder stated: 'The subcommittee has received disturbing reports that while our British allies were supposed to eradicate . . . 12,000 acres of opium poppy, they are barely off the ground in Helmand and have done almost nothing in Nangarhar.' Furthermore, he complained of internal difficulties within the Bush administration: 'Let me be clear: if it is true that there is some degree of foot dragging by the British in this complex matter, the US Department of Defense comes off far worse.'[21]

Charles's testimony exposed the conflict between both INL and Britain and within the US government over the best approach to eradication. He calculated that for eradication to be successful, the allies needed to eradicate 35,000 ha[22] – although this was eventually revised up to between 60,000 and 90,000 ha.[23] Not only were the targets arbitrary and devoid of scientific rationale but they also grossly exaggerated what could be achieved given poor Afghan capacity, insecurity and corruption in the provinces. In the coming years, both the US and UNODC used these arbitrary targets to shape policy.[24] Foremost among Charles's concerns was Britain's insistence on only eradicating where farmers had access to alternative livelihoods:

> it appears that our point of disagreement . . . is that we believe . . . if there is heroin poppy there, which needs to be eradicated, we shouldn't be picking and choosing . . . we shouldn't be making it conditional upon providing an instant and available income stream.[25]

He went on to note: 'of course, we all want alternative development . . . But we cannot make our eradication efforts conditional on pre-existing or . . . the necessity of parallel development.'[26]

To achieve his target, Charles placed Lesley Pallett, Ryder's successor, under considerable pressure to agree to substantial amounts of eradication.[27] Frustrated by a perception of British weakness on the issue, Charles's testimony was a specifically crafted strategy to coerce Britain into more forceful action. If the rift were aired publicly, the reasoning went, Britain would have little alternative but to accede to INL's demands. A State Department official recalls:

> We tried privately again and again . . . to get the British to change their policy and cooperate on . . . creating more disincentives. If you say something publicly, people then have to be accountable, then they have to say, well all right, we should do something on the disincentive side as well.[28]

Charles's congressional testimony did not have the desired impact: instantaneous support for wide-scale eradication. It did, however, initiate a gradual shift of attitude in the FCO where Britain was willing to accept stronger eradication methods in the hope of forestalling aerial eradication. Nevertheless, British politicians were privately incensed at Charles's testimony, and informed their US counterparts of their displeasure. A British minister observed:

> We did not take kindly to our principal allies criticising us publicly . . . we got very pissed off when they did that . . . and we pushed back very robustly and said: bugger off we have the lead responsibility on this and we have expended an awful lot of political capital supporting you . . . and you are making life more difficult for us.[29]

In public, however, British politicians' demonstrated restraint as FCO Minister Bill Rammell down played the conflict, simply saying: 'there have been some differences of emphasis'.[30] Not all politicians thought the best course of action was to downplay the rift publicly, a minister commenting: 'I often argued internally, that there was political merit in airing some of that publicly.'[31] To do so, however, would have inflamed an already delicate situation between INL and FCO officials and caused more damage to the wider Anglo-American alliance at a time when the coalition was fighting on two fronts, with the one in Iraq already extremely unpopular. The wider Bush administration were also aware that

Charles's comments did little for the unity of the special relationship, and the NSC let Charles know of their displeasure through back channels. A State Department official recalled:

> they didn't like the fact about publicly stating [criticism. The view was] we need to hang together, or we are going to hang separately. This is not easy stuff. We all need to be on one page to get it done.[32]

Notwithstanding, Charles's comments demonstrated that, as the dominant partner, some within the US had no hesitation in publicly cajoling Britain into a policy reversal. As the junior partner, Britain was more sensitive to the criticism of – as General Sir David Richards later referred to the US – 'big brother'.[33] Senior British diplomats were attuned to this form of alliance politics as British Ambassador to the US David Manning later recounted about Britain's role in the special relationship: 'At the best of times, Britain's influence on the US is limited. But the only way we exercise that influence is by attaching ourselves firmly to them and avoiding public criticism where possible.'[34]

On 15–16 April, Blair was in the US to hold talks with Bush.[35] In general, the British government felt embarrassed by its poor performance on counter-narcotics, especially with reports of a record crop.[36] With Britain clearly unable to combat the narcotics industry on its own, Blair used the opportunity to petition Bush for assistance. Khalilzad stated that: 'President Bush agreed at Blair's request to involve the United States more actively on the counter-narcotics front.'[37] But that still begged the question of how they would engage, and if it transpired that aerial eradication was to be urged, there were going to be even more problems.

By mid-2004, as the debate over the forthcoming US counter-narcotics strategy accelerated, Britain came under increasing US pressure to step up its own efforts. A British official noted that whilst, 'the US was putting pressure on Britain, Britain was also putting pressure on itself ... there was a lot of impatience in London ... [Coming] from the prime minister downwards to get a grip on the problem.'[38] This pressure, on both sides of the Atlantic, reached fever pitch as the UNODC got ready to announce the results of the 2004 crop and, more importantly, the new planting season loomed.

US counter-narcotics strategy: policy discussions

Notwithstanding accusations of electoral impropriety, the 2004 Afghan presidential elections – that confirmed US-backed Hamid Karzai as President – were considered an important milestone in Afghanistan's transition to democracy. Despite this achievement, one issue cast a long shadow over post-conflict Afghanistan: soaring opium cultivation. A month after the elections, the UNODC confirmed that a record 131,000 ha of opium was under cultivation, a 64 per cent increase on the previous year.[39] Moreover, cultivation had spread to all of Afghanistan's provinces, some of which had no previous history of cultivation.[40] Over the coming weeks, discussions about what action the US should take to combat this dominated the interagency process.[41]

The development of a counter-narcotics strategy, however, remained divisive with all levels of the policymaking apparatus at odds over how best to proceed.[42] The issue was widely discussed in the director-level Afghanistan Interagency Operations Group (AIOG) – formed in August 2003 and co-chaired by the State Department and NSC[43] – which met weekly to discuss policy matters.[44] Sitting above the AIOG was the Afghan Steering Group, a Deputy Assistant-level body. Issues were then raised to the Deputies Committee, which was a Deputy Secretary-level body. From there issues went to the Secretary-level Principals Committee, which was chaired by the Deputy National Security Advisor for Iraq and Afghanistan. Finally, the NSC was a Secretary-level Committee chaired by the President.[45] Throughout all of the bodies, the key issue remained aerial spraying and above all it proved a constant source of tension over the next four years, causing bitter exchanges within the Bush administration and in the wider Anglo-American alliance. However, Charles was convinced of the need to employ an aggressive eradication campaign and took further steps to promote it.

During an AIOG meeting, Charles pitched his plan to transfer aircraft from Colombia to southern Afghanistan to carry out aerial eradication. Concerned about the implications of this, a military official from the Joint Staff sternly asked Charles about INL's provisions for rescuing shot-down pilots and its plan to prevent aerial eradication colliding with ground patrols. Charles responded confidently that aerial eradication would be wholly coordinated with military activities. Next, United States Agency for International Development (USAID) and DEA officials made it clear to Charles that they did not have the capacity to offer alternative livelihoods to those affected by eradication – something they argued was essential. Pentagon officials also raised concerns about the need to convince farmers that the US was not launching chemical warfare against the rural population and the difficulty in winning hearts and minds while destroying farmers' livelihoods. Angered by these responses, Charles said:

> these famers are criminals, period. They are breaking Afghan law. We are not there to win the hearts and minds of criminals. We are there to restore stability and rule of law to Afghanistan and not let it become a narco-state![46]

Charles also knew that for his plan to succeed, he needed Afghan support. He assembled a team of experts to travel to Afghanistan to sell his idea to Karzai and demonstrate that a version of herbicide glyphosate – which is used to kill domestic garden weeds – could deliver instant results with no serious health risks.[47] However, this was far from certain as the safety of herbicide glyphosate was hotly contested around the world. Alarmed about negative health risks, the Ecuadorian government called for a UN study to examine Colombia's aerial spraying programme near its border. Demonstrating the politicised nature of the debate, US Ambassador to Colombia and future Ambassador to Afghanistan William Wood noted: 'a UN study is unnecessary and duplicative from a scientific perspective for this widely used, 40-year-old herbicide . . . [it would also] . . . invite further politicization of a technical issue, which would damage vital U.S. counter-narcotics efforts in Colombia'.[48] Throughout its usage in Latin America, no irrefutable scientific evidence was presented to conclude the debate. In the end, Charles did not get the opportunity to brief Karzai, as Khalilzad blocked his country clearance. Charles was informed: 'it's a crowded time so let's put that off'.[49] A State Department official commented: 'it's almost unprecedented . . . it highlights the level of tension that existed [over aerial eradication]'.[50]

   Whilst Khalilzad was not against aerial eradication in theory, he understood that in the Afghan context it could have disastrous consequences,[51] not least turning an insurgency into an insurrection. In his fight against the introduction of aerial eradication,

Khalilzad had the support of McNeill's replacement as Commander of Combined Forces Command-Afghanistan, Lieutenant General David Barno. Prior to deployment, the General, like his predecessor, was warned by the Defense Department that counternarcotics was not the military's mission. Barno was also aware of the potential 'dangers of aerial eradication . . . [and] thought it would be immensely counterproductive'.[52] A view reinforced during conversations with British military officers.[53] An NSC official commented: 'General Barno was against aerial eradication for sure. I think he was not against eradication per se because it took place whilst he was there but eradication that was unimpeded by common sense: yes.'[54] With the two most powerful Americans in Kabul, plus Commander of CENTCOM General John Abizaid[55] against the introduction of aerial eradication, Charles's job of convincing the administration to adopt the controversial policy was looking increasingly unlikely.

One of Congress's most active drug warriors, Republican Dana Rohrabacher, did get the opportunity to brief Karzai over the issue. Whilst on a visit to Afghanistan in 2003, Rohrabacher had asked the president to sign a letter approving aerial eradication that could, if necessary, be presented before Congress to generate support. Rohrabacher also hinted that Congress might cut aid to Afghanistan if significant action was not taken to quash the opium trade. Surprised by this, Karzai responded that his government was working hard to control opium cultivation and it had made progress. His Chief of Staff Sayed Jawad also expressed concerns regarding the environmental damage that aerial eradication would cause.[56] At the time, the issue stalled, and no conclusive action was taken. However, before long, the issue was at the centre of White House discussions.

Despite hostility from the Pentagon, the British and the Afghans, Powell tried to sell Plan Afghanistan to the president at a war Cabinet meeting in November 2004. Powell illustrated the narcotics problem vividly and made a persuasive argument. Bush seemed concerned about the issue and was encouraging of aerial eradication.[57] Charles, also present at the meeting, was overjoyed at the president's response, believing his plan was now approved. However, Rumsfeld used Bush's declarations simply as the start of the debate. And when his objections failed to close down the possibility of the president authorising the plan, he continued his opposition 'through back channels'.[58] Not only did Rumsfeld

agree with his military commanders that introducing aerial eradication would endanger US forces in rural communities, in general
the Pentagon wanted to downgrade the counter-narcotics effort,
not accelerate it.[59] The Pentagon's view chimed more with their
transatlantic counterpart than with their State Department colleagues. In broad terms, the State Department and its INL and
DOD occupied opposite ends of the policy spectrum with the
British somewhere in-between. In its effort to stop aerial eradication, the Pentagon was helped by the fact that they had an ally in
Khalilzad.

Despite his own opposition to aerial eradication, Khalilzad
nevertheless had a job to do; this meant acting as an intermediary
between Karzai and Bush. When discussing the issue with Bush,
the president was unequivocal in his support, declaring: 'I am a
spray man.'[60] This posed Khalilzad with a problem. According
to him, the president's view was conditioned by the perceived
success of US aerial eradication efforts in Colombia – which
Bush was a fan of. Back in Kabul, Khalilzad, accompanied by
the British Ambassador Rosalind Marsden, informed Karzai of
Bush's offer: to arrange a discussion with Colombian President
Alvaro Uribe. Bush predicted that it would ease Karzai's concerns
over aerial eradication (it is unclear whether Karzai spoke to
Uribe). But Khalilzad thought that Bush's hopes were misplaced
and so it proved. The Afghan president was also unequivocal in
his view: he adamantly opposed aerial eradication. Karzai vigor-
ously argued that if it was introduced 'it would undermine the
war effort in the eyes of the Afghan people' and it 'would turn the
liberation into an occupation'. Furthermore, Karzai contended
the measure would amount to – literally – the deployment of
chemical weapons against the Afghan people.[61]

Shortly afterwards, Khalilzad briefed Bush for a final time in
Washington.[62] Bush remained committed to the idea of aerial
eradication,[63] but Khalilzad made a convincing argument that
Karzai was willing to cooperate on all aspects of the counter-
narcotics programme, apart from aerial eradication. A compromise was reached which saw aerial eradication dropped on
the condition that if the alternative strategy did not produce
results in one year, the US would have the right to introduce
it. Karzai also promised to front the counter-narcotics effort
by delivering a robust anti-opium message to a conference of
Afghan elders.[64]

Despite believing in the merits of aerial eradication, Bush never entered the fray decisively to end the inter-departmental squabbling and, in any case, congressional and alliance politics made the likelihood of decisiveness in this policy area elusive for anyone, even someone as powerful as the president. In addition, with the Pentagon largely shaping policy and Rumsfeld's ability to outmanoeuvre his opponents politically, the probability of State Department success in this area was constrained. Likewise, Bush's decision not to override Khalilzad on this aspect of policy was also partly a consequence of his presidential style: Bush was results driven – less concerned in the specifics of policy than achieving the overall goal.[65]

There was suspicion in INL that Khalilzad, influenced by his relationship with Rumsfeld, had dissembled in what he did. Instead of trying to persuade Karzai to adopt aerial spraying, he had done exactly the opposite. An aggrieved State Department official recalled the intervention:

> Khalilzad had a stick that he could put in the wheel of everyone else's policy ... he was an obstacle to progress ... and was a puppet of Rumsfeld's idea that – I am oversimplifying things – we don't need a [counter-narcotics policy] we will just pick up terrorists.[66]

In fact, whilst Khalilzad considered aerial eradication a sub-optimal policy, he was pragmatic, knowing that the chances of introducing it against the wishes of Karzai, the Pentagon, intelligence community and British was unrealistic.[67] Nevertheless, Khalilzad's intervention was crucial: there would be no aerial eradication.

Less than a month after Powell briefed Bush, Charles learned that a watered-down version replaced his strategy, despite commanding the president's approval during the Cabinet meeting; it saw aerial spraying abandoned in favour of manual eradication.[68] This came largely because of opposition orchestrated by the Pentagon and Khalilzad.[69] This episode further damaged relations between the State Department and Pentagon – and was another example of friction between Rumsfeld and Powell over foreign policy. Once again, the counter-narcotics agenda was shaped by individual agency with the Pentagon and its fellow-travellers pursing policies that suited their aims and objectives. As detailed below, for most of Bush's time in office, counter-narcotics policymaking was fractured, with individual strength of character a key determinant in policy debates. This did little for the construction of effective counter-narcotics policies.

At a 17 November 2004 briefing, Charles outlined a new, and for the first time, comprehensive US counter-narcotics strategy, which had five pillars: public information, law enforcement, alternative livelihoods, interdiction and eradication.[70] Whilst it is true that the Pentagon and Khalilzad had successfully torpedoed aerial eradication, they did not win the entire policy debate as the new strategy represented a significant increase in US counter-narcotics efforts. A State Department official explained:

> The Defense Department [did not] win the whole policy debate on the US counter-narcotics strategy … eradication remained part of the strategy and [it] was approved. The US had a substantially robust counter-narcotics strategy … that went to Congress and was largely funded. [There was] a huge increase in the amount of money for a US counter-narcotics strategy.[71]

US counter-narcotics funding for the upcoming year increased significantly. The US spent $782 million on counter-narcotics in 2005, up from $380 million between 2002 and 2004.[72] As the US stepped up its efforts and funding, the dynamics between the Anglo-American partners changed. Britain was still lead nation on counter-narcotics, but by virtue of the disparity in funding levels – in 2005, Britain committed £100 million (approximately $182 million)[73] – the US now held considerable sway over the policymaking process.

With the threat of aerial eradication hanging over him, Karzai gave his resolute support to the counter-narcotics drive. In December 2004, at a counter-narcotics conference in Kabul, he declared a jihad against the narcotics industry describing it as a 'cancer' more dangerous than the Soviet invasion and terrorism.[74] Pledging to eliminate it in two years, Karzai highlighted the vital role provincial governors would play and threatened to sack them if they did not comply with his directive.[75] Around the same time, Britain also attempted to 'raise the profile of counter-narcotics' by upgrading the CND into the Ministry of Counter-Narcotics (MCN).[76] Whilst the Anglo-Afghan efforts were a step in the right direction, the US demanded more.

Renewed efforts

In February, still under pressure from Washington, the Afghan government produced the 2005 Counter-Narcotics Implementation Plan. The plan, in theory, would provide the framework to accelerate Afghan and coalition efforts to tackle narcotics. It consisted of eight pillars: building institutions; information campaign; alternative livelihoods; interdiction and law enforcement; criminal justice; eradication; demand reduction and treatment of addicts; and regional cooperation.[77]

The Afghans were not the only ally in Washington's sights. According to a British military officer, some US actors were: 'pretty disparaging of the British lead on counter-narcotics [and] I think they had every reason to be'.[78] After all, under Britain's watch opium cultivation had spiralled to record levels. Embarrassed by this,[79] and in response to US criticism, Britain reinvigorated its counter-narcotics approach.[80] As such, Britain was under no illusion that they now had to *lead* on counter-narcotics.[81]

To give its campaign a boost, Britain launched a series of counter-narcotics measures in 2005. In February, a new counter-narcotics unit was established within the FCO, the Afghan Drugs Inter-Departmental Unit (ADIDU), headed by Peter Holland, and consisting of seventeen staff.[82] A Cambridge University and London School of Economics graduate, Holland was an intelligent and thoughtful head,[83] who quickly set about trying to implement the government's – unrealistic – ten-year plan, conceived several years previously. The under-resourced and overwhelmed BEDT was also upgraded; in the space of a year, the team nearly doubled in strength rising from thirteen[84] to twenty.[85] Reflecting Blair's personal interest in a successful counter-narcotics mission, both teams reported to Number 10 on a bi-monthly basis.[86] To improve Anglo-American coordination, the partners commenced formal bi-annual counter-narcotics talks – the Counter-Narcotics Strategy Group[87] – in Washington or London to share analysis and agree upon strategy for the coming year.[88] This was accompanied by the establishment of the Joint Narcotics Analysis Centre (JNAC), housed in the Old War Office in London.[89] The centre's aim was to improve counter-narcotics intelligence sharing with the goal of building a comprehensive picture of the narcotics trade. JNAC fed information to the Anglo-American Interagency

Operation Coordination Centre in Kabul to produce 'targeting packages' for interdiction efforts by British, American and Afghan law enforcement agencies.[90]

Around this time, the DEA also boosted its capacity by deploying military trained, Foreign-deployed Advisory and Support Teams. The teams worked with military forces, and the US-trained National Interdiction Unit, to disrupt narcotics organisations, opium stashes, heroin processing labs and precursor chemical stockpiles.[91] Efforts were also underway to create a court system where those arrested during interdiction missions, especially high-value targets, could be tried. The Central Narcotics Tribunal was established to 'hear cases involving more than 2 kilograms of processed opiates or 10 kilograms of opium'.[92] The US, Britain and UNODC were among several donors that funded a Criminal Justice Task Force to train investigators, prosecutors and judges to try counter-narcotics cases. Despite being regarded as one of the most competent arms of the counter-narcotics apparatus, the court system was plagued by political interference, resulting in very few high-level prosecutions.[93]

In the meantime, there was still a persistent tension in the alliance over eradication. The core of the problem – as expressed by Charles the previous year – was that British efforts were considered half-hearted. INL was ploughing considerable resources into eradication, awarding private contractors DynCorp – who delivered aerial eradication in Colombia – a $50 million contract to train the Central Poppy Eradication Force (CPEF).[94] That said, Britain attempted to temper INL's urges for wide-scale eradication, by establishing the Central Eradication Planning Cell. The unit's purpose was, in the words of FCO Minister Bill Rammell, to 'ensure that eradication by the CPEF is targeted in a way which takes account of alternative livelihoods'.[95] The policy was best summed up as targeting 'the greedy, not the needy'.[96] Although, in the face of mounting US pressure, Britain's ability to maintain this policy diminished.[97]

Notwithstanding, by this stage, Britain had committed to help the Afghans eradicate a sizable amount of opium – 20,000 ha or 15 per cent of the total poppy per year.[98] Therefore, demonstrable progress was needed. In May, a leaked cable from the US Embassy in Kabul complained that Britain was '"substantially responsible" for not eradicating more acreage'.[99] The cable did acknowledge, however, that the real issue was poor Afghan leadership and political will. The CPEF, like many Afghan police units, were under-manned, unreliable, corrupt and unwilling to engage in eradication.[100] Governor-led eradication, which ran alongside the centrally administered force, faced similar, if not worse, problems. Prior to 2005, there was no impartial mechanism to verify how much eradication occurred, often leading to over-reporting. Eventually the UNODC assumed that role but, for some time, questions remained about the reliability of its data.[101] Despite the cable acknowledging that the real problem lay with the Afghans, not all within the US administration considered criticising the British as compatible with the maintenance of the special relationship. A State Department official commented:

> It was very damaging to the US relationship with Britain at the more senior levels where they were cooperating ... not just with Afghanistan but with other issues, [such as] Iraq ... The US government wanted to cooperate with Britain. If the lead wasn't enough from the Brits, we were going to have to do more. We don't have to go around bashing them ... [criticism of this kind] does not do much for trust and cooperation.[102]

Amid this continued criticism, Blair chaired a ministerial meeting in July that doubled ADIDU's annual budget from £25.3 million to £46.8 million. This was part of an £115 million increase, which swelled the overall British counter-narcotics budget to £270 million over three years – from 2005 to 2008.[103] Although the funding was considerable by British standards, realistically Britain did not have the resources to make substantial headway against the opium industry. Of course, Britain's counter-narcotics budget, like the conflict in general, was constrained by Iraq. A British official reflected that '[that] was the tragedy of the international effort in Afghanistan ... It was never going to be easy but if it hadn't been for Iraq, Afghanistan would have been in a better place.'[104] Given this constraint, in October, Britain established the Counter-Narcotics Trust Fund (CNTF). The UN administered fund was designed to increase international contributions, facilitate Afghan ownership of the funding stream and improve the transparency and accountability of counter-narcotics funding.[105] As the CNTF was designed to be an ambitious $900 million trust fund, Jack Straw and Clare Short's successor as Development Secretary, Hilary Benn, travelled the world attempting to generate support.[106] Britain, naturally as lead nation, was the principal contributor donating $44.3 million; however, it failed to encourage other nations to support the initiative. By 2008, reflecting the lack of international willingness to deal with counter-narcotics, donors had only committed a measly $83 million.[107]

The testing ground: Nangarhar Province

In 2005, Nangarhar Province provided the testing ground for increased US counter-narcotics efforts. The province was both of significant strategic value to the US – given its proximity to the Pakistan border and large presence of US troops – and one of the largest opium producing provinces in the years prior to and including 2004.[108] Nevertheless, Nangarhar was relatively stable, experiencing low levels of violence and high levels of reconstruction aid. After the establishment of a US-led Provincial Reconstruction Team (PRT) in 2003, several infrastructural projects were launched, including the development of roads, bridges, irrigation systems, health clinics and schools.[109] With ISAF confined to Kabul during the first two years of the conflict, PRTs were civilian–military units designed to spread the 'ISAF effect' into the provinces without formally extending ISAF throughout Afghanistan. PRTs comprised 60–100 military personnel, Afghan advisors and officials from civilian development agencies.[110]

It was against this backdrop that the Provincial Governor Haji Din Mohammed implemented a successful opium ban in 2005. A variety of external and internal factors coalesced to make the implementation of the ban achievable.[111] Internationally, there was strong backing to make tangible progress to prevent a perceived failure in the state-building project.[112] Locally, the population and governor were also fully behind the implementation of the ban. In particular, Haji Din Mohammed embraced Karzai's warning to dismiss those who failed to comply with his directive. The governor then used Karzai's threat to remind district leaders that their own positions would also be in jeopardy if the ban failed.[113] Generally, the population was supportive of the government's state-building agenda, having played their role in electing Karzai the previous autumn.[114]

The prevailing economic environment also helped the situation. Wheat prices in the province had increased by 49 per cent between October and November 2004, inducing fears among the rural population of food insecurity. Additionally, opium prices had fallen from $320/kg in May 2003 to $136/kg in May 2004. Both factors impacted farmers' decisions not to plant opium.[115] More importantly, to encourage the population to agree to the ban, provincial governors, the government and the international community made promises of development aid.[116] The flow of development aid and promise of future funding proved a significant reason in persuading farmers not to plant poppy. Across Afghanistan, USAID expanded its Rebuilding Agricultural Markets Programme to provide alternative employment opportunities for those reliant upon opium cultivation, to the sum of $17.9 million.[117] This was accompanied by a $408 million alternative livelihood programme, which included cash-for-work projects 'that increased the agricultural income and provided much needed infrastructure investments, including rehabilitation of roads and canals'.[118]

The governor's strategy to implement the ban was influenced by the Taliban's 2000 prohibition. As Mansfield states, the governor

> co-opt[ed] both formal and informal institutions into the process. Negotiation and political bargaining were at the forefront of Haji Din Mohammed's strategy to reduce opium production; the reward of increased development assistance formed an integral part of the dialogue between the governor and the rural population.[119]

Emphasis was placed on preventing farmers from planting opium at the start of the season as opposed to concentration on eradication once the poppy was planted. Eradication was utilised where the conditions allowed but targeted to prevent violent resistance.[120] Of the 4,000 ha eradicated in 2005, Nangarhar accounted for 46 per cent and Helmand 26 per cent.[121] Nevertheless, it was in this quid pro quo environment that the ban was successfully achieved. As a result, opium cultivation in the province fell a staggering 96 per cent, from 28,213 ha to 1,093 ha.[122]

The north-eastern province of Badakhshan was also a key focus of Anglo-American counter-narcotics efforts. The province had a long history of opium cultivation and was the third largest opium producer in 2004 – producing 15,600 ha, which accounted for 12 per cent of the national area cultivated.[123] Britain's strategy – implemented by DFID – focused on creating alternative livelihoods for poppy farmers whilst improving the coordination and implementation of development and counter-narcotics programmes.[124] Britain funded a £4 million alternative livelihoods project, part of which included the construction of an irrigation canal to facilitate the transition to alternative crops.[125] After Nangarhar, Badakhshan was the second largest recipient of USAID development funding in 2005[126] receiving $47.3 million.[127] Little eradication was needed in the province as the threat of eradication proved a potent enough threat to deter poppy planting in the first place.[128] Compared to the previous year the province experienced a 53 per cent reduction in opium cultivation.

The successful reduction of cultivation in Nangarhar and Badakhshan was replicated, to varying degrees, throughout Afghanistan. A reduction of cultivation was observed in nineteen provinces[129] and the overall amount of land dedicated to opium cultivation in 2005 decreased 21 per cent from 2004 – although favourable weather conditions meant production was only down 2.4 per cent to 4,100 tons.[130] The number of poppy-free provinces increased from zero to nine.

One of the primary reasons for the first reduction in opium cultivation since 2001 was Karzai's influence exerted on governors to adhere to his nationwide opium ban, which was for the first time actively backed by the entire Anglo-American alliance. Buoyed by the reduction, Afghan officials confidently declared that opium cultivation would also be reduced the following year. The Afghan Deputy Minister of Interior for Counter-Narcotics General Mohammed Daud boasted that cultivation could be reduced by 40 per cent in 2006. However, this optimism was contradicted by the UNODC who predicted that the 2006 opium crop would exceed 2005 levels. Reportedly, Daud simply dismissed out of hand a UNODC report forewarning of an increase in cultivation.[131] Nevertheless, it remained to be seen if the reduction was a sustainable outcome of a rejuvenated counter-narcotics campaign or a momentary triumph.

8 Afghanistan's Poppy Capital, 2005–2006

In 2005, ISAF announced its decision to assume operational command for the whole of Afghanistan by October 2006. Hitherto, ISAF was responsible for Kabul and the northern and western regions, with the US in command of Afghanistan's southern and eastern provinces.[1] Under the US's lead, however, the campaign had stagnated as attention and resources were directed towards Iraq.[2] This oversight had allowed the Taliban, particularly in the south and east, to re-emerge as a potent force and intensify its violent campaign.[3] Progress had also stalled at the political level as the Karzai government failed to extend its writ into southern Afghanistan, thus leaving the population caught between a resurgent Taliban and ineffective and corrupt provincial authorities. Compounding matters, for the first five years of the conflict, relatively few troops were stationed in the south – despite the region being a Taliban heartland. Only 3,000 troops, headquartered at Kandahar Airfield, were responsible for covering nine provinces.[4] Even Afghanistan's largest province of Helmand, which is three times the size of Wales and has approximately one million residents, only had approximately 150 coalition troops.[5] Moreover, development projects in Helmand, such as reconstruction of roads and regeneration of electricity and water supplies, were also limited. Even when projects were due to commence or conclude, the lack of security prevented the implementation of alternative livelihoods. In 2004, a major USAID sponsored project to rejuvenate agriculture in the south was not fulfilled because of insecurity in the region. The following year, the project was halted in Helmand after the Taliban executed several labourers.[6]

As part of NATO's move southwards, Britain, Canada and the Netherlands had volunteered to deploy forces to the three provinces of Kandahar, Helmand and Uruzgan. During the decision-making process, the Canadians insisted that they assume control of Kandahar, the south's most strategically significant province. The Canadians had calculated that by taking charge of the spiritual home of the Taliban, its military would have the greatest opportunity to demonstrate its value beyond peacekeeping. Britain, therefore, was left with Helmand, the south's second most strategically significant province and poppy capital of Afghanistan.[7] This chimed well with Blair's eagerness to combat Afghanistan's narcotics trade and became an important but secondary reason to take charge of Helmand.[8] Although some military officers were frustrated about deploying to the less important province of Helmand,[9] largely the British were enthusiastic about playing a significant role in the expanding effort.[10]

Despite broad support for the mission, troop levels were intentionally set low at 3,300 to enable the policy to pass through Cabinet without generating significant resistance. The military, having 'their own sense of "what the [political] market would bear"', also agreed to this. Of course, Britain's commitment in Iraq dominated discussions and proved the largest factor in capping troop numbers.[11] At any rate, the deployment to Helmand represented a substantial increase in military resources. The two previous British-run PRTs in Mazar-e-Sharif, Balkh Province (2003–6), and Maymaneh, Faryab Province (2004–5) only had a combined total of approximately 150 troops.[12]

Unfortunately, the deployment to Helmand was characterised by poor planning and inadequate knowledge of the province.[13] There was a dearth of information on the vital features of the province: the insurgency, the narcotics industry, tribal politics and the relationship between them. The minimal intelligence available indicated a growing insurgency, which was then used to strengthen the argument for going to Helmand to invigorate the campaign before it was too late,[14] but few if anyone really knew what awaited British forces there.

The British were aware, however, that the incumbent Provincial Governor Sher Mohammed Akhundzada was alleged to be involved in the narcotics trade. Suspicions about the governor's illicit activities grew when a British minister visited Helmand on a fact-finding mission in June 2005. During a meeting at the US-run PRT in Lashkar Gah, the minister was briefed by intelligence operatives that not only was Helmand awash with poppy, but Akhundzada was one of the largest narco-barons in the province. The minister's meeting with US officials was then followed by an almost comical encounter with the controversial governor. During their conversation, Akhundzada protested that 'he had been mistakenly identified as the godfather of the opium industry [in Helmand]'. Akhundzada then, in a puerile attempt to deflect attention, argued that 'there are an awful lot of Mohammed's in Helmand and they have got the wrong one'. The minister left Helmand with 'very dark feelings and intimations about what was going on [as] it was clear that [narcotics] corruption went right to the top of the Helmand administration [and] Kabul government'.[15] Several weeks later, the intelligence indicating Akhundzada was a narco-baron was confirmed when he was caught with nine tons of opium in his office during a combined Afghan and DEA raid.[16] Appointed as governor in 2002, Akhundzada epitomised the rapacious, anti-Taliban warlord that gained power in the post-intervention government. Akhundzada, supported by equally repugnant associates, terrorised the Helmandi population through a campaign of abuse, extortion and extrajudicial killings.[17] Despite this, the governor was a close personal ally of Karzai – not least because his grip on the province prevented a full-scale return of the Taliban. Nevertheless, Akhundzada's anti-Taliban prowess did little to assuage British concerns that his illegal activities would undermine their forthcoming deployment to Helmand. As a result, the British petitioned Karzai for his removal. Grudgingly, the president agreed, removing him in December.[18] Akhundzada's removal, however, proved a constant source of tension between Karzai and the British, with the president later complaining that this had made his government 'look like a puppet of the British'.[19]

Akhundzada's replacement as governor was Engineer Mohammed Daoud, a Helmandi technocrat and relative of the Minister for Counter-Narcotics.[20] To the British, Daoud was a model governor: free from links to the narcotics trade and corruption. Whilst Daoud's credentials were impeccable by western standards, by Afghan standards he lacked the necessary tribal affiliations to provide strong leadership in a province of extensive tribal networks.[21] Although removing Akhundzada was the correct decision, it soon had sinister implications for the British campaign in Helmand. The outgoing US PRT (and SAS) considered Akhundzada as the vital component in maintaining stability within the province and, as such, were disgruntled at his removal.[22] It was not long before US fears were realised: far from improving stability in the province, removing Akhundzada fuelled insecurity. ISAF commander General Sir David Richards noted: 'They [the Taliban] were there – they were in a lot of those southern provinces – but there was a marriage of convenience between them and the drug lords and Akhundzada, and there was very little violence.'[23]

Removing Akhundzada also highlighted a fundamental difference of approach in the Anglo-American alliance. Throughout the campaign, the US had demonstrated its willingness to work with Afghans involved in illegal activity. The British, on the other hand, were more squeamish, as former British military officer Frank Ledwidge notes: 'the British approach might essentially be summed up in the phrase "we want nothing to do with such people"'.[24] By interfering with the political landscape, Britain had unwittingly made its mission in the province more difficult by upsetting the delicate balance of power. Moreover, as detailed later, the move into Helmand was the pivotal moment in Britain's campaign and had far-reaching consequences for its other objectives, namely counter-narcotics and the stability of both Afghanistan and the Anglo-American alliance.

Nevertheless, on 26 January 2006, during a statement to the House of Commons, Defence Secretary John Reid continued the narrative that the elimination of narcotics was an important but subsidiary reason for Britain's involvement in Helmand and linked it to domestic policy:

> We are also working to make sure that our goals are Afghan goals, too. Assisting Afghan counter-narcotics initiatives is an obvious example. If we help them, we help ourselves at the same time. As I mentioned earlier, 90 per cent of the heroin injected into the veins of young people in this country originates in Afghanistan. Helmand Province is the largest single source of opium in Afghanistan.[25]

Several days after Reid's statement, an international delegation convened in London and counter-narcotics was high on the agenda.

The Afghanistan Compact

The London conference was convened to redefine the framework for international collaboration with Afghanistan and inaugurate what was known as the Afghanistan Compact. The compact marked the conclusion of the 2001 Bonn Agreement and set out a new five-year partnership focusing on three interdependent pillars: security; governance, rule of law and human rights; and economic and social development plus a crosscutting counter-narcotics agenda which was linked to the pillars.[26] The Compact also replaced the system of lead nations with partner nations, with Afghanistan assuming lead nation status and the international community in support. International donors pledged more than $10 billion (£5.7 billion) in reconstruction aid over five years, with Britain, as partner nation on counter-narcotics, announcing a £500 million aid package over three years.[27]

In the years that followed the Bonn conference – as opium cultivation reached unprecedented levels – counter-narcotics became a highly controversial issue in the special relationship. The significance the US Embassy in Kabul (and US departments) placed on making headway against rampant opium cultivation was illustrated by a cable sent to Colin Powell's successor, Condoleezza Rice, prior to the London conference. The cable stressed the severity of the situation and the importance of using the conference to cajole Karzai into action:

> The next few months are critical; they determine the success or failure of the program. Your message to Karzai must be direct: Opium cultivation remains the single most significant threat to his government and to Afghanistan's successful reconstruction and he must bring the full prestige of his office to bear in this effort.[28]

The cable further noted that reference to eradication must be included in the Afghanistan Compact. Eradication was not only considered the most effective law enforcement tool, but also a morally just tool in achieving demonstrable progress against opium cultivation. The view, however, was not shared by the Afghan government as they omitted eradication during the drafting of the Compact. Concerned by this, Ronald Neumann, Khalilzad's successor, raised the issue during a 10 December 2005 meeting with the Afghan government and fellow G8 Ambassadors. He highlighted eradication's centrality: 'strongly call[ing] for its inclusion as a statement that both donors and the GOIRA [Government of Islamic Republic of Afghanistan] accept both the legitimacy and practical necessity of eradication as one of the tools to fight

Afghanistan's narcotics scourge'.[29] Whilst the language regarding counter-narcotics was 'strengthened' in the Annex of the document, the Kabul Embassy reported that: 'we are inclined to push back once more on the language in the cover document'.[30] At a 24 December meeting to review the latest version of the document, the issue was again raised with the Afghan government. A cable from the Kabul Embassy noted: 'we have gained much of what we wanted in this latest revision, notably including specific references to counter-narcotics program "eradication" efforts in both the Chapeau and Annex I benchmark text'.[31] The Kabul Embassy exerted enough pressure and won the debate: eradication was included in the final document.

The conference was also used to launch the government's new ANDCS. The strategy, first fashioned in 2003 then updated in 2006 (and subsequent years), had four priorities: targeting the trafficker; strengthening and diversifying legal rural livelihoods; reducing the demand for illicit drugs and treatment of problem drug users; and developing state institutions at the central and provincial level. In addition to these principal elements, eight pillars were identified: public awareness; international and regional cooperation; alternative livelihoods; demand reduction; law enforcement; criminal justice; drug eradication; and institution building.[32] The strategy presented a framework to tackle the narcotics trade, highlighting some important requirements, such as a prerequisite for alternative livelihoods to be present before eradication was implemented and the complete rejection of aerial spraying[33] – a fact that was ignored by State Department and White House officials over the coming months.

As a strategy, however, the ANDCS failed in certain aspects. It did not take into consideration the regional variants of opium cultivation, nor did it target the most significant opium cultivating provinces. There was no provision for resource distribution or indeed resource approximation for correct execution of the strategy.[34] Moreover, the edicts laid forth in Kabul policy documents did not reflect the political realities in the provinces, where the government failed to extend its authority and a myriad of local actors were also pursuing competing and often conflicting agendas.

One of the main challenges confronting the ANDCS was the application of the aims and goals in practice. The first goal of the ANDCS was to disrupt the narcotics trade through attacking powerful traffickers, whilst recognising that many farmers cultivated opium out of economic necessity.[35] However, the government's record on this was extremely poor, failing to arrest, prosecute or remove high-level traffickers from office. The majority of those who were convicted or punished were low or mid-level narcotics traffickers with no political connections, whereas high-level narcotics traffickers with political connections were able to avoid punishment. Successful implementation required the government to display political will, which was lacking most evidently in its failure to stop protecting powerful narcotics traffickers.

The ANDCS stipulated that farmers would be able to access alternative livelihoods to alleviate the financial distress caused by adhering to governmental poppy bans or the eradication of their poppy crop. However, like the other pillars of the strategy, what was set forth in the ANDCS and what was implemented did not always coincide.[36] Furthermore, as will become clear, in many cases those who had forgone poppy cultivation for the promise of alternative livelihoods were not rewarded with employment or financial reimbursement.

The ANDCS also acknowledged the problem of domestic narcotics consumption by stating there was a need for improved harm reduction policies. However, the Afghan government was slow to improve services and, in some cases, prevented new narcotics treatment services from being implemented. Publicly there was still a great deal of stigmatisation towards narcotics users, which was one reason why treatment and rehabilitation policies were given little priority. Rather unsurprisingly, at the time of writing, narcotics use is more prevalent than ever.

The conference's triumphant but wishful tagline was 'Building on Success'. However, this was more optimistic than realistic, especially as by 2006 evidence of a resurgent narcotics industry, rising violence, poor governance and rampant corruption were all apparent.[37] The conference was, according to US Principal Deputy Assistant Secretary for INL Thomas Schweich, a 'grand event mired in deception, at least with respect to the drug situation'.[38] As always in Afghanistan, success levels were contested, or the longer-term trend questioned. Schweich correctly complained those in attendance failed to face the reality of a predicted record opium harvest and instead highlighted the reduction in cultivation the previous year.[39]

Another record opium crop

With the US pushing eradication as the main element of its counter-narcotics effort, Karzai responded by promising increased eradication to achieve a 20 per cent reduction in cultivation in 2006.[40] Under pressure from Washington to maintain the reductions of the previous year, Neumann visited Helmand to emphasise to the governor that a successful campaign was *crucial* given the level of international scrutiny.[41] In part, domestic political realities drove the ambassador's desire to achieve substantial progress with the eradication campaign. With the White House, INL and Congress all pushing for more, eradication became an important measure in determining whether the counter-narcotics campaign was successful. Therefore, if not achieved with manual eradication, a lack of progress would lend weight to calls for aerial eradication. Although believing eradication an important tool, Neumann nevertheless opposed aerial spraying. Not for the first time in his two-year tenure, Neumann had to cajole the Afghans and British for *just enough* eradication to keep Washington and Congress content but, at the same time, not inflame Afghan or British sensitivities over the issue.[42] This was indicative of Neumann's diplomatic style: knowing when to force the issue when possible, but likewise, draw back when necessary. The veteran diplomat's approach was designed to 'keep policy in his hands'.[43] Although Neumann was well acquainted with the complexities of Afghanistan – having visited the country when his father was US Ambassador in the 1960s and 1970s – it was in Washington that many of his problems arose.

Congress, as the world's leading financer of counter-narcotics efforts, was able to promote eradication as the main component of the US's strategy by allocating it more funds than any other pillar. Congress had also constrained the ability of the US administration to deliver financial aid to the Afghan government if it did not implement substantial eradication. Neumann commented:

> there was a provision for a waiver that the administration was forced to use, but the Congressional pressure to increase restrictions was real. Both our war-fighting and development efforts could be endangered if we did not make enough progress to keep these restrictions from being triggered.[44]

Congress, for the most part, was guided by the view that narcotics in Afghanistan was filling the coffers of the Taliban. As such, a British diplomat explained, 'when questions arose about drugs policy, the instinct in Congress was to ask was it tough? Not does it work? It was very "hawkish".'[45]

During his visit to Helmand, Neumann indicated to Governor Daoud that it was vital that the rebranded Afghan Eradication Force (AEF) partake in the campaign.[46] The State Department had spent considerable money training the AEF and Congress insisted on its involvement.[47] Under instruction from London, Marsden was also anxious for the AEF to deploy and, crucially, to conduct the campaign in a pre-decided zone to circumvent any hostile reactions British troops might face on their forthcoming arrival to Helmand.[48] The Anglo-American partners agreed that areas selected for eradication should be: (1) poppy fields directly benefiting from irrigation projects, (2) poppy fields exceeding 1 ha (2.5 acres) in size and (3) poppy fields being grown on government-owned land.[49] As with most years, the allies and Afghan government launched a public information campaign to inform the population of the impending eradication process. This included commissioning radio adverts and billboards and distributing thousands of posters, stickers and booklets.[50]

In April 2006, British troops arrived in Helmand during the eradication campaign.[51] The insurgency used the unfortunate timing of their arrival to disseminate propaganda claiming the British *invaders* were in Helmand to eradicate the province's poppy crops.[52] Moreover, the British landed at the beginning of the traditional fighting season, which also coincided with the presence of Pakistani farm labourers in Helmand to harvest poppy. The point being as British General Sir Nicholas Houghton noted: 'They are very happy to stay on as guns for hire if there is a local tribal fight in which they can earn some money . . . In many ways, the poppy eradication gave them a cause.'[53] From the outset, the Taliban used Britain's colonial past and efforts as partner nation on counter-narcotics to foster anti-British sentiment in the province. For many, especially in southern Afghanistan, British participation in three Anglo-Afghan wars was still remembered and unfavourably so.[54]

More than 1,000 Afghan police and Afghan National Army (ANA), supported by US contractors DynCorp, deployed into the province to conduct the annual eradication campaign.[55] A cable from the US Embassy in Kabul cautiously pointed to the fact that the campaign represented 'an improvement over last year's in absolute numbers if not percentage of . . . ha cultivated'. The seven-week effort also saw the first deployment of a combined ANA and police operation – although its success was limited as security only briefly improved in some locations and was offset by security deteriorating in other areas.[56] Moreover, the cable further noted that in Helmand's 'poppy belt', where over 70 per cent of the province's poppy was cultivated, little, if any, eradication was conducted.[57,58] As routine, wide-scale corruption marred the eradication efforts, with local officials and the AEF striking deals to prevent its implementation. In a vivid example of Afghanistan's lawlessness, it was reported that 'significant numbers of police deserted their posts to work as day laborers in the poppy fields' in Helmand.[59]

Despite these setbacks, the Anglo-American allies and UNODC reported that eradication was, in fact, a success. This blatant over-reporting did not go unchallenged as Britain's own satellite imagery revealed that eradication was less than half of what was claimed. When a British contractor confronted the head of the BEDT with evidence disputing the claims, the diplomat was adamant that the scientifically rigorous imagery was wrong. By supporting inflated eradication numbers, the head of the BEDT hoped that he could cement a close relationship with the US Embassy in Kabul[60] – a key actor demanding increased eradication. It seemed, from a British perspective, the maintenance of the special relationship trumped all in Afghanistan.

The counter-narcotics 'success' of the previous year proved short-lived as several opium bans collapsed. In 2005, rural populations adhered to the national ban, predominately on the condition that development aid would be forthcoming and, in part, offset the financial hardship associated with forgoing opium cultivation. However, alternative livelihoods failed to alleviate the economic distress of farmers. Many of the programmes were quick impact, cash-for-work schemes that were unable to meet the financial demands of living costs and debt repayment. Furthermore, USAID-planned cash-for-work programmes were either late in starting, did not run for their projected duration or failed to provide farmers with significant loans.[61] All of which prevented the implementation of another nationwide opium ban and resulted in cultivation rising by 59 per cent – setting a record of 165,000 ha.[62]

Britain deploys to Helmand: reality sets in

The British deployed to Helmand with the aim of concentrating its efforts around the provincial capital, Lashkar Gah, and Gereshk to create a 'lozenge of security'.[63] The strategy, known as ink-spot, would in theory allow the gradual dispersion of security and reconstruction from the centre throughout the province (replicating the gradual expansion of an ink-spot), extending the authority of the Afghan government.[64] In essence, the strategy was defensive: substituting the pursuit of the Taliban for enhancing stabilisation and security, providing reconstruction and countering the narcotics trade.[65] However, after a matter of weeks, the commander of 16 Air Assault Brigade Brigadier Ed Butler came under pressure from Daoud and Karzai to change strategies and deploy his forces to northern Helmand, in what has since been named the 'platoon-house strategy'. The Afghans demanded the British re-establish government authority in northern Helmand – an area rich in opium growing and trafficking – by regaining control of districts that had fallen under Taliban influence.[66]

Given the limited resources on the ground, the military realised this plan was unsustainable but, after all, Daoud was *their* man in the province so they gave way to political pressure.[67] The reformulated strategy deployed soldiers to the districts of Musa Qala, Now Zad, Kajaki and Sangin.[68] From the outset, British forces came under intense daily attack, a situation exacerbated by the fact that only 650 out of the 3,300 troops deployed were combat soldiers.[69] The remaining troops were in Afghanistan to facilitate the key tasks of the mission: reconstruction and development. Under-resourced and ill-equipped to deal with the insurgency, British forces found themselves dragged into a bloody conflict.[70] That was in stark contrast to the well-documented and misinterpreted comment by the Defence Secretary John Reid, who hoped that British soldiers could complete their mission without firing a single shot.[71] As a result of the spiralling violence, Britain abandoned the original mission – to increase stability and security, provide reconstruction and counter the narcotics trade.[72]

This had disastrous consequences for Britain in Helmand. By

failing to deliver development aid and reconstruction, the population had seen little material improvement in their way of
life; further undermining the military's attempts to win hearts
and minds. A frustrated David Richards accused DFID of 'not
living up to our expectations and their own promises'.[73] DFID,
however, argued that its efforts were impeded by a hostile security
environment, resulting in very few DFID officials being deployed
to Helmand.[74] Whilst the military's complaint was not without
merit, the argument exposed the difficulties of civilian organisations operating in conflict zones. Understandably, given its structure, DFID's first and overriding priority was the protection of its
staff – and if that came at the expense of implementing development then so be it. A minister noted that:

> This was always a huge weakness ... our [DFID] representatives
> [were] trying to persuade poppy farmers to grow pomegranates and so
> on [then] the Taliban would turn-up and sabotage the project or kill
> somebody. It was simply impossible ... for them to continue with that
> work until there was a military guarantee of [protection].[75]

Another minister recalled the quagmire:

> it was not like rebuilding Germany after the end of World War II,
> where there was control from the allies until the domestic political
> capacity was built up. It was a lot more complicated that than. It was
> a difficult task, and that's the truth: it was a difficult task![76]

In addition to navigating an insecure operating environment,
some DFID officials were still dubious about the counter-narcotics
mission. As previously noted, many in the department viewed
counter-narcotics – given that farmers had an income – as incompatible with DFID's core mission of poverty reduction. An FCO
official recalls: 'DFID was always deeply uncomfortable [with
counter-narcotics. If they could] they would have been happy to
give us a chunk of development money and let us do development without them.' With counter-narcotics still a priority for
Blair, DFID had little choice but to remain, albeit reluctantly,
signed up to the mission. Theoretical considerations aside, DFID
was also concerned about the balance between short and long-
term interventions. In an effort to engender local support, both
the military and FCO supported 'quick impact projects' that

delivered instantaneous results. However, DFID officials argued that short-term initiatives, by their very nature, did not provide a sustainable means to transition poppy farmers out of opium cultivation.[77] Despite this view being underpinned by sound logic, for the first two years of the Helmand campaign, development work was focused on 'quick wins'.[78] As a result, development projects failed to deliver substantial or lasting benefits to poppy farmers.

One of the most controversial moments of Britain's first year in Helmand was its withdrawal from the district of Musa Qala in October 2006. After experiencing months of intense fighting, Daoud had brokered a peace deal that saw the British and Taliban withdraw from the town and the district elders placed in charge.[79] Britain's departure, whilst far from ideal, was deemed necessary to allow its forces to regroup and redeploy on a more mobile basis.[80] However, both the Afghans and the Americans were sceptical of making a deal with the Taliban. Karzai, for his part, used the opportunity to try and reinstate Akhundzada as Governor of Helmand, arguing he would 'bring the situation back under control'. The international community held firm and rejected Karzai's alternative plan of action. The US Embassy in Kabul was also deeply concerned about the agreement but nevertheless tried to make it work. A cable from the embassy suggested that if Musa Qala was subject to counter-narcotics measures it could provide a 'bridge toward normal governance in the district'.[81] At the military level, the US expressed their views more candidly: the agreement was tantamount to surrender.[82] A NSC official recalled an equally downbeat mood in Washington:

> [the deal] was a source of tension between our government and the British . . . I tried to put the British position in context with the folks that I worked with and said that this wasn't a surrender . . . it wasn't just giving up and running away.[83]

Given that the primary focus of both special relationship partners in Afghanistan was the defeat of the Taliban and al-Qaeda, it is of little surprise that the withdrawal – tactical or not – raised questions about British efforts. American concerns were justified as the agreement only lasted 143 days until 2 February 2007 when the Taliban re-entered the town, which according to the British military was against the wishes of the local population.[84]

9   The Lesser of Two Evils, 2006–2007

After identifying organised crime as a strategic threat to Britain, the Home Office restructured its antiquated multi-agency approach by creating the Serious Organised Crime Agency (SOCA), effective from 2006.[1] As part of this process, SOCA – described in the media as Britain's Federal Bureau of Investigation[2] – replaced HMCE as Britain's key law enforcement agency in Afghanistan. SOCA's primary function was disrupting the flow of narcotics to Britain through intelligence collection on narcotics traffickers and networks, interdiction and developing the capability of the Afghan police.

Like its predecessor, SOCA's 'leading partner' in Afghanistan was the DEA; the initial relationship, however, proved far from cordial. SOCA officials found the DEA a difficult and uncooperative partner, which led to a 'few very heated discussions'. In those discussions, while the point was made that 'we are all on the same side, so we have to work together',[3] the problem remained that the DEA, like other US agencies in Afghanistan, was under pressure from Washington to demonstrate its value to the counter-narcotics campaign. As a result, the DEA was concerned that another law enforcement agency would claim credit for its counter-narcotics successes.[4] More broadly, both organisations were separated by widely different operating cultures and at the outset this did not augur well. The DEA, on one hand, had a quasi-military culture, with some of its operatives having undergone intensive commando-style training. This military culture led a SOCA official to describe the DEA as not exactly 'gung-ho' but, 'they were certainly strong for aggressive deployments'. SOCA, on the other hand, whilst not technically a police force, was a civilian law enforcement organisation. During interactions, SOCA officials felt their American partner was dismissive of alternative points of view and unwilling to listen to their policy proposals.[5] Despite this early friction, the two agencies were able to manage their differences, and ended up cooperating closely on policy formulation and implementation.[6] Although SOCA and the DEA participated in the bi-annual counter-narcotics meetings, most of the interactions were conducted bilaterally – without the involvement of the FCO – either in London or Washington.[7]

Coinciding with improving relations between the British and American counter-narcotics enforcement agencies, the DEA and US military also resolved some of their initial difficulties. Throughout 2006, the US military slowly began supporting counter-narcotics activities, in particular, interdiction missions. Prompted by record levels of opium cultivation and concerns of a narco–insurgency nexus forming,[8] the military increased its airlift support to DEA interdiction operations. Although the Pentagon had agreed to provide airlift support in 2005, in reality they refused most DEA requests. The most significant factor for this was resource constraints; the military did not have enough helicopters to deploy at short notice.

By 2006, as counter-narcotics rose in significance and more resources became available, cooperation between the partners improved. In the first six months of the year, the military had granted twelve out of seventeen DEA airlift requests.[9] Additionally, the Pentagon also provided the Ministry of Interior (MOI) with helicopters to be used for counter-narcotics missions.[10] Reflecting on the alleged friction between the DEA and military over counter-narcotics, a US Embassy Kabul official noted that was 'an exaggerated urban legend'.[11] That said, at the tactical level, there were still occasions when the military refused to support counter-narcotics missions, fearing that doing so would damage the army's attempt to win the hearts and minds of the rural population. In Nangarhar Province, US Lieutenant General Benjamin Freakley aborted all DEA and Afghan counter-narcotics missions, complaining they were obstructing military missions.[12] Nevertheless, as time went on, both the counter-narcotics and military missions became more closely aligned.

The lesser of two evils: ground-based spraying

The record crop once again pushed the issue of aerial eradication to the forefront of Anglo-American counter-narcotics discussions.

As was the case in 2004, INL officials petitioned their FCO counterparts for stronger action by pointing to their failure to control opium cultivation. But by late 2006, not only were FCO officials under immense pressure to agree to some form of aerial eradication, the tone of the debate had changed. This came largely because of record amounts of opium and the change of leadership at INL the previous year. Influenced by her time as US Ambassador to Colombia, Anne Patterson, Charles's successor, championed the introduction of aerial eradication.[13] The highly respected diplomat was able to throw more political weight behind the drive than Charles – who, whilst vocal, was nevertheless a State Department outsider.[14]

Notwithstanding Patterson's diplomatic reputation and expertise deployed in favour of aerial eradication, it was her deputy, Thomas Schweich, who proved the key actor in the unfolding drama. A graduate of Yale and Harvard Law Schools, Schweich was an intelligent but temperamental former chief of staff to three US ambassadors to the UN, including Patterson.[15] Schweich's zeal for advocating an aggressive approach to the Afghan narcotics problem, specifically aerial eradication, resulted in several heated confrontations with his British counterparts in London, Kabul and Washington.[16] At one meeting in Kabul, a British Embassy official recounted, Schweich was 'difficult to deal with and was very assertive and insistent that a more aggressive policy needed to be pursued, including spraying'.[17] Even among his own colleagues, Schweich's approach was considered aggressively abrasive, to the point of a 'rabid dog'. During several Anglo-American counter-narcotics meetings when Schweich was in full flow, US officials felt 'uncomfortable', and 'didn't like sitting on the American side of things when that was going on'.[18]

With Schweich at the helm, relations between the Anglo-American allies over counter-narcotics policy had changed since the beginning of the decade, from 'a wholly cooperative one, where disagreements were worked around' to one where the fundamental difference on aerial eradication had 'become impossible to fudge any longer'.[19] As a result, the counter-narcotics relationship showed considerable strain and, over the following year, deteriorated further. What Schweich's view failed to appreciate, however, was the intersection between counter-narcotics and the wider Anglo-American agenda. Although counter-narcotics was an important objective for both Blair and Bush,[20] it was only one component of a multifaceted relationship. The British had deployed significant resources and expended considerable political capital supporting the US in two wars, with one widely unpopular. Time and again, Britain had demonstrated its value to the US campaign in Afghanistan, the most recent example of which was by playing a significant role in NATO's expansion into southern Afghanistan. Considering this support, Schweich's attempts to coerce Britain, in a direct and forceful way, to agree to aerial eradication undermined collegial relations with the US's most important partner. This point was not entirely lost among Americans. During a conversation with Schweich, a US Embassy official highlighted Britain's broader value to the US mission:

> You can . . . say all this stuff about the Brits . . . we are going to take over and we are going to crush the Brits . . . but you need to understand the British effort supporting the US government in . . . Afghanistan is huge. If it were not for the Brits being there . . . the American government would have tremendous problems in this region [with it] looking like . . . the Americans doing their will and imposing themselves. The Brits are hugely important to Bush and the US government beyond this narcotics thing. So, if you think this narcotics thing is something you are going to use to get the Brits put down by the US government, it ain't [sic] going to happen, so you are wasting your time.[21]

Nevertheless, Schweich, with evangelical enthusiasm, continued to press for aerial eradication.[22] The situation, however, was compounded by Britain's deployment to Helmand, which inserted another dynamic into Anglo-American discussions and strengthened Britain's resolve to reject aerial spraying and, more generally, wide-scale eradication. Like their US counterparts, the British military considered any policy, such as eradication, that attacked farmers' livelihoods a recipe for unrest and were fearful that if associated with widespread eradication in Helmand, Britain's soldiers would be in the firing line.[23] The military were clear: eradication was incompatible with winning the hearts and minds of the rural population. Consequently, the military became a powerful voice in resisting eradication in 'their' province, even though the British government, as partner nation on counter-narcotics, supported a limited and targeted manual eradication approach. The FCO were left with an impossible task: how to balance INL's visceral demands for more eradication, including aerial spraying, against the military's demands for less. This led to further tensions arising across the British foreign policy bureaucracy. A British diplomat in the Kabul Embassy explained, 'when we were in Helmand there was a lot more internal dispute about how to conduct the counter-narcotics effort . . . you had the military, in large numbers and at senior levels, saying we must not stir things up with counter-narcotics'.[24] An FCO official further elaborated:

> The same fault lines that you saw in the American government existed in Britain and the military was always suspicious of counter-narcotics. There was never an entirely consistent view across government [and] the military obviously had a rather different view to Number 10, and ideally would have downgraded our counter-narcotics to zero if they had their way.[25]

The Afghans too were still equally opposed to the introduction of aerial spraying. During a September meeting with Neumann, Karzai was still 'vehemently against aerial spraying'.[26] In her memoirs, Condoleezza Rice noted Karzai's objections: 'He did not want to even acknowledge the possibility of dramatic measures such as crop destruction through aerial spraying. This issue would be a source of tension between our two countries for the remainder of President [Bush's] term.'[27]

As the battle intensified between the allies, it was realised that some sort of compromise was needed. With strong backing in Washington, Neumann supported the implementation of a ground-based spraying (GBS) programme. The scheme would be a middle ground between the previously unsuccessful manual eradication and the much-opposed aerial eradication. Neumann championed the proposal in the hope that, if successful, it would provide a bulwark against the aerial eradication zealots in INL. Pressure was building in Washington that wide-scale eradication *must* take place, and the ambassador attempted to contain this tide by demonstrating enough progress through GBS. Whilst Washington formulated the broader direction of policy, Neumann had to some extent a degree of autonomy over implementation of details. More importantly, for the White House and State Department to be able to force through a controversial policy in Afghanistan, Neumann had to be onside.[28] As evidenced by Khalilzad's opposition to aerial eradication in 2004, it was very difficult to reach agreement if America's top diplomat in Kabul did not support the policy. This led to disagreement with INL, who championed a more aggressive policy than Neumann was willing to adopt.

During a 1–3 November 2006 trip to Kabul, Bush's NSA Stephen Hadley, who had succeeded Rice the previous year, sought to impress on Karzai the need to adopt GBS and persuade him to sell the idea to the public.[29] A cable from the US Embassy in Kabul suggested that Hadley gain the Afghan Minister of Counter-Narcotics Habibullah Qaderi's insight on the best way to get Karzai to approve GBS.[30] It is unclear if Qaderi did in fact offer Hadley any advice. Nevertheless, the US planned to first reach agreement with the British and ISAF, then approach Karzai to approve the plan. Three days later, on 6 November, the US Principals Committee approved GBS. It was now the job of US officials to convince their allies.[31]

On 8 November, at a working lunch organised to discuss donor support, the new British Ambassador to Afghanistan Stephen Evans expressed his concerns about spraying. He contended that the allies *had* a strategy in place, but it needed time to be effective, with Britain's position being 'that priority should be given to fully implementing Afghanistan's National Counternarcotics Strategy rather than introducing a new policy (eradication)'. He went on to say 'that progress on implementing the strategy is inhibited by security problems, but it should not be abandoned'. However, the Assistant Secretary of State for South and Central Asian Affairs Richard Boucher responded 'that efforts to reward reduction in cultivation are strengthened when backed by increased eradication – including spraying'. He further noted 'that poppy production is highest in some of the regions where there is the highest expenditure on alternative livelihood programs'.[32]

The issue was raised again when the Deputy Assistant Secretary of State for Pakistan, Afghanistan and Bangladesh John Gastright met with FCO, MOD and Cabinet Office officials in London on 14 November. During the meeting, the British delegation informed Gastright that Karzai had agreed to the introduction of GBS 'provided 1) that it was the agreed international position, 2) the programme was implemented throughout the country, and 3) he could say the international community forced it on him'. A cable from the US Embassy in London noted, however, as there is no capacity to conduct full GBS in all provinces this coming season, it was not clear whether Karzai was trying to set an impossible condition or merely saying that the GBS should be seen to be applied fairly.

Gastright suggested that GBS be implemented in Helmand and Badakhshan;[33] at this point, the British remained silent on whether they would support conducting GBS in Helmand. Less than a week later, however, Karzai confirmed his willingness for Helmand and another province to be the testing ground.[34] Now convinced that GBS would find approval, the US moved equipment and glyphosate into Kabul.[35] Unfortunately, whilst Karzai seemed to have agreed the plan for GBS, his Cabinet had not, and there lay a problem.

Aware of the mounting tensions in London, Washington and Kabul, FCO officials knew that they were running out of options to fend off the State Department and INL attempts to introduce aerial eradication. An FCO official reckoned: 'with the pressure of the Americans for more radical solutions, we felt under pressure . . . [so GBS] was certainly something that we embraced'.[36] FCO officials felt they had little choice but to back the proposal and submitted it to ministers for consideration, who subsequently approved it.[37] However, fearful of violent reaction from poppy farmers, Britain refused to support a pilot in Helmand; it had to be elsewhere. FCO officials gambled that agreeing to GBS would at the very least postpone the introduction of aerial eradication; at best, it would prove sufficiently successful to eliminate it as a policy option. Another FCO official elaborated:

> What we agreed to do was a pilot . . . not a full campaign. I couldn't see how Britain could resist GBS because the impact was not going to be that different to any other ground eradication. We knew there was going to be a showdown over aerial spraying . . . so this seemed a way of at least postponing it. Our policy through all of this was frankly to avoid aerial spraying.[38]

Underpinning this thinking, however, was the stability of the Anglo-American relationship. Agreeing to the proposal, in the words of an FCO official, 'showed a level of willingness to cooperate with the Americans'. The US was the main actor in Afghanistan and, for Britain to be successful in implementing policy, FCO officials needed to 'have a relationship' with INL. The official further stated:

> I couldn't afford to not be able to pick up the phone to the Americans ... The US were the biggest players, they were the people that could make the biggest difference and cause the biggest amount of trouble. So, we had to manage that.[39]

Despite being partner nation on counter-narcotics, Britain did not have the resources or manpower to drive forward the counter-narcotics campaign alone; as such, US support was crucial. However, throughout many US departments, a preference existed for robust action, making the US a difficult interlocutor and complicating the policymaking process. Even when these preferences ran contrary to its favoured approach, Britain still had to find a way to make the relationship work. As a result, FCO officials felt that since 2004, 'tempering bad policy' and 'trying to exercise damage control' characterised their interactions with their INL counterparts.[40] The discussions over introducing GBS followed a similar trajectory. Another FCO official reflected:

> it's a slightly arrogant British way of expressing it but certainly as far as the aerial debate was concerned [tempering bad policy] was true. Extending the point, there were plenty of us who were sceptical that ground-based spraying would achieve very much but we were willing to try it out as a less bad option than aerial.[41]

INL and, more generally, US policies were, in the minds of FCO and other British officials, forthright and aggressive; it was Britain's job to continue the long-held tradition – however, spurious that tradition was – of improving US policies. This stemmed from the asymmetry between both partners; altering US policies was the best Britain could hope for.

Whilst in one respect Britain was tempering American policy, in another it showed the considerable sway that the US held over the policy debate vis-à-vis Britain, which was partner nation on counter-narcotics. For two years, Britain's eradication policy had been under pressure, and by agreeing to GBS, demonstrated that Britain had to bend to American will. By doing so, FCO officials had gambled it would kill the prospect of aerial eradication; it appeared, however, that the gamble had failed. While the British thought that they were tempering US policy, the Americans simply saw it as preparatory groundwork for eventually doing what they really wanted to do. A report from the US Embassy in Kabul noted: 'more importantly, [ground-based spraying] is designed as an icebreaker to get acceptance for other than mechanical and manual means'. In other words: aerial eradication.[42] As Britain's eradication approach became more aggressive through approval of GBS, ironically it made the prospect of aerial eradication more not less likely.[43]

Despite the Anglo-American partners having reached an agreement in December 2006, the debate over where to conduct GBS continued. Boucher concluded that while it was reasonable that Britain was concerned about Helmand, they should view the bigger picture and not just concentrate on 'their' province. Afghan National Security Advisor Zalmai Rassoul complained that Britain's attitude was indicative of the narrow focus of NATO countries towards 'their' provinces, unlike the wider focus of the coalition.[44] At a 10 January 2007 meeting with Boucher, Karzai also complained about Britain's narrow focus on Helmand. Boucher noted that he would impress on the British the need to sanction GBS in Helmand[45] when they were in Washington in several weeks' time.[46]

On 21 January, agreement on GBS came when Neumann, British Embassy officials and others met with Karzai and his Cabinet to discuss its introduction.[47] Although Karzai had tentatively agreed to GBS, there was no guarantee it would find broader Cabinet support. This fact was not lost on a US Embassy official who recalled a previous conversation he had with Faizullah Kakar, the Deputy Minister for Public Health. Holding a master's degree in toxicology from Indiana University and PhD in epidemiology from the University of Washington,[48] Kakar challenged the official: 'when DDT was [prevalent throughout] the US, how did that work out? How many birds [and] species did you lose as a result of DDT poisoning?'[49] During the meeting, Kakar argued his point forcefully: glyphosate use would result in damaging health and environmental consequences.[50] The Cabinet needed little cajoling: there would be no GBS in 2007. The episode left Neumann convinced that spraying, of any kind, would never find approval in Afghanistan. If the US could not persuade a small group of educated and westernised Afghans, then there was little hope of convincing a larger group of less-educated, rural Afghans.[51]

With the GBS proposal vetoed, Neumann still needed to demonstrate progress on eradication to placate the White House and Congress. He devised a plan to manually eradicate 10,000 ha – a politically viable number that he could peddle in Washington.[52] A considerable eradication campaign, focused on government-held territories, was launched in Helmand. Overseeing the operation was the province's new Governor, Assadullah Wafa, the previous Governor of Kunar and Karzai's distant relative.[53] His predecessor, Engineer Daoud, was dismissed after the British, once again, petitioned Karzai to remove a member of the provincial leadership. This time, the British lobbied Karzai to remove Akhundzada's brother Amir, as deputy Governor. What the British failed to anticipate was that Karzai, under the pretence of maintaining the delicate tribal balance, also fired 'their' man in the province, Daoud, although David Richards suspected the move was designed to demonstrate that Karzai, not the British, 'called the shots' in Helmand.[54] Before the campaign, Wafa demanded that eradication not only focus on 'friends of the government' but also be extended to Taliban-controlled areas in Northern Helmand. However, for that to happen a major military operation was needed, something that could not be mobilised without significant planning.[55]

The Helmand eradication campaign once again brought the US Embassy in Kabul into conflict with the British military, as the latter feared improperly targeted eradication would drive insecurity. The previous year, David Richards had suggested that eradication was postponed for twelve months to prevent an increase in violence and allow alternative livelihood programmes to reach more farmers. However, Neumann declined his suggestion, fearing it would destabilise eradication programmes throughout the country – and, of course, incur the wrath of Congress.[56] With the ambassador pushing for eradication, the British military sought to limit where and when the eradication force could deploy, complaining that 'the AEF has set back security progress in Helmand by 12 months . . . [and] the AEF drives residents into the arms of the Taliban and interferes with critical security operations'.[57] According to a US Embassy official, the British military were obstructive throughout the planning phase of the operation: 'There were questions about where they [the AEF] could operate. There were a lot of discussions with the British military about this and every time they said not that area. There was a no to every proposal, but no counter proposal.' The official further noted that during discussions:

> There was a lot of left-over criticism of the British effort to buy the crop . . . it was old news, it added to the scrappiness because people were scoring points. I remember us having friction rather than intellectual debates about the past . . . there were issues about eradication . . . particularly in Helmand where we had to have consent from the British.[58]

With the British military stonewalling American Embassy officials, Neumann had to mediate and take the issue to Richards. He explained that he needed to make progress with eradication to satisfy domestic political pressures from the White House and Congress. After Richards appealed to the British military, a compromise was reached, and Britain agreed to allow the AEF to operate in certain locations.[59]

Notwithstanding the agreement, the episode demonstrated the waning of collegiality as efforts to halt opium cultivation failed. The quest for more eradication was fed from Washington into the US Embassy in Kabul which in turn fed it onto its British allies. The process shows the degree to which domestic political realities informed policy implementation and how this impacted broader alliance politics. The counter-narcotics alliance showed considerable strain, with policy discussions disintegrating into counterproductive recriminations instead of meaningful debates. That in turn meant senior British officials had to defend their positions robustly, creating a self-reinforcing circle of discord and mutual resentment, all of which prevented the advancement of constructive policy solutions. As US officials pushed for stronger eradication, it fostered resentment within the alliance and added to the sense that the British were being bullied and cajoled into accepting a policy that was neither prudent nor commensurate with their objectives. This was particularly pronounced as British soldiers were dying to stabilise Helmand. It was not long before predictions of a massive opium crop surfaced, and relations deteriorated further.

10   The Showdown over Aerial Eradication, 2007

In January 2007, with alarm mounting over the prospect of another record opium crop, a crisis Cabinet met at the White House. Acknowledging that the previous counter-narcotics strategy had failed, the Deputy Secretary of State John Negroponte and Director of the White House Office of National Drug Control Policy John Walters assembled an interagency committee to reformulate strategy.[1] The man charged with fronting the interagency strategy was Schweich, who, after Patterson's recommendation, was promoted to ambassadorial rank.[2] Holding him in high regard, Patterson considered Schweich a 'formidable' operator and someone that had the necessary 'juice within the interagency' process to push through INL's agenda.[3]

As the discussion gathered pace, Congress again attempted to shape the debate. In February 2007, members of Congress wrote to Rice and the new Defense Secretary Robert Gates regarding rampant opium cultivation. Gates, a twenty-seven-year intelligence veteran and former President of Texas A&M University, placed more weight on the counter-narcotics mission than his predecessor.[4] This was hardly surprising given that Rumsfeld was one of the strongest opponents to a full-scale counter-narcotics campaign in Afghanistan. It was Rumsfeld's handling of the Iraq War, however, that eventually proved his downfall. Amid widespread discontent about the conflict, the Republicans lost control of both chambers of Congress in the 2006 midterm elections; the following day Rumsfeld was forced to resign.[5] The letter implored the administration to increase its efforts and underscored the need for domestic and international unity:

> The open and public dispute with our British allies on opium eradication methods, along with the many different and often conflicting

views of NATO, our Defense Department, the Drug Enforcement Administration, and other US agencies on how to best handle the narcotics challenge, does <u>not</u> bode well for success in taking on a major source of the financing for the Taliban and other anti-coalition militants.[6]

Whilst Schweich set about developing his strategy, recurring difficulties appeared in Helmand. The complexity of balancing Britain's objectives in Afghanistan was again brought to the fore when the military's dislike of eradication exploded. In March and April, fearing local anger, Britain's Task Force Helmand distributed pamphlets and commissioned radio announcements that stated ISAF was not involved in the anti-poppy campaign.[7] The leaflets read: 'ANA and ISAF will not destroy your poppy fields. Poppies serve as the only tool of economy and benefits for the farmers and we don't want to stop your source of feeding and income.' A radio announcement further stated: 'that ISAF and the ANA know that many Afghans have no choice but to grow poppy and ISAF and the ANA do not want to affect their livelihoods'.[8] Understandably this provoked a political outcry from the civilian agencies that wanted to promote the counter-narcotics strategy.

Karzai and the MOI complained that the messages 'undermined the [GOIRA]'s counter-narcotics operation' by implying that ISAF permitted opium cultivation. The Deputy Minister of Interior for Counter-Narcotics Mohammed Daud informed ISAF officials that they were in Afghanistan supporting the GOIRA, and therefore were duty bound to declare opium cultivation illegal. ISAF attempted to gloss over the issue by explaining the communications were designed to inform farmers of the purpose of Operation Achilles: a military offensive against the insurgency – not eradication of poppy fields.[9] Angered by the misjudged messages, Schweich flew to Brussels to show the leaflets to the Supreme Allied Commander Europe (SACEUR).[10] The British were in the direct political firing line and Schweich lodged a formal complaint with the FCO and British Embassy in Kabul.[11] The leaflets not only exposed inter-governmental tensions but they also exposed domestic pressures between ADIDU and the military over Britain's objectives. An FCO official commented: 'they put out a very silly leaflet that said: don't blame us! The commander got hauled over the coals; it was absolutely out of line.'[12]

More broadly, the incident highlighted the growing tension

between the British military and the US over Helmand. During a March meeting with Walters, the new ISAF commander, General Dan McNeill said he was: 'dismayed by the British effort' and that they had 'made a mess of things in Helmand'. Citing the failed Musa Qala agreement, which had led to the recapture of the town, McNeill stated: 'That agreement opened the door to narco-traffickers in that area, and now it was impossible to tell the difference between the traffickers and the insurgents.' Moreover, given Britain's lead role in Helmand its efforts needed to be vastly improved.[13] A US military officer commented that: 'Musa Qala was a terrible deal, it was not good for anybody. It was not good for the Alliance, it was not good for the British and it damn sure wasn't good for Karzai.' However, the military officer was equally adamant that while the deal was fundamentally flawed, the British were still up to the job:

> I'm not saying the British were not up to the task, I'm saying that choice of tactic . . . was ill advised . . . The closest friends the US has are the British. Sometimes they are awfully hard to be friends with, but they are the best friends we have got.[14]

In late 2007, Britain, with the help of the US, recaptured control of the town.

In the same meeting McNeill also raised concerns about Karzai's commitment to counter-narcotics, describing him as 'the missing ingredient'.[15] By 2007, American and British officials thought that Karzai was at best wilfully ambivalent to the narcotics trade or at worst deliberately obstructive, viewing his rhetoric as shallow and deceptive. Publicly, Karzai declared that opium cultivation contravened Islamic law and acknowledged the corrosive effects on the state. Privately, he also made similar statements when meeting with western officials. Rice noted that when she discussed the issue with Karzai, the president always put a positive spin on his assessment of the narcotics problem: 'we're making real progress'. This was a case of Karzai's political charm ignoring the hard evidence. Karzai's contentions left Rice unsure whether: 'Karzai believed what he was saying or just thought that we might.'[16] However, despite his statements about fighting the narcotics trade, he took very little action to seriously address the issue.

Karzai's action against the narcotics industry during his first eighteen months in power was replaced with a realistic recognition that he needed the support of the powerful networks involved in the narcotics industry and a more nuanced approach if success was to be achieved. Power in Afghanistan, even for the president, was conditional on continuing support. Karzai had to rely on the use of patronage as a tool to cement his power base and if that meant turning a blind eye to some of his followers' connections to the narcotics industry so be it. Additionally, Karzai was fearful that wide-scale eradication would drive farmers into the arms of the insurgency.[17] There was also a larger economic concern that compromised preventive action: the IMF noted that 'a successful [counter-narcotics] campaign could adversely affect GDP growth, the balance of payments and government revenue'.[18] Opium cultivation was a symptom of the broader problem, therefore Karzai was restricted in his action until a comprehensive structure was in place to deal with the issues of poor governance, corruption, security, rule of law and economic development. The lack of unity of action within the special relationship to agree on the best methods to counter the narcotics trade allowed Karzai to forgo stronger action. This was a catch-22 situation. Karzai could not afford to suppress narcotics until a viable economy and system of governance were in place, but for them to function effectively strides against the narcotics industry were needed.

The push for aerial eradication

The pressure to force aerial eradication onto the agenda intensified when another Colombia veteran, William Wood, succeeded Neumann in April 2007. Wood, a career diplomat with thirty years' service, had overseen one of the US's largest counter-narcotics programmes in Colombia and championed aerial eradication as an effective tool in the fight against narcotics. Proponents of aerial eradication were optimistic at his appointment as he favoured strong measures.[19] This approach became evident to the British Embassy in Kabul early in Wood's tenure. Meeting a British official at a diplomatic event, Wood complained: 'what the British were doing on drugs was half-hearted and inadequate'. The official recounted: 'I reacted quite strongly to that and we traded blows for a moment.' Wood's comments belittled British efforts, as the official further commented: 'the thing that startled me was, frankly, the rudeness with which he made this point about a programme on which the FCO was spending roughly £50 million a year, so it was not a minor effort for us'.[20]

Coinciding with Wood's arrival was the appointment of Sir Sherard Cowper-Coles as the new British Ambassador to Afghanistan. An Oxford University graduate and former Ambassador to Israel and Saudi Arabia, Cowper-Coles was considered a diplomatic heavyweight. His arrival signalled an escalation in the campaign as Britain sharply increased its civilian resources to complement the increase in military resources.[21] Cowper-Coles's task was complicated by the fact that the military was now confronting a full-scale conflict and the counternarcotics effort had gone from bad to worse.[22] In response to rising cultivation, the FCO also increased the size of the counternarcotics team in Kabul and restructured it to focus on purely narcotics-related matters (as opposed to previously focusing on rule of law as well). A British diplomat at the Kabul Embassy recalled the urgency in London: 'there was a lot of pressure from the centre to show some progress'.[23] During Cowper-Coles first meeting with his US counterpart, Wood discussed replicating what he saw as the successful aerial eradication programme implemented in Colombia. The next day, Wood laid forth his proposal for wide-scale eradication in Helmand to Cowper-Coles[24] – Schweich also reported that Wood sent an email advocating an aerial eradication campaign to destroy 80,000 ha of opium in Helmand.[25] Convinced of glyphosate's safety, Wood boasted he would have himself sprayed to demonstrate its harmlessness[26] – a stunt he had reportedly performed in Colombia.[27] Relations between both ambassadors were extremely cordial, but over the coming months Cowper-Coles was under pressure from Wood to agree to aerial eradication. As Cowper-Coles recalled: 'He looked to me to swing HMG [Her Majesty's Government] behind such an approach.'[28] Given Wood's support for aerial eradication, Cowper-Coles mischievously christened him 'Chemical Bill', a play on 'Chemical Ali', the notorious Iraqi official who ordered thousands of Kurds to be gassed in 1988.[29] Likely unaware of the origins of his nickname, Wood, on occasion, even referred to himself as 'Chemical Bill'.[30]

The bureaucratic battleground over the issue became more entangled, as Number 10 intervened to pressure Kabul Embassy officials to agree to some form of spraying. When it was evident that counter-narcotics policies had failed to make a significant dent in the narcotics trade, Blair was reportedly 'depressed' by the lack of progress.[31] Cowper-Coles recounted: 'As the debate raged back and forth . . . [there was] pressure from 10 Downing Street for us to agree to some spraying.'[32] Adding to the pressure, Bush's support for aerial eradication did not go unnoticed on the other side of the Atlantic. Cowper-Coles recounts: Bush attempted to engender support for the policy by mentioning the issue – on more than one occasion – to the prime minister, 'urging us to support' the policy.[33] If the British were onside, it would perhaps help the president win the policy debate against the influential Pentagon naysayers.

Meanwhile Schweich's new counter-narcotics strategy was developing in Washington. In an effort to confirm the policy, the senior director for Afghanistan at the NSC, Anthony Harriman, submitted it to the Deputies Committee in May 2007. At that point, Harriman also instructed Schweich to compose an unclassified version. DOD reaction was predictable: it attempted to derail the policy's rite of passage and stall the release of the unclassified version. Members of the DOD threatened Schweich with professional retribution if he disclosed the unclassified version to the public. When the Pentagon failed to prevent the release, they used back channel methods to kill off the policy by allegedly disclosing the classified version to British Defence Attaché and Head of the Defence Staff in Washington Major General Peter Gilchrist.[34] The British had consistently opposed aerial eradication and Gilchrist informed Schweich that its position had not changed. A British military officer commented, 'I think this was aimed by the DOD to kill aerial eradication once and for all.'[35] Britain, of course, was only too willing to capitalise on the opportunities that alliance with the Pentagon presented. An FCO official relates how Britain used the alliance to undercut INL's plans for aerial eradication: 'I would . . . lobby different parts of the American system to oppose what we thought INL wanted to do. The Pentagon absolutely were our allies in that because [it] did not want to do aerial spraying.'[36] On 26 July, word reached Cowper-Coles that the US were preparing to push through aerial eradication against the wishes of the Afghan and British governments, as well as both sides' military establishments. In response to this danger, he was determined to work with the Afghan government to stop aerial eradication. 'We had a fight on our hands, a fight which we would win only by telling the Afghan Government that HMG would support it in resisting US pressure to agree to spraying.'[37] The Pentagon's plan to derail aerial eradication from the new strategy by feeding information to the British had yet to come to fruition.

In August, the new Labour Prime Minister Gordon Brown also intervened when he telephoned Bush and asked him not to coerce Karzai into accepting aerial eradication when he visited the US.[38] From the outset, the relationship between Brown and Bush was less close than had been the case with Blair. During the prime minister's first visit to Camp David the previous month, the atmosphere was tense as Brown made a point of distancing himself from the overtly friendly relations displayed by Blair.[39] Despite Bush's praise for Brown at the conference, it was later reported that the president had concerns about Brown's suitability as prime minister – after the latter had berated Rice in a previous encounter.[40] The situation was compounded by Brown's decision to reduce Britain's commitment in Iraq, at the time of the US surge.[41] That said, while the partnership had cooled, Brown was still committed to foster good Anglo-American relations. Crucially though, this had to be done 'without [Brown] doing a Tony'.[42]

Notwithstanding the cooling of relations between Bush and Brown, these developments illustrate vividly the dynamics of the complex policy formulation process in the Anglo-American alliance in Afghanistan. There was a veritable roundabout of pressures from INL to the Pentagon to the British and on to the Karzai government with several pressure flows back onto the US government not to adopt aerial spraying. In detail, this involved INL battling the British and Afghan governments to adopt its policy proposal. At the same time, it had domestic constituencies undermining its attempts, notably the Pentagon, which in turn on this occasion found a marriage of convenience with Britain helpful in the Washington bureaucratic turf war, as both were opposed to the introduction of aerial spraying. The policy landscape was fractured between INL's hard-line approach forged in Colombia, the Pentagon's reluctance to engage with counter-narcotics and Britain's approach somewhere in-between. It is also fair to say that, in the face of objection from most of their domestic and international partners, INL's pursuit of aerial eradication was almost ideological. This acrimony between the key actors regarding eradication was prejudicial for attempts at building a cohesive counter-narcotics approach, and more importantly, allowing the existing policies space and time to take effect. In the face of rising opium cultivation, counter-narcotics policy suggestions became reactive, with many in the US administration urging policies that they hoped would yield instantaneous results.

In August 2007, Schweich's interagency team published its unclassified Counter-Narcotics Strategy. It supported the first five points of the ANDCS: public information, alternative development, elimination/eradication, interdiction and law enforcement/justice reform.[43] The strategy emphasised the need to dramatically increase assistance to provinces that had reduced opium cultivation, whilst simultaneously intensifying both interdiction and eradication operations.[44] To meet this need, INL and Britain established the Good Performers Initiative to donate financial aid to provinces that reduced poppy cultivation significantly or completely. The budget for the programme was between $25 million and $50 million. A further incentive was the delivery of development aid to compliant governors.[45]

Unsurprisingly, in addition the revised strategy advocated a robust eradication plan, with the option of introducing aerial spraying.[46] Schweich was critical of the Afghan government's record on eradication and stated that manual techniques could only eradicate 10 per cent of the overall crop, a figure Schweich – and UNODC officials – contended would have to increase to 25 per cent to act as a tipping point for success[47] (however, the evidence to justify why 25 per cent would act as a tipping point was unclear). Schweich also wanted to double the amount of poppy-free provinces from six to twelve by the following year.[48]

In reality, the strategy differed very little from the US's first counter-narcotics strategy and notably one that had already failed to produce significant reductions in the level of opium cultivation. The strategy drew criticism from members of the House Committee on Foreign Affairs, Representative Tom Lantos and Representative Ileana Ros-Lehtinen: 'What the plan lacks is the recognition that Afghanistan is approaching a crisis point, and that immediate action is required . . . so we can reverse the country's steady slide into a potential failed narco-state.'[49] The plan represented a shift in tactics as opposed to a shift in strategy.[50] All this was beginning to look like a political quandary that was sucking away the energy required for developing effective policies.

The situation reached a crescendo when the UNODC's 2007 Afghanistan Opium Survey confirmed that there had been a record 193,000 ha of opium planted, leading to a concerted effort by the State Department and INL to force aerial eradication onto the policy agenda. In the survey's summary, UNODC Executive Director Antonio Maria Costa claimed: 'opium cultivation in Afghanistan is no longer associated with poverty – quite the opposite'. An assertion that was later rejected by the UNODC's own Independent Evaluation Unit.[51] Nevertheless, Costa's justification for such a claim was that: 'Helmand, Kandahar and three other opium-producing provinces in the south are the richest . . . while the much poorer northern region is abandoning the poppy crops.'[52] This theory, unsurprisingly, was endorsed by the State Department who also pointed to the fact that Helmand Province accounted for 53 per cent of opium cultivation in Afghanistan and was one of the wealthiest. Furthermore, they stated if Helmand was a country it would be the fifth largest beneficiary of US aid in the world[53] receiving $400 million between 2002 and 2007.[54] This, according to the US Embassy in Kabul, stood in direct contrast to Karzai's claims that farmers were driven to cultivation as a result of poverty.[55] However, the overall picture was complex. The accuracy of such claims was refuted and indeed, in many circumstances, poverty was a key factor in opium cultivation.

Costa also claimed that opium cultivation was inextricably tied to the insurgency.[56] Again, this argument found State Department and INL support, who pointed to reductions in the north, where there was minimal insurgent activity and increases in south, where insurgent activity was high.[57] Since 2003, INL had unsuccessfully pushed the narco–insurgency narrative, but, by 2007, the theory had gained currency across the US administration.[58] Conditioned by its experience in Colombia, INL highlighted the financial relationship between the Taliban and narcotics industry as evidence of this nexus replicating itself in Afghanistan. To combat this, INL contended wholesale eradication would bankrupt the Taliban by taking away a key source of its income. More importantly, the reasoning went, it would weaken the Taliban's long-term capacity to continue its insurgency. A State Department official noted that – although it took seventeen years – Plan Colombia was instrumental in bringing FARC to the negotiating table. Therefore, aerial eradication was not only a weapon to be utilised against narcotics trafficking, but it could be used to defeat terrorism and install the rule of law.[59]

David Kilcullen, a counter-terrorism expert advising the State Department, contended that since 'areas of major narcotics activity have increasingly become geographically aligned with areas of Taliban influence', wholesale forced eradication would not alienate the local population. He added: 'even the harshest efforts to eradicate the poppy would be highly unlikely to alienate anything like the majority of the population, except in areas that already firmly support the Taliban and are therefore already alienated anyway'.[60]

Whilst State Department and UNODC officials were convinced of the convergence of the Taliban and narcotics traffickers, British officials disagreed. Although they identified a loose relationship between the two groups, there was a dearth of evidence to conclude that both organisations were one and the same. An FCO official recalled: 'there was analysis to try to understand any relationship between the insurgency and the drugs trade and frankly, at that stage, we weren't able to show very much ... although we knew there was some money moving around'.[61] SOCA officials also concluded that whilst both organisations were connected, narco-traffickers were not fully paid up members of the insurgency.[62]

In short, the parallels between the Taliban and FARC were over-exaggerated, and did not reflect the fluid, local and decentralised nature of the Taliban's relationship with the narcotics industry.[63] In fact, neither the State Department nor UNODC could accurately estimate how much money the Taliban generated from narcotics.[64] The Taliban did not gain the majority of its funding from taxation of the opium industry, as international observers claimed. Moreover, officials with either direct or indirect ties to the government were just as much, if not more, involved in the narcotics industry than the Taliban.[65]

Despite the evidence being disputed, State Department and INL officials used the narco–insurgency narrative to buttress their arguments to introduce aerial spraying. Recalling this pressure, an FCO official noted that in the coming weeks and months there was an enormous 'amount of activity which went up to ministerial level'.[66] The US was pushing aerial eradication in every counter-narcotics conversation in London, Washington and Kabul.[67] INL's argument was simple as a British military commander recalled:

we have given you every chance ... you have completely failed! Ground eradication isn't working, alternative livelihoods isn't working, criminal justice system is not convicting enough people, and interdiction is doing well but not well enough. What are you going to do about it?[68]

In other words, if not aerial eradication, what do you suggest?[69] Given that Britain had failed to prevent record amounts of opium cultivation, this was not an entirely unreasonable question. However, INL officials were 'evangelical' in their belief that opium cultivation was illegal and required dealing with as such.[70] This viewpoint was myopic and failed to appreciate the complexity of transitioning farmers out of opium cultivation. Not only would aerial eradication inflame rural tension, but it would not provide a sustainable solution to the opium problem. Nevertheless, a high-impact solution was needed to prevent the derailment of the Afghan state-building project.[71]

By autumn 2007, INL, State Department and White House officials began ramping up pressure on their European and Afghan allies over the issue.[72] This increased Anglo-American tension in Kabul, but as a British diplomat recalled: 'they pushed hard – but we also pushed back hard'.[73] Around this time, INL had thrown its considerable weight behind the drive to introduce aerial eradication by spending $6 million researching herbicidal eradication techniques and purchasing spray equipment.[74] The previous year, in 2006, Schweich had also conducted extensive research on the best method to get 'spray planes' into Afghanistan, whether that be manufacturing new planes or reconfiguring existing aircraft.[75] All this amounted to sustained pressures for aerial eradication that were difficult to resist.

Karzai and his government colleagues, like the British and Europeans, had been under heavy pressure from US officials to support aerial eradication; numerous members of the Bush administration spoke to them several times. Wood, Rice, Hadley, Walters, Boucher, Schweich and others attempted to persuade Karzai to adopt aerial spraying. Wood and Boucher pressed Karzai over the issue, but he continued to refuse until, in the words of a State Department official, 'he had something to offer the farmers. But at that point, we were not giving him anything else to offer the farmers.'[76] During a September meeting with Karzai, Boucher suggested conducting aerial spraying in Taliban-controlled territories and manual eradication in government-controlled ones. Attempting to evade the issue, Karzai 'gave no reaction'.[77] After it was clear that he would not discuss aerial eradication, the US again suggested introducing GBS to persuade the Afghans of the effectiveness and safety of spraying, which might then make aerial eradication acceptable. Karzai remained unenthusiastic about the idea.[78] Nevertheless, his reluctance did not deter those pushing for aerial eradication and the debate in the US gained momentum.

The failure to control opium cultivation was now a pressing concern for both the interagency Deputies Committee and the more senior NSC. A State Department official explained the sense of urgency both committees felt:

> I don't think it was something that could be put off. We had to find a way to get at the [opium] problem [and] . . . spraying was the only thing that we had seen be successful elsewhere and so we should give it a try.[79]

By late 2007, the plan for aerial eradication had gained so much traction within the administration that the NSC approved it. A cable reported that Washington had 'reached . . . internal consensus' over the issue,[80] but the claim of internal consensus disguised feebly continuing reservations elsewhere in the administration, most notably at the Pentagon. A State Department official recounted the range of views present:

> There was widely shared wild enthusiasm for it! [There was] consensus but everybody had to agree or at least drop their objections. The military begrudgingly came along and said we want to make sure that the areas where we are about to conduct operations are not suddenly going to be sprayed . . . So, everybody had a caveat on it but by and large our goal was to start spraying . . . You might say we are all united with different levels of enthusiasm.[81]

The plan was to launch a pilot programme in Nangarhar Province, where the US had a significant presence. The scheme aimed to destroy 4,000 to 5,000 ha whilst informing the public the plan would only be utilised against rich, corrupt farmers. The pilot programme would then roll out across Afghanistan.[82] The US Embassy in Kabul had reached an agreement with Nangarhar Governor Gul Aga Shirzai to conduct the pilot[83] – he had also been in favour of GBS.[84] With the US having reached something approaching internal consensus over the issue, it was now the task of officials to sway their British allies. During a counter-narcotics meeting in Washington, Schweich confronted FCO officials over the issue. The British remained steadfast in opposing aerial eradication, but Schweich, convinced of the US's supremacy over the policymaking process, retorted: 'it doesn't matter what you Brits think because the president is going to agree' and that meant it would happen. In efforts to pre-empt the forthcoming State Department onslaught, FCO officials submitted a policy proposal to Foreign Secretary David Miliband recommending the rejection of aerial eradication.[85] The policy submission was bolstered by the fact that at the point US support for aerial eradication in Afghanistan reached peak pressure,[86] the Colombian government downgraded aerial eradication in favour of manual eradication.[87] A diplomat in Kabul recalled when embassy staff discovered the news before attending an Afghan Cabinet meeting over aerial eradication: 'it felt that morning as if Christmas had arrived early'.[88]

Despite this boost, word reached the FCO that Bush had agreed with the NSC and approved the policy.[89] The president had remained a supporter, albeit somewhat passively, of aerial eradication since Powell pitched Plan Afghanistan in late 2004. When the issue went to Bush, he sought the opinion of Wood and McNeill. Predictably, Wood was 'all for it'. McNeill, however, was more cautious, arguing that whilst it would be 'helpful', the plan if implemented contained certain risks, namely:

> the day you spray, the next morning standing in front of the international press will be some insurgent holding a badly deformed infant and he will say this is what they did to us. [So] we have to be able to live with that.[90]

Bush's decision was that the 'Brits and Afghans had to line up' behind the policy.[91] However, given the cool relations between himself and Brown, Bush was unwilling to raise the issue with the prime minister fearing it may 'undermine the Anglo-American relationship'.[92] Therefore, to get the British 'to line up', Rice scheduled a call with Miliband to press the issue. As Miliband had only been in office for a matter of months, officials were unsure if he would back them or give in to American pressure for aerial spraying. Despite being ambivalent towards the counter-narcotics mission, Miliband immediately recognised that the introduction of aerial eradication would be counterproductive to the international community's efforts in Afghanistan. When the telephone call came, Miliband told Rice that Britain would not support aerial eradication in Afghanistan.[93]

Frustrated, the US now targeted Karzai in an attempt to finally coerce him into agreeing to the plan. They could then, in turn, use his compliance to defeat British opposition. A State Department official recalled: 'we knew that the British had lined up against it [but] they had to say well if Karzai agrees then I guess it is okay'.[94] The British, however, had other ideas. From the moment that Pentagon officials informed Gilchrist of the INL and White House's intention to force through aerial eradication, Britain launched a counteroffensive. The plan was simple but effective: they forewarned Karzai of the developments and pledged their support against the introduction of aerial eradication. When Rice and Wood pressed Karzai to support the new policy, Anglo-American disunity gave Karzai, who was also supported by his Cabinet,[95] the perfect excuse to refuse by pointing to British opposition.[96] Although unimpressed by British efforts in Helmand, and angered about the removal of Akhundzada, Karzai used the triangular policy relationship between himself, Britain and the US to suit his own ends. When under pressure from the State Department and White House to agree to aerial eradication, he used Britain's reluctance to strengthen his own case against adopting the policy.[97] The feud led to Anglo-American friction in Kabul as a British Embassy official recounted: 'Wood complained because we told Karzai what was coming without telling the Americans and they got upset; there was quite significant pressure.'[98]

When raising aerial eradication for a final time with Karzai during a videoconference, Bush said, 'we think that aerial spraying is the only way to get at the narcotics problem'. Karzai then 'went through his arguments that it was going to alienate more people that it was going to help. [Instead] we needed to go in with alternative livelihoods and until we could do that we should not spray.'[99] Although a US military officer believed other factors prevented Karzai from adopting the plan,

> He would not verbalise it in terms of political base but he kept hinting to me in other terms this is where my support is, I don't want to spray down there and alienate what is a large political base for me.[100]

A State Department official recounted why Bush did not force the policy upon Karzai:

> He [Bush] very much felt like his dialogue with the Afghans had to be president-to-president like he would have a dialogue with another government and he had to show them respect . . . Ultimately . . . the overall American goal was to create an Afghan government that could take responsibility and so that meant we had to respect the Afghans when they took responsibility for the decision. I think President Bush understood that.[101]

By December 2007, aerial eradication had been defeated. Ultimately, several factors blocked the State Department and INL's push for aerial eradication, despite support from the White House. First, the US was the only NATO member advocating aerial eradication and, as such, had no support from the international community. British resistance thwarted or at least hindered American plans, as Britain fought an embattled position to prevent its introduction. This opposition to aerial eradication became more pronounced when British troops deployed to Helmand Province, and the military argued such a move would jeopardise the safety of its soldiers. Whilst the issue reached a climax in late 2007, aerial eradication had dominated counternarcotics discussions for nearly four years. A British military officer summed up this ever-present threat: 'we spent the whole time from 2004 to 2007 fighting aerial eradication but we fought it tooth and nail'.[102] This opposition illustrates that Britain fulfilled an active role within the alliance; despite heavy pressure, it did not concede to US demands. That said, the US held considerable sway over the policymaking process, even though Britain was partner nation on counter-narcotics. Moreover, Britain had to make substantial concessions along the way – namely, GBS and a more forceful eradication policy – to prevent the introduction of aerial spraying.[103] Nevertheless, if, as some participants and later analysts believed, the US dominated the policy landscape, it should have been able to coerce Britain into accepting aerial eradication in 2007. The basic fact was that in the event it could not. But this was not just because of British opposition.

Second, the Pentagon was ardently opposed to aerial eradication and did all within its power to prevent its introduction – even colluding with the British against their own colleagues in INL.

The policy landscape, even within Washington, was, in other words, fragmented. DOD's opposition reflected broad opposition to becoming involved in counter-narcotics, and especially aerial eradication, because that was considered the most damaging policy to winning hearts and minds. In addition, the Colombian government downgraded aerial eradication, which also deflated INL's plan. An FCO official noted: 'it therefore, became very difficult for the Americans to claim this had been a success in Colombia as they had done previously'.[104]

Third, and the most important reason for the failure to implement aerial eradication, however, was Afghan resistance to the issue. Karzai was crucial in preventing its introduction, and British support bolstered his opposition. It would have been politically unviable and extremely controversial for the US to override the Afghan government's wishes given the drive to *Afghanise* policy. An FCO official made a telling point concerning the dynamics of policy formulation: 'if you turn that around, if the US had got Karzai's support, it would have become difficult for us to argue that you should not do it'.[105] Although the decision was concluded definitively, some US actors were still committed to the introduction of aerial spraying. In a February 2008 US Embassy cable, Wood argued that strong measures, including aerial eradication, may have to be deployed to make progress against 'Afghanistan's special problem'.[106] His ambitions, however, were never realised as the debate was quickly overtaken by events. Many of the chief protagonists pushing this policy, including Schweich, soon left government.[107] Then, as detailed shortly, the Obama administration ended all hope for the introduction of this controversial practice.

11 Counter-Narcotics in Transition, 2008

With aerial eradication dead in the water, the counter-narcotics mission had to rely on manual eradication and the ability of provincial governors to implement an effective ban: reductions in other parts of Afghanistan had demonstrated that governors could play an important role.[1] Two provinces once again dominated the counter-narcotics landscape: Helmand and Nangarhar. The latter had effectively implemented an opium prohibition during 2005 when cultivation fell to 1,093 ha but, by 2007, opium cultivation rebounded in the province to 18,739 ha.[2] Given its lead role and large troop presence in Nangarhar, the US was determined to implement a successful opium ban in the province. The US was aided in its quest by having the support of a willing partner: Gul Aga Shirzai. The governor firmly supported counter-narcotics measures in the knowledge that such support increased his standing with the international community – those who oversaw reductions in opium cultivation were regarded as 'good' governors – and furthered his chances at career progression.[3] But as an outsider in the province, Shirzai's ability to enforce the ban was completely contingent upon good relations with local officials and tribal powerbrokers. Cognisant of this fact, the governor had set about cultivating connections with influential former mujahideen, businessmen and tribal elders since his arrival in Nangarhar in 2005.[4]

The broader security and economic situation in the province also favoured the implementation of a ban. The number of insurgent attacks across Afghanistan had spiralled from 1,558 in 2005 to 4,542 in 2006, with violence further increasing by 27 per cent between 2006 and 2007.[5] In an attempt to quell the violence and reverse the Taliban's momentum, large numbers of US and Afghan troops flooded into Nangarhar. This had practical benefits for the implementation of an opium ban as the number of checkpoints and house searches increased, thus projecting the authority of the government into rural spaces, which had hitherto been ungoverned. The governor was also able to manipulate farmers' perceptions by implying that US forces were in the province for counter-narcotics purposes not counterinsurgency ones.[6] Accompanying the uptick in US forces was an increase in development aid to the province, delivered by both the military and USAID. Moreover, development projects that had been started several years previously were coming to fruition, with roads providing good transport links to central markets. Lastly, opium prices plummeted to 1990s levels and food prices rose prompting concerns about food shortages.[7] All of these factors coalesced to produce a successful reduction in opium cultivation in Nangarhar. Success was so pronounced, the UNODC declared the province opium free in 2008.[8]

The reduction of opium cultivation in Nangarhar Province reflected the national trend in 2008. Throughout Afghanistan opium cultivation declined 19 per cent from 193,000 ha in 2007 to 153,000 ha in 2008, and the number of poppy-free provinces rose from thirteen to eighteen.[9] Helmand Province, however, stood in sharp contrast to Nangarhar, as opium cultivation rose to a record 103,500 ha, accounting for 66 per cent of the total opium cultivated in Afghanistan.[10]

In March 2008, against the backdrop of exploding opium cultivation in the province and British complaints that the Governor of Helmand Assadullah Wafa was ineffective, Karzai appointed Gulab Mangal as his successor.[11] An experienced technocrat and former Governor of Paktika and Laghman provinces, Mangal's arrival was considered positive in an otherwise beleaguered campaign.[12] In particular, from his first moments in office, Mangal signalled his commitment to combating the narcotics trade. In July, two of Mangal's international advisors proposed a counter-narcotics strategy for the forthcoming growing season.[13] The international advisors, however, were former military men with no experience in counter-narcotics, rural development or Afghanistan – this lack of expertise in counter-narcotics later proved to have disastrous consequences.[14] The strategy, which came to be known as the Helmand Food Zone (HFZ), prescribed a variety of incentives and disincentives based around alternative livelihoods, interdiction, eradication and public awareness campaigns.[15] The programme's objective was to deliver development aid, such as wheat seed and fertiliser, in exchange for farmers consenting to halt opium production. Farmers were required to sign an agreement to this effect, with those breaking the contract punished by eradication. During its first year, the HFZ provided 33,000 households in central Helmand with subsidised wheat seed.[16]

However, among counter-narcotics and development experts, the HFZ was considered a 'retrograde step'.[17] Simple crop-substitution plans, in this case wheat for opium, had been widely discredited in the development community for more than a decade. Whilst crop substitution was a necessary intervention, legitimate crops on their own could not address the fundamental deficiencies with the Afghan ecosystem – market access, transport links and non-farm income opportunities – to transition farmers out of opium cultivation.[18] More importantly, substituting wheat for opium confused the role that both played in the rural community; wheat is a food crop, whereas opium provides 'cash, credit, or access to land'.[19] Conditionality, where aid is tied to reductions in cultivation, was also a widely discredited concept. In a difficult operating environment, it was not always possible to enforce the conditions of the contract, therefore undermining the legitimacy of the agreement. For example, the local authorities did not always have the capacity to conduct eradication if farmers cultivated opium.[20]

Undeterred by these design flaws, and committed to reducing cultivation in the province, Mangal continued to promote the plan. It also found favour with the British-led PRT and international community.[21] Despite his commitment to counter-narcotics, Mangal's hold on the governorship was precarious given his less than favourable relationship with Karzai. Moreover, Karzai still equated the rising violence in the province as a direct consequence of the dismissal of Akhundzada and favoured recalling the controversial governor at Mangal's expense. But if Mangal made progress on counter-narcotics, he would gain British and American support, thus bolstering his position in Kabul.[22] The British, fearful of Akhundzada's return to the governorship, were only too happy to help and used every opportunity to petition Karzai to keep Mangal as governor. In one 2008 meeting with Karzai, Gordon Brown repeated his robust support for Mangal.[23] For the time being, Mangal remained.

Helmand, like Nangarhar, was the focus of international efforts in 2008. The province was the epicentre of insurgent violence and the largest area of opium cultivation in the world, both of which did not reflect well on the British. By this time, Britain's failure in Basra was also well established, therefore success in Helmand took on another level of importance – not least to restore the military's reputation with its special relationship partner.[24] In the aftermath of the 2003 invasion of Iraq, Britain took charge of four southern provinces, including Basra. Whilst things had started well for the British, before long, the army was under daily attack. This spiralling violence did little to improve public support for an already widely unpopular conflict. As a result, a decision was taken in London to expedite the transfer of security to Iraqi forces and withdraw British troops from Basra city. The withdrawal had disastrous consequences: Basra was overwhelmed by sustained insurgent attacks. Although Iraqi forces eventually recaptured the city,[25] to many at the time, and later, the British withdrawal amounted to defeat.[26] Faced with an equally perilous situation in Helmand, Britain responded by increasing troop numbers, armoured patrol vehicles and civilian resources. The US also deployed additional troops to the province in support of its British counterpart.[27]

Despite these developments, British efforts in Helmand were widely criticised in a series of US diplomatic cables. In November 2008, the Afghan Foreign Minister Rangin Dadfar Spanta complained to Wood that British troops were 'not ready to fight as actively as American soldiers'.[28] The following month Karzai shared this view when he met with Senators John McCain, Joe Lieberman and Lindsey Graham. The president told the senators that he was grateful US Marines were being sent to Helmand instead of more British troops.[29] A cable from the US Embassy in Kabul was even more scathing in its criticism, noting: 'we and Karzai agree that the British are not up to the task of securing Helmand'.[30] With Britain struggling to maintain both its mission of stabilising Helmand and position as partner nation on counter-narcotics, something had to give.

Counter-narcotics loses its profile

By mid-to-late 2008, as the conflict deepened, counter-narcotics slipped down Britain's policy agenda, as an FCO official notes: 'I think there's no question the priority of counter-narcotics declined ... by ... 2008. Counter-narcotics had gone from being one of our top priorities in Afghanistan to and pretty explicitly a second order priority for us.'[31] Another FCO official recalls: 'counter-narcotics ... was something that ticked along and there was a lot of effort, but it did not have the same profile. It very quickly lost its profile.'[32] Two reasons precipitated this shift.

First, as the premiership transitioned from Blair to Brown, Number 10's interest in counter-narcotics diminished significantly. That is not to say that Brown was unsympathetic to counter-narcotics as a strategic priority, but nevertheless he did not exhibit the same zeal as his predecessor. Blair had, after all, made counter-narcotics an important objective in the Afghan campaign and was 'personally invested' in the mission.[33] Brown's apathy towards counter-narcotics was very quickly expressed to Whitehall officials. During the first Cabinet Office, Afghanistan Senior Officials Group meeting after Brown assumed office, an FCO official recalls: 'there wasn't an explicit "counter-narcotics isn't a priority", [but] there was an explicit "there's a new prime minister so we can't assume that any of the policy we had before now remains"'.[34] Whilst the message was conveyed in ambiguous terms, it soon became clear that counter-narcotics would not be the priority it was under Blair. In practical terms, this meant that the regular meetings and conversations between Number 10 and ADIDU – which happened bi-monthly – very quickly stopped and Number 10 'didn't exert itself as much [with regards to counter-narcotics]'.[35]

Brown's different take on things obviously impacted on officials. An FCO official explained: 'that views changed when the prime minister's view changed'.[36] More importantly, Number 10's disinterest gave officials who were opposed to counter-narcotics the freedom to openly question whether or not counter-narcotics should remain a priority for the government.[37] Whilst many Whitehall officials were sceptical about counter-narcotics during Blair's tenure, the prime minister's personal investment in the mission ensured it remained a top priority.[38] However, Blair's departure transformed the parameters of the debate. An FCO official noted under Brown one could pose the question: Was partner nation on counter-narcotics the right strategy for Britain? But 'while Blair was there, nobody would have dared ask that question, it would not have been countenanced. So, there was no point. The door definitely opened when the prime minister changed because everyone knew this was fundamentally driven by [Blair].'[39] Whilst many officials were committed to counter-narcotics, there were equal amounts of scepticism across all departments and at all levels of officialdom. The debate was not simply confined to traditional interdepartmental wrangling between the FCO and DFID or indeed between civilian agencies and the military. No department was ever completely sold on the counter-narcotics mission. Even within the FCO some officials thought: 'god [do] we have to do this?' Drawing a contemporary parallel, an FCO official notes: 'it is not too dissimilar . . . to Brexit . . . you are not going to find very many civil servants signed up to it . . . [but] they're good civil servants, [so] people get on and do it'.[40]

Moreover, the aversion to counter-narcotics permeated the political ranks of government, with many ministers unconvinced that Britain could score a success against the narcotics industry. Successive Foreign Secretaries Jack Straw, Margaret Beckett and David Miliband were, at best, ambivalent towards Britain's role as lead and partner nation.[41] Summing up this feeling, a British minister reflected: 'Those three Secretaries of State were vastly more concerned with the politics of Kabul than they were with . . . counter-narcotics. I think counter-narcotics was way down the list of priorities in reality – although they paid lip service to it.' The minister went on to note that, as the conflict dragged on, this also 'went for me as well . . . because I could see what was happening on the ground'.[42] Equally, DFID ministers were also convinced that the counter-narcotics mission was a forlorn hope.[43]

Second, as the deteriorating situation in Helmand dominated the debate, the Afghanistan Strategy Group launched a review of policy. By this stage, the conflict had descended into a full-scale war and British forces were left ill-prepared to stem the violence in Helmand. Therefore, the most pressing objective, in the words of a British diplomat in Kabul: 'became to limit the damage to British forces . . . and the goal of aggressively pursuing a counter-narcotics effort was inconsistent with that'.[44] Britain did not have the resources to focus on stabilising Helmand let alone the intractable problem of counter-narcotics. For example, a US $45 million rural livelihood programme was abandoned in most of the province because of insecurity.[45]

Resource inadequacies aside, it was also evident that after six years of counter-narcotics efforts little progress had been made. The opium problem was a symptom of the disorder not a cause, and without addressing a range of underlying problems – security, the rural economy, rule of law, corruption and governance – progress could not be made. Recognising this, a British Embassy official commented that dealing with counter-narcotics: 'might shift the furniture around but we wouldn't really deal with the fundamental problem'.[46] Although many within the FCO had originally questioned the feasibility of a ten-year timeline to eliminate opium cultivation, by 2008 (the halfway point) there was little doubt that meeting this target was impossible.[47] It is important to note that Blair's high ambition for counter-narcotics prevented a more measured approach from being adopted. Consequently, Britain downgraded counter-narcotics to a second order priority. Although this did not have an immediate impact on British efforts, it opened a gateway for London to reconsider its long-standing commitment to counter-narcotics.

As Britain shifted focus in Afghanistan, US officials expressed doubts about Brown's leadership credentials. Cables from the embassy in London revealed that US officials considered the prime minister to have an 'abysmal track record' as he staggered from 'political disaster to disaster'.[48] The cables further predicted Brown's tenure as Labour leader could be short-lived. In the year since Brown became leader, the broader Anglo-American relationship had altered. The prime minister had distanced himself from the US, but he failed to do so without alienating himself from Bush and his administration. From the moment Brown assumed office, US officials, on both sides of the Atlantic, questioned his suitably; noting that the Labour 'party . . . seem[ed] increasingly to miss Blair's charisma'.[49] Despite this, the long-standing history between the two special relationship partners endured, as another US cable concluded: 'Britain is our closest and most important ally', further noting that Brown: 'wants – and knows that Britain needs – a strong relationship with the US administration'.[50] This feeling of distance in the special relationship did not escape the attention of US officials. During a meeting with shadow Foreign Secretary William Hague, US officials asked: Was the relationship still special? Hague replied that

the [opposition leader, David] Cameron, and Shadow Chancellor George Osborne are all "children of Thatcher" and staunch Atlanticists but acknowledged that the network of ties once binding the British public to America may not be as thick for all citizens of Britain.[51]

As the conflict deepened and the US elected a new leader, the Anglo-American relationship continued to cool.

ISAF and the narco-insurgency nexus

Meanwhile, there was a limited but nevertheless significant shift in NATO's willingness to undertake counter-narcotics work. Since 2005, FCO officials had spearheaded a campaign for the Alliance to redraw its restrictive rules that prevented ISAF from participating in counter-narcotics work, specifically interdiction activities. However, this was complicated by the lack of unity among member states, as most European nations – in particular Germany – who were responsible for provinces, were uneasy about anything that endangered the hearts and mind campaign.[52]

This, of course, was bolstered by the US military's resolute opposition to counter-narcotics work since 2001. However, by 2008, attitudes at the Pentagon had altered, as the narco–insurgency nexus theory gained acceptance. Several factors facilitated this change in policy. First, Rumsfeld's departure as Defense Secretary removed one of the greatest obstacles to this theory gaining traction in the Pentagon. Crucially, his successor Robert Gates placed more weight on these arguments and supported expanding ISAF's mission to include interdiction activities.[53] The theory had also – the previous year – risen up the policy agenda, with its supporters claiming greater evidence that it captured reality. A Department of State Inspector General report stated that the 'links between poppy cultivation, the resulting narcotics trade, and funding of insurgency groups became more evident in 2008'.[54] This view was further supplemented by the UNODC's 2008 Afghanistan Opium Survey, which stated:

98 per cent of all of Afghanistan's opium is grown in just seven provinces in the south-west – Helmand, Kandahar, Uruzgan, Farah, Nimroz, and to a lesser extent Daykundi and Zabul – where there are permanent Taliban settlements, and where organized crime groups profit from the instability.[55]

Addressing the North Atlantic Council (NAC), UNODC Executive Director Costa also argued for expanding ISAF's role to include counter-narcotics.[56]

Attitudes among US military commanders also gravitated towards embracing the narco–insurgency theory. In June 2008, outgoing ISAF Commander McNeill was reported to have said 'that narcotics pose a greater challenge in RC [Regional Command]-South than does the insurgency, and . . . when he sees a field of poppy, he sees the Kalashnikovs and improvised explosive devices that the poppy will fund'. To combat this, McNeill recommended that the NAC debate whether ISAF's remit should be widened to allow it to provide force protection for Afghan-led eradication and interdiction activities against narco-traffickers linked to the insurgency.[57] On 11 June, in an effort to swing NATO policy, SACEUR Bantz J. Craddock promoted an amendment to the Counter-Narcotics Annex of the ISAF Operations Plan (OPLAN) to permit its forces to interdict narcotics production and trafficking capabilities. However, even with US support, the plan stalled in NATO's Military Committee due to 'objections from key allies'.[58] In September, attempting to break the deadlock at the NAC, Craddock argued:

> It is clear that narcotics fund the insurgency and fuel corruption in Afghanistan. Afghan counter-narcotics forces can only respond to 1 in 4 narcotics targets. Afghan capabilities will remain minimal for the next 1 to 2 years. ISAF must be authorized to take more action in combating narcotics until Afghans have more adequately developed their own indigenous capability. Regarding expanding ISAF's counter-narcotics mission . . . the increased tactical authority will achieve a strategic level affect.[59]

Nevertheless, several European nations including the French, Dutch, German and Italians remained resistant to change. In response to Craddock's comments, Germany's Permanent Representative to NATO Ulrich Brandenburg argued that whilst the opium industry was a problem, it was not ISAF's job to deal with it.[60] At Condoleezza Rice's request, US officials were instructed to launch a lobbying campaign to sway member states to support the policy. Britain also embarked on a démarche to encourage several keys allies to support amending the OPLAN to grant ISAF interdiction capabilities.[61] An FCO official commented:

'It was a massive effort to persuade, no to educate, countries
[about the dangers of the narcotics trade] . . . Britain and the US
worked in tandem – and pretty well together actually – speaking
to people [and] lobbying Europe.[62]

Ironically, however, the US complained that *even* Britain
was not committed to a 'broader approach' and sought to 'set
conditions on interdiction operations based on the availability
of intelligence demonstrating a clear nexus between a specific
counter-narcotics target and the counterinsurgency campaign'. By
stipulating this, the US argued it would 'effectively paralyze ISAF
interdiction operations due to the need for legally "iron clad"
evidence'.[63] Britain, however, was convinced of the need to follow
due process: the narco–insurgency nexus could only be confirmed
after sufficient evidence was gathered.[64] The British were also
guided by practical considerations – aware that NATO countries
would only support so much. In the end, the US backed this more
limited approach. The démarche of the Anglo-American allies
worked as the French and Dutch, among others, now promised
support for increased ISAF involvement in interdiction activities.[65] The German government, however, facing stiff domestic
opposition, remained non-committal. The discussions took place
in the lead up to a Bundestag vote to extend the army's mandate
for participating in ISAF. The Germans, therefore, were 'loath
to support' changing ISAF's OPLAN, which would then require
altering the mandate passing through the Bundestag. Instead the
Germans advocated interpreting the current OPLAN 'as broadly'
as possible. This, they suggested, could be restructured to allow
countries to 'opt in' as opposed to 'opt out' if countries were
against involvement, consequently allowing the German army
to avoid involvement in interdiction activities without having to
submit a formal national caveat.[66] At an October 2008 meeting in
Bucharest – after a three-year campaign – NATO agreed to 'take
action in concert with the Afghans against facilities and facilita-
tors supporting the insurgency as provided for in the existing
operational plan'.[67] Gates was described as 'extremely pleased
that . . . NATO has decided to allow ISAF forces to take on the
drug traffickers who are fuelling the insurgency, destabilizing
Afghanistan, and killing our troops'.[68]

As concerns about the narco-insurgency nexus grew in the US
administration, the NSC established the Afghan Threat Finance
Cell (ATFC). Based on a similar unit in Iraq, the ATFC was

tasked with identifying and disrupting the networks that were supporting the Taliban and other insurgent groups. The ATFC discovered that far from being separate entities insurgents, narcotics traffickers and government officials were partly connected through finance networks. The ATFC helped to build the allies' knowledge of the illicit economy in Afghanistan.[69] In December 2008, the Defense Department relaxed its rule of engagement to allow the US military to accompany US and host nation officials in counter-narcotics missions.[70] Primarily this was focused on targeting narcotics traffickers who provided the insurgency with material support.[71] It was not long before US policy in Afghanistan underwent revision as President Barack Obama came to office. The period also ushered in the third, and final, phase of the counter-narcotics campaign.

Part 4

12 Obama and Shifting Anglo-American Relations, 2009

Several problems confronted the US in Afghanistan as President Obama came into office, all hinging on the fact that the security situation remained unresolved and was deteriorating. Under the Bush administration, the conflict in Afghanistan had deepened as the insurgency gained strength, and violence reached levels not seen since 2001.[1] In part, this was a result of resource constraints, with approximately 65,000 troops deployed in Afghanistan, compared to 150,000 troops in Iraq.[2] Before any decision was taken on strategy or resources, the new Secretary of State Hillary Clinton announced the appointment of Richard Holbrooke as special representative for Afghanistan and Pakistan (SRAP).[3] Having served every Democratic president since the late 1960s, Holbrooke's list of diplomatic achievements was extensive, including overseeing the negotiations that resolved the Bosnian conflict. Holbrooke's influence, however, was directly related to his close personal relationship with Clinton, whom he had supported in her presidential bid the previous year.[4] With few friends outside the State Department, Holbrooke's combative and overbearing style eventually led to friction in the interagency process. Britain, acknowledging the appointment of Holbrooke, appointed its own SRAP – who would act as his British equivalent. The man assigned to this task was the incumbent Ambassador to Kabul, Sir Sherard Cowper-Coles.[5]

Although Obama campaigned to send more troops to Afghanistan during the election, he wanted to contextualise any troop deployment in a broader strategy for the war.[6] In order to codify this, Obama commissioned Bruce Riedel, a former CIA official and Afghan expert, to conduct a sixty-day strategic review of policy in Afghanistan.[7] As the administration reviewed its strategy, Britain attempted to influence the policymaking process of its special relationship ally.

Between January and March, senior British officials, including Brown's foreign policy advisor Simon McDonald, travelled to Washington to participate in the US review process.[8] At the SRAP level, Cowper-Coles also considered his 'first, and overriding priority' was to influence Holbrooke and the administration's thinking on Afghanistan.[9] To do this, Cowper-Coles and his aide, FCO Political Director Adam Thomson, travelled extensively throughout the US and Europe to meet with Holbrooke and other important figures in this embryonic stage of planning. Among those taking part in the review on the US side was Professor Barney Rubin of New York University. Rubin, a distinguished Afghan expert, was a close confidant of Holbrooke and was responsible for influencing his thinking – especially on counter-narcotics policies. For his part, Cowper-Coles engaged in a series of meetings, and written communication with US officials to further his objectives. He wanted to:

> persuade [the] Obama administration . . . [that] . . . plunging on with a strategy of pouring in more troops and more money, without doing something about governance and about [political offerings] to the Afghan people, and something to engage the regional players, was a recipe for eventual failure.

Cowper-Coles also briefed ministers before they interacted with US officials, but his efforts were in vein as he concluded: 'seldom if ever did we get much by the way of reaction or reply'.[10] Cowper-Coles was frustrated in his attempts to craft an effective British position that he could urge on to the Americans. This clearly would have implications for Britain's ability to influence US thinking, especially Holbrooke's, on counter-narcotics policy.

Cowper-Coles's lack of success was symptomatic of a broader shift in relations. A Cabinet Office official recalled that the Anglo-American relationship under Obama was 'less close'. Further noting that:

> [Bush's NSA] Steve Hadley used to phone [Simon McDonald] to shoot the breeze, and say, we have a problem what do you think? That was never [done with] the Obama administration . . . We had less influence . . . we were [just] another coalition partner, we were dependable – you can always rely on the Brits – but the atmospherics of the relationship changed.[11]

A key reason for the shift in relations was the close personal connection that characterised the Anglo-American alliance under Bush and Blair faded as Brown assumed office. It is worth noting that while Blair enjoyed close relations with Bush, his *actual* influence on US policies was limited, other than at the margins. Relations became even cooler after Obama became president, and several issues – unrelated to the war in Afghanistan – made the new relationship with Brown tense, namely a divergence of views over the BP oil spill and the release of the Lockerbie bomber. Neither Brown nor Obama had the warmth in personal relations that had characterised the Bush–Blair friendship. Further complicating matters were several public relations disasters – again not directly related to the conflict – at high-profile meetings during 2009.[12] Britain, naturally, remained the US's closest partner in the conflict but the special relationship was more muted than had previously been the case. This demonstrated just how important close leader relations were for the maintenance and success of the special relationship.

Before the Riedel review was completed, Obama was forced to deploy 17,000 more troops to Afghanistan to protect the upcoming presidential elections from the predicted Taliban assault.[13] The president later endorsed sending a further 4,000 troops to train the ANA, coupled with another 10,000 later in the year. Of the original 17,000, the first 8,000 Marines were sent to rural Helmand, which provided a boost to the embattled British. Accompanying the increased military personnel was a substantial increase in civilian officials deployed to Afghanistan.[14]

During the review process, the Bush administration's counter-narcotics policies – which saw cultivation rise from 74,000 ha in 2002 to 157,000 ha in 2008, an increase of 112 per cent – were also re-evaluated.[15] For several years, Holbrooke had been an outspoken critic of Bush's record on counter-narcotics,[16] and in March 2009, he stated the strategy '[was] the most wasteful and ineffective programme I've seen in over 40 years in and out of the government'.[17] As detailed below, the outcome of the Riedel review, along with Holbrooke's thoughts, provided the blueprint for the forthcoming US counter-narcotics strategy.

On 27 March 2009, using the Riedel review as a basis, Obama outlined his vision for the conflict: 'we have a clear and focused goal: to disrupt, dismantle and defeat al-Qaeda in Pakistan and Afghanistan, and to prevent their return to either country'. He further noted that 'to succeed . . . we must reverse the Taliban's gains, and promote a more capable and accountable Afghan government'.[18] As part of this strategy, the US also increased its efforts to implement a fully resourced counterinsurgency campaign.[19] During his speech, the president identified the destabilising effect of the narcotics industry: 'Afghanistan has an elected government, but it is undermined by corruption . . . [And] the economy is undercut by a booming narcotics trade that encourages criminality and funds the insurgency.'[20]

The issue of strategy and resources, however, was not settled for long. During his confirmation hearing, the new ISAF commander General Stanley McChrystal indicated that the additional 21,000 troops commissioned for deployment three months previously might prove inadequate to reverse the gains of the insurgency. McChrystal was instructed to conduct his own sixty-day assessment of the war, allowing him to evaluate both strategy and troop levels.[21] Another lengthy review, however, disrupted British plans, as a Cabinet Office official explained:

> there was this enormously drawn out period where they reviewed their strategy, which had an impact on . . . what we were about to do. When your key ally is going through a lengthy internal process it meant . . . things significantly slowed down.[22]

Gordon Brown also recounted his frustration:

> President Obama's review created huge difficulties for us. What Obama ultimately decided was pivotal to everything we did: while Afghanistan and Pakistan represented Britain's greatest overseas commitment, our contribution was still small compared with that of America; and, ultimately, only the US had the political and military authority to broker real change. The series of reviews took the best part of 2009. For all that time, the uncertainty left me trapped between the British military's demand for more troops, which I knew could only make a difference as part of a wider American surge, and the American position, which was to wait for the results of the review.[23]

Both the review process and the adoption of a well-resourced counterinsurgency strategy had direct implications for the third phase of the counter-narcotics campaign.

We are downgrading our efforts to eradicate crops

In June 2009, influenced by the Riedel review, Holbrooke crystal-lised many of the ideas that formed the basis of the forthcoming US Counter-Narcotics Strategy. In short, the strategy contained three main points: to break the narco-insurgency nexus by refocusing interdiction; increase assistance to farmers and integrate alternative development programmes into general agricultural assistance; and de-emphasis eradication.[24] To be successful, the strategy would have to recognise the link between counter-narcotics and counterinsurgency, and wider process of stabilisation, economic development and rule of law efforts in Afghanistan.[25] Speaking before the House Committee on Oversight and Government Reform, Holbrooke summed up the strategy: 'if I had to give a headline, I would say, a massive increase in agriculture . . . [and] downgrading our efforts to eradicate crops'. He further cautioned that the US was not 'downgrading narcotics' instead only 'downgrading crop eradication'.[26]

Ostensibly the most dramatic shift in policy was the downgrading of eradication and the disbandment of the Poppy Eradication Force (previously known as the AEF). The move was orchestrated by Holbrooke and his advisor Rubin, both of whom considered eradication as a fruitless and counterproductive exercise.[27] In fact, Holbrooke complained that eradication 'hasn't hurt the Taliban one iota' as the insurgency received money irrespective if the poppy crop was destroyed or not. Moreover, he contended that eradication was responsible for driving rural support for the Taliban.[28]

Despite being only one component of a five-pillar plan, eradication had formed the main component of the US's counter-narcotics strategy from 2004 to 2008, with the other aspects receiving less attention.[29] In saying that, the pivot away from eradication was more nuanced. Whilst Holbrooke and Rubin were instrumental, the process had actually commenced towards the tail end of the Bush administration when it was clear that eradication efforts were highly ineffective yet, crucially, financially expensive. From 2005 to 2009, the centrally led eradication force only managed to eradicate a combined total of 9,446 ha.[30] For this, DynCorp, the contractors overseeing the process, received an annual payment of $35 to $45 million.[31] Some officials considered the policy an expensive waste of resources. Such views chimed well with arguments put forward by Holbrooke. A State Department official commented:

> The Poppy Eradication Force itself was already being curtailed at the end of the Bush administration, mostly for reasons that it was not believed to be that effective and . . . particularly for the amount of funds being expended. There was already a significant shift in the direction to governor-led eradication . . . it was not a cut-off; it was more a turning of the valve in a slightly different direction . . . Was it [eradication] the best way we could spend scarce resources? It wasn't [an] economically effective way to spend taxpayers' bucks.[32]

Nevertheless, and unsurprisingly so, some INL officials contended that while eradication had proven ineffective in Afghanistan it still constituted an important element of *any* counter-narcotics strategy. After all, INL had emphatically championed the policy in Afghanistan and Latin America for several years. During the policy discussions that ensued, in the words of a US official, Holbrooke 'was in an argument with INL and . . . INL tried to push [eradication] into the budget'. Holbrooke then had to 'find [the document] in the Secretary of State's office and zero out the different lines for eradication'. Reflecting on the tension, the official noted: 'it wasn't perfectly congenial policymaking'.[33] It is important to note that Holbrooke, at least in the early part of his tenure, held considerable sway over counter-narcotics policies. A US official confirmed that Holbrooke was: 'just about in complete charge as you could be'.[34] That said, as the campaign progressed and a rift opened between Holbrooke and the White House, his influence over policy was minimised. In this complex myriad of policy changes, differences also emerged in the Anglo-American counter-narcotics relationship.

In a paradoxical reversal of events, some British officials felt that Holbrooke's stance on eradication was too passive.[35] This proved particularly ironic as, for four years, the issue of eradication had proven a bitter source of tension between London and Washington.[36] Overly aggressive eradication was the one thing the British had never wanted, but many British officials also thought that properly used eradication was an important tool. A British diplomat noted the flaws with downgrading eradication: 'there was some balance in the middle . . . I thought totally removing all threat of eradication was wrong; there were some people who needed it, they couldn't just get away with it scot free – it was a symbolic thing'.[37]

As discussed in previous chapters, this curious British policy position must be placed in a wider context. Since 2004, Britain had been under immense INL and State Department pressure to agree to aerial eradication and, in order to prevent its introduction, had to gradually shift its eradication policies to accord more with INL and State. An FCO official summed up this almost contradictory position:

> Holbrooke came in and leapfrogged the Brits and the Brits were left stranded looking like they were the pro-eradication crowd – but they weren't. This was a consequence of the very difficult negotiations between Britain and the US to avoid aerial spraying and [Britain] trying to avoid being seen as weak on eradication.[38]

However, whilst Britain ended up looking like the 'pro-eradication crowd', in fact the shift in policy brought the Anglo-American relationship on counter-narcotics closer than had been the case under the Bush administration. An FCO official commented the reversal of policy 'removed . . . the bone of contention . . . To put it in simplistic terms, the question of eradication was eradicated from the agenda of the bi-annual meetings.'[39] The official wishfully concluded that: 'the Americans, if you want to put it this way: they were falling into line with our view on eradication'.[40] In reality, this harmonisation of policy came more through happenstance than design. Britain had little, if no, influence over the process, as Cowper-Coles complained: 'Britain had reluctantly to go along with these virtual unilateral changes.'[41] Therefore, Holbrooke changed a major component of US counter-narcotics policy without consulting the British. This pointed to a slightly cooler, not closer, period in the Anglo-American counter-narcotics relationship.

It was not only the Brits who were sidelined; the Afghans also complained: 'when you [the US] are announcing policy positions that affect us, your friends, so directly, we expect that you will consult with us in advance'. The Afghans further argued 'that the US was going from one extreme to another'.[42] Whilst the US defunded centrally led eradication, it did not end the practice completely; after all, it was enshrined in the ANDCS.

Cowper-Coles recounted that Holbrooke was concerned about the Afghan authorities' ability to implement eradication, but nevertheless conceded that the US would not block GLE.[43] A US Embassy cable summed up the philosophy of the administration towards Afghanistan, 'our motto is: Afghan leadership, Afghan capacity, Afghan sustainability'.[44]

Interdiction and agricultural development

The Riedel review concluded that a key objective in Afghanistan was to break the link between the narcotics industry and the insurgency, as both were inextricably connected as well as driving corruption and distorting the legal economy. To accomplish this, Holbrooke reallocated the money intended for eradication to interdiction and law enforcement activities.[45] Whilst the narco–insurgency narrative had gained traction towards the end of the Bush administration, its inclusion in the US's strategy for Afghanistan represented a significant shift in policy. Thus, the rationale of attacking the narcotics industry would, in theory, weaken the insurgency by reducing the funding, support and corruption that sustained it.[46] Furthermore, a controversial decision was taken to place narcotics traffickers with ties to the insurgency on an official 'kill list' called the 'Joint Prioritized Effects List. The Senate Committee on Foreign Relations reported that fifty top narcotics traffickers who contributed funds to the insurgency were placed on the list in 2009.[47] A Pentagon spokesman commented: 'it is important to clarify that we are targeting terrorists with links to the drug trade, rather than targeting drug traffickers with links to terrorism'.[48]

The final key component of the strategy championed by Riedel and Holbrooke – who started his career as a USAID officer during the Vietnam War – was a massive increase in agricultural assistance to bolster the legal economy. More importantly, the Riedel review noted:

> in a country that is 70 per cent rural, and where the Taliban recruiting base is primarily among under-employed youths, a complete overhaul of our civilian assistance strategy is necessary; agricultural sector job creation is an essential first step to undercutting the appeal of al-Qaeda and its allies.[49]

Holbrooke's enthusiasm was not shared in the wider Anglo-American alliance. Cowper-Coles remained sceptical that building up agriculture alone was the solution to opium cultivation or preventing unemployed men from joining the insurgency. Cowper-Coles recounted a meeting when Holbrooke argued that 'we must all put all our efforts into building up the Afghan agriculture this year: that is how we are going to beat the insurgency'. Cowper-Coles noted disappointingly: 'I was frankly flabbergasted. All our efforts to persuade Holbrooke that the fundamental problem in Afghanistan was political seemed to have made no impact.'[50]

Whilst outwardly the new counter-narcotics strategy developed by the Obama administration was dissimilar to its predecessor, in reality it was not a radical departure to that of the Bush administration's. The key difference was a focus on interdiction of Taliban-linked traffickers, a move away from eradication and being more competent at delivering alternative livelihoods to rural Afghans. A State Department official contended that the shift in counter-narcotics strategy was more nuanced than dramatic:

> in some of the rhetoric ... [there was] a clear pivot away from US support for eradication ... So, if you think of counter-narcotics policy beginning and ending with eradication there was a huge change but ... not so much in other realms.[51]

That said, the most important change under Obama was a massive increase of resources and attention. Like the previous US counter-narcotics strategies, it was constrained by an expectation to produce instantaneous results. The question remained, however: would a massive increase in resources deliver results and, if so, would the results be sustainable? As the allies moved closer together on counter-narcotics, on the ground in Helmand the relationship between the militaries deteriorated.

The special relationship in Helmand

The summer of 2009 marked an escalation in the conflict as an extra 4,000 US Marines and 3,000 British soldiers were deployed in counterinsurgency operations in southern and central Helmand.[52] Although the British military were in desperate need of help, the influx of US troops changed the dynamics of the Anglo-American relationship as the Marines became the dominant force, outnumbering British soldiers by 10,672[53] to 9,000.[54] Relations between the partners soon disintegrated as the Marines, conditioned by a 'can do attitude', deplored Britain's acceptance of Taliban-controlled territory believing that this had allowed the insurgency to gain momentum.[55] A State Department official noted: 'Marines . . . tend to sprint, while my sense of British forces is that they had a marathon mind-set.'[56] Friction with the British-led PRT was even more pronounced, as the PRT and Marines clashed over how best to reconstruct Helmand. This tension was underscored by infighting over 'who owned the policy space about what Britain and the US were doing in Helmand'. The British official also noted that: 'the dynamic between the PRT and Marines was often very difficult' as the latter disregarded the former's policy advice.[57] The relationship between the Marines and PRT was important because it later affected the delivery of counter-narcotics policy on the front line of Afghanistan's poppy capital.

On 19 June, the British launched phase one of a two-part coalition offensive against the Taliban. The operation, named 'Panther's Claw', aimed to drive the Taliban out of an area of Green Zone between Lashkar Gah and Gereshk, which included the districts of Babaji, Malgir and Spin Masjid. In doing so, the British hoped to provide enough security for the area's 80,000 residents to vote in the upcoming presidential elections. The offensive, which was the largest British operation to date, was also the deadliest, costing ten soldiers their lives. Despite official claims of success, the operation fell short on several critical levels. Not only did it fail to completely clear insurgents and hold the areas, it also failed to enable significant numbers of Afghans to vote.[58] In the end, turnout was so poor that only 150 out of approximately 50,000 villagers from Babaji district voted.[59] The US operation, however, proved more successful.

On 2 July, the US Marines launched operation 'Strike of the Sword', to clear the Taliban from the southern Helmand districts of Nawa, Garmser and Khan Neshin. During the offensive, the Marines deployed in large numbers allowing them to station men between each village and make their presence felt by conducting routine patrols.[60] Significantly, the visible physical presence of coalition forces – checkpoints, roadblocks and military bases

– with a strong governor-led counter-narcotics message helped to reduce opium cultivation in Nawa and Garmser in the 2009/10 planting season.[61] A key component of the counterinsurgency plan was to remain in the areas after the insurgents were cleared 'to show that government could do more for the people than the Taliban could'.[62] This included working with the local population on alternative livelihoods. In the wake of the operation, development aid streamed into the province, with USAID expanding the Afghanistan Voucher for Increased Production in Agriculture (AVIPA-Plus) – a programme distributing agricultural resources. There was also substantial investment from the British government as DFID funded a 'US $45 million programme of investments in infrastructure and private sector development, aimed at promoting economic growth – the Helmand Growth Programme, and the Commanders Emergency Response Programme'.[63] The influx of coalition troops, along with a change in the price of wheat and opium, led to a substantial reduction in opium cultivation in Helmand.[64]

The Helmand Food Zone

As outlined in the previous chapter, there was considerable Anglo-American enthusiasm regarding the establishment of the HFZ in 2008. The results of the scheme, however, were not confirmed until the autumn of 2009. They appeared extremely positive, as cultivation in Helmand decreased by approximately a third, to less than 70,000 ha. The situation in Helmand was replicated across Afghanistan, as opium cultivation decreased from 157,000 ha in 2008 to 123,000 ha in 2009 – a fall of 22 per cent. Buoyed by what was the largest drop in cultivation since the intervention, the UNODC's Afghanistan Opium Survey confidently declared: 'the bottom is starting to fall out of the Afghan opium market'.[65] In particular, the report extolled the 'dramatic turnaround in Helmand' as a pivotal reason for the nationwide reduction in cultivation. The success was attributed to strong counter-narcotics measures, competent provincial leadership and the introduction of the HFZ.[66]

It was perhaps unsurprising that the UNODC was quick to praise the HFZ; it had, after all, contributed to the first reduction in the province since 2003.[67] Convinced of its success, the

Minister of Counter-Narcotics Zarar Osmani even called for the HFZ to be replicated throughout Afghanistan.[68] However, attributing the reduction in cultivation to the HFZ and Mangal's leadership overinflated the ability of the governor (and state) to enforce the ban.[69] More importantly, it also oversimplified the prevailing economic situation. Between mid-2007 and late 2008, the cost of wheat rose by 133 per cent (from 15 Afs/kg to 35 Afs/kg) as opium prices fell by 42 per cent (from US $120/kg to US $70/kg).[70] Consequently, between 2008 and 2009, the amount of land dedicated to wheat rose by 50 per cent, as farmers grew concerned by 'food security and their ability to purchase wheat in the local bazaar'.[71] These shifting patterns occurred even in districts where wheat seed and fertiliser were not available from provincial authorities and where eradication was unlikely. In subsequent years, farmers still opted to cultivate more wheat than opium to offset food shortages, leading to a sustained decline in opium cultivation.[72] This economic principle was not lost on a British Embassy official: 'we were quite lucky . . . I would love to claim success, but the true story was there was a glut in opium production combined with a shortage of wheat worldwide.' The official noted, however, that the reduction did take 'the pressure off a little'.[73]

Like most previous counter-narcotics interventions in Afghanistan, the HFZ was plagued by implementation problems. The public information campaign (one of four pillars of the HFZ – along with interdiction, eradication and alternative development) proved particularly ineffective – although it did improve in subsequent years. Part of the problem was the governor's reliance on a British military escort to travel throughout Helmand, thus giving the impression that the state was unable to secure the province. This resulted in tribal elders, fearing the authorities could not protect them from Taliban retribution, refusing to disseminate the governor's public information message.[74]

The alternative development aspect of the programme also ran into difficulties during the first year of its implementation. The lack of security throughout the province meant that seeds were not distributed to every part of the target area, with outposts limited to provincial centres. In the autumn of 2009, as security improved due to coalition military operations, the number of centres expanded throughout the target area.[75] Whilst the incidences of bribery and corruption affecting GLE decreased, its implementation was still hampered by a focus on remote, marginal areas. Nevertheless, things improved in subsequent seasons.[76]

Predictably, pervasive corruption marred the distribution of the aid, with the list of beneficiaries rigged in favour of those with connections to the governor. Provincial authorities also charged recipients a percentage of their aid or sold stolen aid in the bazaar.[77] The programme was further brought into disrepute as many of its employees were engulfed in a corruption scandal. It was discovered that officials made fraudulent claims resulting in illicit profits of tens of thousands of pounds. It was also alleged that members of the project had replaced high-quality seed with low-quality seed whilst charging the funders for top grade and stealing the difference.[78] The seed was of such poor quality many who received it did not plant it. Notwithstanding the implementation problems, many in the counter-narcotics community continued to lavish praise on the HFZ. However, little did they realise that the HFZ set in train a combination of events that contributed to opium cultivation exploding across the province.[79]

More broadly, as the conflict entered a new phase, so did the Anglo-American relationship. Although the partners moved closer together on policy matters, notably counter-narcotics, at a wider, political level, the relationship had drifted. This was largely to do with the change of leadership in the US, as Obama placed less emphasis on the special relationship than Bush. There were also important differences of opinion regarding levels of blood and treasure to be committed to Afghanistan. Just as Obama was gearing up to increase US commitment to the conflict, Brown was unenthusiastic about significantly expanding British efforts. The key problem was that Brown, described as 'an extremely reluctant war leader',[80] neither had the strategic capacity nor the desire to inject much needed leadership and resources into the faltering Helmand campaign. Although the prime minister, after several requests from the British military and US pressure, did eventually agreed to a small troop increase,[81] the fundamentals of the situation remained unchanged: Brown was not looking to substantially increase British efforts in Afghanistan. Similarly, in London, Brown was not alone in his disinclination towards the eight-year-old conflict. As Whitehall grappled with how to make the best of a bad situation in Afghanistan, focus turned to Britain's counter-narcotics brief.

13   A Poisoned Chalice, 2009–2011

After eight long years, public support for the conflict was waning. At the outset of the Anglo-American military campaign in October 2001, an ICM poll for *The Guardian* and *BBC Newsnight* recorded 74 per cent of those surveyed were supportive of the mission, with only 16 per cent opposed.[1] By July 2009, a similar poll revealed that support for the conflict had fallen to 46 per cent and opposition to the conflict had risen to 47 per cent. Likewise, a small majority, 42 per cent, supported an immediate withdrawal of British troops, and 36 per cent stated troops should stay as long as necessary.[2] With support falling and a major military offensive underway, ministers became increasingly convinced that the counter-narcotics mission was a distraction to Britain's most immediate goal in Afghanistan: securing Helmand. Even the FCO minister responsible for counter-narcotics, Mark Malloch-Brown, questioned the desirability of continuing as partner nation and 'was quite clear that Britain ought to be getting out'.[3] Around that time, during testimony to the House of Commons Foreign Affairs Committee (FAC), Malloch-Brown expressed his frustration:

> Certainly the G8 partner thing has become a little redundant, in the sense that it is not the formula for sharing out roles in Afghanistan . . . Certainly, we feel that we are doing that more because someone has to than because we are hugely enthusiastic about it, so if others wanted to take it on credibly we would help them do it . . . Yes, it is not a comfortable position to be in. It is not great PR to be in charge of counter-narcotics, but as I say, it is an important part of this.[4]

This disillusionment was also evident at official level, as one official remarked that counter-narcotics was seen as the 'ugly step-child' of the Afghan effort.[5] Consequently, at all levels of government, 'there was zero commitment to resource being the partner nation during this period'.[6] Given that the Afghanistan Compact – the framework that initiated the system of partner nations – was due to conclude in 2011, a debate opened within Whitehall as to what would come next. Whilst the decision-making process was fragmented, most officials were guided by a realistic assessment of what had been achieved and what was likely to be achieved in the near term: very little. Most officials agreed that Britain could not and should not continue its commitment to counter-narcotics. This was conditioned by several distinct but related reasons.

First and foremost, with the death toll spiralling out of control in Helmand – and the government under intense media scrutiny – reducing casualties was top of the agenda. In the space of fourteen months – June 2008 to August 2009 – British casualties doubled from 100 to 200.[7] It was proving impossible to sustain equal levels of commitment to stabilising Helmand and partner nation on counter-narcotics. Primarily, this was driven by financial, personnel and intellectual constraints. There was also a fundamental tension between the counter-narcotics and military missions. During 2009, British officers stationed in Nad-e-Ali took the unusual step of participating in an 'informal lesson' in opium harvesting. By doing so, officers reasoned that they could assuage farmers concerns that the British army was not in Helmand to eradicate poppy. British officer Mike Martin recalls the fall-out: 'the FCO in London . . . were appalled. How could British troops, representing the lead on counter-narcotics in the international coalition, do such a thing?' Martin further noted that: 'it was gently explained to [the FCO] how conflicted the twin policies of counterinsurgency (aim: win the population) and counter-narcotics (result: drive the population away) were'.[8]

Second, with media attention fixated on rising casualties, the FCO were under pressure to counteract this with good news stories.[9] Although cultivation had decreased for the second consecutive year in 2009, this did little to counter the broader cultivation trend since the intervention, which was moving upwards. Concerned by this, many FCO officials considered counter-narcotics to be a 'liability' and that Britain should end its commitment.[10] Third, and as previously discussed, it was widely accepted that Britain's original timeline to eliminate opium cultivation by 2013 was due to fail.[11] Ultimately, Afghanistan's opium problem was judged too difficult and too long-term to solve. In August, the FAC delivered a blunt assessment of Britain's role as partner nation:

> We conclude that in accepting the role of Afghanistan's 'lead' international partner in respect of counter-narcotics, Britain has taken on a poisoned chalice. There is little evidence to suggest that recent reductions in poppy cultivation are the result of the policies adopted by Britain . . . it is clear that success . . . [is] beyond the control and resource of Britain alone. The scale of the problem . . . makes any . . . achievement of the aspirations set out in the Bonn Agreement highly unlikely. We further conclude that the lead international role on counter-narcotics should be transferred away from Britain.[12]

Responding to the FAC's withering assessment, an FCO official concluded: 'Was this a poisoned chalice? Frankly, I think it was. You could not fix that in a decade – it is a multi-generational programme.' The official further noted that, 'people didn't like it but . . . you don't like answering those types of questions as they expose truths'.[13] Shortly after, the Afghanistan Senior Officials Group submitted a proposal to ministers recommending that Britain should end its commitment to counter-narcotics.[14] On 2 November 2009, the National Security, International Relations and Development subcommittee agreed that Britain should relinquish its position as lead international nation on counter-narcotics after the conclusion of the G8 partner mechanism in 2011.[15]

With a decision reached, some officials argued that it was incumbent on Britain not to abandon counter-narcotics without, in the words of an FCO official, 'placing counter-narcotics on a more sustainable footing'.[16] Or in other words, Britain should not walk away without finding its own replacement. This would allow Britain, in the minds of some at least, to 'do the honourable thing'.[17] Counter-narcotics expert David Mansfield, however, argued that the move amounted to little more than window-dressing Britain's departure.[18] Whatever Britain's true intention, the UNODC was the obvious choice to assume the role – given its history of drug control in Afghanistan and, more importantly, the lack of an alternative.[19] However, given the UNODC's weak funding structure – approximately 90 per cent comes from voluntary contributions and only 10 per cent comes from the regular UN budget – and poor capacity, concerns were raised about its ability to take on the role, especially by 2011. Nevertheless, with options limited, Britain had no choice but to focus on building the UNODC's capacity.[20]

In early December, during a counter-narcotics meeting in Washington, FCO officials informed their US counterparts of their decision.[21] An FCO diplomat recalled that US officials did not voice 'strong objections' to Britain relinquishing its role but raised concerns about the UNODC's suitability.[22] The US was also anxious that Britain would honour its pre-existing commitments. With the narco–insurgency nexus high on the administration's list of priorities, DOD officials were particularly keen for Britain to continue supporting interdiction activities.[23] Britain did sustain its commitments in the short term but then slowly reduced its counter-narcotics resources. In 2008–9, the FCO's counter-narcotics programme totalled £49.1 million, the following year it decreased to £24.5 million,[24] by 2011–12 it was slashed to £16 million.[25]

The surge

Coinciding with the Anglo-American counter-narcotics meeting, President Obama unveiled his new strategy for Afghanistan. The strategy was conditioned by McChrystal's alarming assessment that if the coalition did not halt the Taliban's momentum within the next twelve months, winning the war might no longer be achievable.[26] To combat this momentum, the president announced a surge of 30,000 troops to Afghanistan (he later authorised sending an additional 3,000 troops). The new strategy was a mixture of a full-blown counterinsurgency and a narrow counter-terrorism effort.[27] Obama stated that the strategy was not state-building; it was narrower than that but aimed to achieve the US's key objectives: 'to disrupt, dismantle, and defeat al-Qaeda in Afghanistan and Pakistan, and to prevent its capacity to threaten America and our allies in the future... [and] revers[ing] the Taliban's momentum and deny[ing] it the ability to overthrow the government'. In order to achieve these goals, the US vastly increased its financial resources to Afghanistan, which enabled a greater military effort and a civilian surge – a move that tripled the number of US civilian personnel in Afghanistan to 1,100.[28] However, during the same speech, Obama announced a timetable for withdrawing US troops – the withdrawal was scheduled for July 2011. Under this timetable, US troops would clear the Taliban from areas then transfer the responsibility to the developing Afghan National Security Forces within eighteen to twenty-four months.[29] In contrast to Bush, Obama placed Afghanistan not Iraq at the heart of his foreign policy agenda.

Paradoxically, whilst counter-narcotics was a higher priority for the Bush administration, it was the sharp increase in resources under Obama that resulted in several counter-narcotics gains. The gains, however, were a consequence of the broader 'state-building project that included efforts to improve governance, security, and development'.[30] As detailed below, the surge of troops and resources were instrumental in achieving this.[31]

The surge and counter-narcotics

In February 2010, McChyrstal predicted that the battle to recapture the central Helmand town of Marjah would be the showpiece of the surge. This was accompanied by a simultaneous British operation in Nad-e-Ali – also in central Helmand. Marjah was considered of great strategic and symbolic value owing to high levels of insurgent activity and narcotics production, and low levels of state control.

The issue of eradication once again complicated matters as the military and counter-narcotics campaign clashed. In the aftermath of the operation – which coincided with the poppy harvest season – US Marines were confronted by high levels of opium cultivation. With a political imperative to act, and cognisant of the fact that forced eradication could undermine their counterinsurgency mission, the Marines launched a compensated eradication plan. Under the scheme, farmers were paid US $300 to destroy their poppy and plant licit spring crops.[32] A member of McChrystal's strategic Advisory Group, Commander Jeffery Eggers, summed up the Marine's position: 'We don't trample the livelihood of those we're trying to win over.'[33] It is unclear if the decision to compensate farmers was sanctioned by either Washington or the US Embassy or was simply an independent decision taken at the operational level.

Inevitably, the scheme was not well received in wider British and American policy circles as, among other things, it contravened existing eradication policy. The scheme exposed divisions between the British-led PRT and the Marines, as the latter did not consult the former during the formulation or implementation process. Upon 'stumbling across it', PRT officials confronted Marine Colonel Michael Killion.[34] A PRT official recounted the meeting:

> The PRT opposed it because there had been a previous [compensation] policy which caused a massive spike in cultivation the next season because farmers thought they were going to get paid a guaranteed amount for their poppies. It was agreed that it had happened now, but it wouldn't be happening again . . . We will never know [the details] because the ranks closed on us.[35]

Also concerned about the negative ramifications of the scheme, British Embassy officials raised the issue with the head of INL in Kabul. Further discussions were also held with CENTCOM, Marine and State Department officials in Washington (via video-conference).[36] With the failures of the 2002 compensated eradication scheme casting a long shadow and the plan flouting an agreed strategy, the Marines subsequently abandoned the policy.[37] A PRT official stated:

> I think . . . we did influence their [the Marines] decision to adjust that policy . . . it is very illustrative of . . . the dynamics of the relationship during the shoulder to shoulder international effort . . . [But] . . . it was not an equal partnership.[38]

Given that American and Afghan government officials also opposed the policy, it is difficult to ascertain exactly what pressure forced the Marines to rescind it, although it is probable that British officials did influence, at least to some extent, the decision-making process. This was another example of Britain attempting to shape American policies for the better. A PRT official recalls:

> There was always a tendency from our Marine colleagues to do something but doing something was not actually always the best thing to do. [So, we had to] steer that energy and intensity in a more constructive, productive way. There wasn't really an option to say: no, don't do anything. That was never going to happen. So, [the question was] what can they do that's going to be helpful – [well], that would be the dream – or at least not counterproductive![39]

Nevertheless, the episode – again – exposed friction between the special relationship allies over eradication. Much like the British military, the Marines considered the FCO's targeted approach to eradication too aggressive. A State Department official noted: 'Britain supported governor-led eradication and a more aggressive counter-narcotics policy. When the Marjah operation began, this caused a degree of friction and disconnect.'[40]

In the end, Marjah failed to be the gold standard operation that McChrystal predicted, at least in the short term as violence increased and governance decreased. Whilst security was not improved, the physical presence of the state – checkpoints, roadblocks, military bases – following the military operations proved vital in reducing opium cultivation in Marjah and Nad-e-Ali. Mansfield explains:

> the act of crop destruction itself is not a major determinant of opium poppy cultivation. Rather, it is the state's ability to establish its presence and outreach convincing the population that the authorities have the capacity to enforce a ban on opium production over a given geographic space.[41]

Coupled to the deterrent effect, the area also received benefits from the HFZ, which supplied 5,500 provincial farmers with fertiliser, wheat and vegetable plant seeds at a subsidised price. Over 90 per cent of farmers took advantage of this initiative.[42] In the end, the amount of land dedicated to opium cultivation decreased from 60 per cent in 2010 to less than 5 per cent in 2011.[43] Across the province, the influx of coalition and Afghan troops contributed to opium cultivation declining from 103,590 ha in 2008 to 63,307 ha in 2011.[44]

In parallel to the Marjah offensive, Cowper-Coles returned to Afghanistan as Chargé d'Affaires until the new Ambassador, Sir William Patey, took up his post. On his return, Cowper-Coles was dismayed that Zarar Osmani, the former Afghan Minister of Interior, was the incumbent Minister of Counter-Narcotics. During his first tour of Afghanistan, for reasons unknown, Cowper-Coles considered Osmani to be one of the most corrupt members of the Afghan Cabinet.[45] Cowper-Coles, fearing Osmani's – alleged – behaviour could undermine the counter-narcotics campaign, directed FCO officials to submit a proposal to David Miliband recommending that Britain sever ties with the minister.

The proposal, however, was problematic on several levels. First, embassy officials could find little definitive proof to substantiate the claims that Osmani was still – if ever – corrupt.[46] Concerned by the lack of evidence, counter-narcotics officials in both London and Kabul judged cutting ties with Osmani as premature. Nevertheless, Cowper-Coles's word carried weight. So, despite their reservations, FCO officials put the veteran diplomat's proposition to Miliband, which he duly accepted.[47] Britain then, in the words of a Kabul Embassy official, 'stopped its financial support to the MCN ... [and] drew down its funding for mentors within the ministry'. The official further explained that British diplomats could 'play an advisory role, meet with counter-narcotics officials and take part in international meetings. But for the bulk of our counter-narcotics work we would not have direct discussions one-on-one with the minister'.[48]

Second, the partner nation on counter-narcotics refusing to work with the lead Afghan counter-narcotics representative presented several challenges, with some having immediate consequences, one of which was approximately a dozen British-funded Adam Smith International consultants, contracted to build the capacity of the MCN, being withdrawn. Predictably, the MCN's capabilities were immediately weakened. The US Embassy in Kabul, however, refused to follow Britain's lead, backfilling the positions and assuming the role of funder. During discussions with the British Embassy, the US, whilst acknowledging British concerns, was clear that supporting the MCN was a crucial element of its counter-narcotics strategy. Moreover, the UNODC and ISAF also concluded that the allegations of corruption were not compelling enough to impact its relationships with Osmani.[49]

Initially, the new British Ambassador Sir William Patey continued his predecessor's policy, but slowly initiated a process to reverse the decision to sever links with Osmani. Partly this was a result of Osmani's commitment to counter-narcotics work and his determination to cultivate a good relationship with the British Embassy in Kabul. A US official commented: 'it was very important for Osmani that the US and Britain believed that he was not involved in illicit activity'.[50] The minister was realistic, knowing that for his policies to have any chance of succeeding, he had to have the backing of both the Americans and the British. More importantly, Britain possessed only circumstantial evidence of Osmani's involvement in corrupt practices whilst at the MOI.

Eventually, Patey commissioned JNAC to investigate any possible wrongdoing, and according to a British official in the Kabul Embassy:

> it became pretty clear that the worst official assessment that anyone could say was that Osmani operated patronage networks. I would suggest if we used that as criteria not to cooperate with Afghan ministers, we would find it difficult to operate with any minister.

The official further noted that: 'there were definitely problems at the Ministry of Interior when he was there around corruption and other issues. But that was the case with every Afghan Minister of Interior before and after my time.'[51] Approximately a year after Cowper-Coles cut ties with the Osmani, Patey resumed contact with the minister.

Meanwhile, in Britain, the recently elected Conservative–Liberal Democrat Government, under the leadership of David Cameron, showed little enthusiasm to prolong the conflict. In June, concerned about the financial and human cost of the conflict, Cameron announced that British troops would be withdrawn from Afghanistan by 2015.[52] Shortly after, NATO announced its decision to complete the transfer of security to Afghan forces by the end of 2014.[53] With western commitment to the campaign low, the conflict entered its final stages.

Implementation of the strategy: interdiction and alternative development

In June 2010, Obama replaced McChrystal as US commander after he gave an ill-thought out interview criticising the president's Afghan review process.[54] He was replaced by General David Petraeus, the officer who was credited with turning the Iraq War in the US's favour. His appointment signalled a continuation of policy, as Petraeus implemented McChrystal's broader counterinsurgency strategy with some refinements. Petraeus's grand vision was the strategy he adopted in Iraq, the generic elements of which could be replicated against any insurgency. The 'Anaconda Strategy' was based around 'squeezing' the insurgents and the materials (such as money, ammunition, explosives, communications, popular support and sanctuaries) they needed to operate.[55]

Forming a key component of his Anaconda Strategy, Petraeus also sought to sever the financial link between narco-traffickers and the insurgency. In testimony to the Senate Armed Services Committee, the General argued: 'this drug money has been the "oxygen" in the air that allows these groups to operate. With the extension of authority granted to US forces to conduct counter-narcotics operations', the US can now interdict narco-dealers.[56] His views meshed with the new counter-narcotics strategy which placed interdicting Taliban-linked traffickers as a top priority.

For several years, concerned by the narco–insurgency nexus, the US military had gradually increased its involvement in the counter-narcotics mission. Nevertheless, DEA agents still complained that they did not receive adequate resources or integration within military operations to disrupt major trafficking networks. Petraeus quickly set about correcting this by incorporating the DEA into his military command. When the head of the DEA in Afghanistan told Petraeus that his organisation had not dismantled any major trafficking organisations because of a lack of resources, the General responded: 'that will change, you will have as many resources as you need'.[57] By this stage, attitudes had also changed in the Pentagon. Once a bastion of opposition to counter-narcotics, senior Pentagon officials were now supportive of an increased role for the US military.[58] Reflecting this, interdiction operations in the south more than doubled from 204 in 2010 to 521 in 2011.[59] Whilst these raids were successful at reducing material support to the insurgency at the local level, they did not affect the Taliban at the strategic level.[60] Moreover, interdiction operations were more successful at destroying narcotics supplies and labs than arresting and convicting Taliban-linked traffickers.[61] Another area where the implementation of this plan fell short was targeting narcotics traffickers with connections to the government. By focusing on Taliban-linked traffickers, the policy strengthened the position of government-linked traffickers by expanding their market share. This failure had ramifications not only for combating the narcotics trade but on good governance as well, as the legitimacy of the state was further eroded.[62]

The other centrepiece of the US's counter-narcotics strategy was substantially increasing alternative development to farmers. Despite this, many USAID programmes launched during this period were focused on stabilisation and 'short-term income generation programmes', not specifically reducing opium cultivation.

In fact, by 2010, one development project abandoned its requirement to produce counter-narcotics progress reports, instead only reporting on its success in growing the legal economy.[63] Further still, other development projects failed to reference opium cultivation at all in their project goals.[64] Launched in the wake of military operations, development and stabilisation programmes were designed to reduce violence and displace the Taliban from cleared areas, whilst laying the foundation for the state to deliver public services. In theory, this would strengthen ties between the government and population, and sever the link between the population and the Taliban.[65]

SRAP Holbrooke's approach to agricultural development was also underpinned by this philosophy: breaking the link between farmers and the Taliban. A central pillar of his plan was to give farmers alternative food sources to grow and provide all the necessary components, such as 'credit and training for farmers, new roads so they could get their goods to market, cold storage ... and processing factories'.[66] However, this plan would take years to produce results; this was unacceptable. Given the time-bound nature of the surge, Holbrooke wanted instantaneous results.

To try to achieve that, Holbrooke championed the recently expanded AVIPA-Plus project in the poppy heartlands of Helmand and Kandahar. AVIPA-Plus offered farmers seeds and fertiliser – at a fraction of the retail price – as a substitute for poppy, whilst providing them with the necessary equipment to undertake the venture.[67] Guided by the opinion that vast spending equalled success, Holbrooke doubled AVIPA-Plus' annual budget from $150 million to $300 million[68] – despite USAID leaders arguing that this far exceeded the amount needed to be effective.[69] The majority of this money – $250 million – was spent on stabilisation initiatives, such as cash-for-work projects and small grants.[70] Typically, projects lasted between thirty and ninety days, and were judged a success on the basis that 'every day that someone was working was a day that he was not emplacing IEDs or fighting'.[71] This rationale was not only short-sighted but failed to appreciate the drivers of poppy cultivation or how to engender long-term support for the state.

In the same way that the US sent the bulk of its forces to Helmand to the neglect of the rest of Afghanistan, Helmand and Kandahar were flooded with cash. AVIPA-Plus was estimated to have tripled or quadrupled the economy of Nawa in Helmand.[72] Whilst providing an instant boost, the injection of vast sums of money created negative consequences. As Nawa was inundated with moneymaking opportunities – typically irrigation canal cleaning or road construction – public servants, such as teachers, abandoned their jobs to earn more as day labourers.[73] Moreover, the programmes failed to provide a sustainable solution to unemployment in the south of the country. Additionally, the artificial economic conditions resulted in tension between communities over resources.[74]

The main objective of the programme was to spend as much money as possible – not to create long-term development.[75] After early scepticism, USAID embraced Holbrooke's spending splurge as they realised that Congress was more concerned about the volume of spending than about sustainability. More importantly, if USAID did not spend its entire budget, it would not receive the same level of funding the following year.[76] The contractor employed by USAID, International Relief and Development, was under strict instruction to spend the full $300 million within the twelve-month contract.[77] However, when it became apparent that insecurity prevented projects rolling out across the two provinces, the contractor was informed that it had to spend as much as possible in the few districts it could.[78] As a consequence, the projects created distortions in the local economy that could not be maintained.

The Senate Committee on Foreign Relations concluded: 'Too much aid can have a destabilizing effect on local communities that are unable to absorb the cash surge.'[79] The influx of large volumes of aid into insecure areas can have two opposite consequences: first, it can have the 'substitution effect', which transfers the loyalty of the population from the insurgents to the authorities. Alternately, it can have the opposite 'income effect', 'whereby development programmes increase the resources available to villagers and lead them to believe that they can improve their prospects of survival by entering into negotiations with the insurgents'.[80] Studies indicate that the delivery of aid projects does not necessarily generate support for the deliverers or for the government.[81] Once coalition troops withdrew after the surge, the artificial conditions created as a result of the programmes collapsed, all in all resulting in unrest amongst segments of the population. A more prudent policy would have been to inject the same amount of money over a longer period, creating sustainable projects which could redevelop agricultural communities and reduce dependency on opium for good.

All this was a sad story of the US throwing large amounts of money at what was a long-term development problem. It was well intentioned, but the dramatic insertion of resources simply created major economic dysfunctions while it provided short-term financial benefits to individuals. Those dysfunctions mitigated against the possibilities of long-term improved and sustainable agricultural economics. Once again problems that the Anglo-American allies confronted were more intractable than policymakers realised.

The transition and beyond

In February 2011, Marc Grossman was appointed SRAP, replacing Holbrooke who had died suddenly the previous December. Largely, Grossman embraced Holbrooke's counter-narcotics agenda; however, the most significant shift was the gradual return of US support for eradication. Grossman, like many others in the State Department, was influenced by his time working on counter-narcotics policies in Colombia and 'believed eradication was part of a deterrent strategy to get people to change their habits and get out of growing poppy'.[82] For eighteen months, 'Holbrooke's view on poppy eradication had cast a shadow across the INL team in Kabul', resulting in the embassy drawing down its support for wide-scale eradication, whilst tentatively providing limited support to GLE.[83] However, soon after Grossman was appointed, INL in Kabul seized the opportunity by increasing funding for eradication.[84] Grossman's support for increased eradication also found support with Osmani. Convinced of its merits, the Minister of Counter-Narcotics toured Afghanistan encouraging governors to increase eradication. His encouragement worked: GLE increased from 2,380 ha in 2010 to 3,917 ha in 2011, representing a 65 per cent increase.[85] By this time, however, Britain's ability to influence events was limited. A British diplomat in Kabul recalls:

[In 2010], the dynamic [between Britain and the US] . . . on eradication was very much in sync. We were always very clear about what we thought was useful: targeted eradication . . . The Americans supported that but as time went on and as American funding for eradication grew and ours [dropped], INL were of the view that targeted eradication wasn't having much impact . . . As our ability and enthusiasm began to dwindle, so this American approach was increasingly influential. The fact that Britain was bringing less focus on counternarcotics also influenced our ability to influence others.[86]

Notwithstanding Britain's diminished influence, its counternarcotics mission faced one last complication. Despite the conclusion of the partner nation mechanism in 2011, the UNODC was unprepared to assume the role of partner organisation. Plagued by funding issues and institutional weakness, the UNODC did not have the capacity or resources to offer the Afghan government sufficient support. With little alternative, the British Embassy in Kabul was forced to continue resourcing the counter-narcotics mission for approximately another twelve months. The situation was also compounded by the competitive nature of the UNODC's and MCN's relationship.[87] At a time when the international community's focus was on developing Afghan institutions, 'the UNODC [instead] was about promoting the UNODC . . . not building the capacity of the MCN'.[88] A particular point of contention was the UNODC's insistence on leading the annual Opium Survey, whilst excluding the MCN from the process. After intensive discussions, the UNODC conceded, making the MCN a partner in the survey.[89] More broadly, however, the UNODC's reliance on year-to-year donor funding meant it was unable to produce the strategic plan the MCN required. Identifying an opportunity, the MCN attempted to bypass the UNODC and secure funding directly from the Americans. The US was only too happy to oblige given its deep scepticism about the UNODC's effectiveness and capacity.[90] Consequently, the MCN and US strengthened ties at the expense of the UNODC – further weakening its ability to assume partner status.

Amid the growing tension between the UNODC and MCN, it was evident that the counter-narcotics gains of the previous years were unsustainable. In December 2011, the UNODC confirmed that opium cultivation increased to 131,000 ha, up from 123,000 in 2010 – the first rise in cultivation for three years.[91] The situation in Helmand provided a stark example of the fragility of opium bans. Although opium cultivation in Helmand fell by 3 per cent, reductions across the province were not uniform. Some urban areas close to provincial centres experienced reductions in cultivation, whereas remote areas still experienced high rates of cultivation.[92] The reductions achieved close to provincial centres – where the state had been historically active[93] – occurred as a result of the influx of troops and resources, diverse income opportunities, access to development assistance and improvements in security.[94] Crucially, the increased numbers of checkpoints and military bases were seen as vital in the population's perceptions of the state's ability to impose the ban.[95] Contrastingly, in remote areas, where the government had a minimal presence, its ability to enforce a poppy ban or eradication was more limited.

Whilst reducing opium cultivation in the target area, signs emerged that the surge and HFZ had also led to an explosion of cultivation elsewhere in the province. The policies had unintentionally resulted in 'a series of socio-economic and political factors that helped change the physical geography of Helmand'.[96] As landed farmers in central Helmand turned away from opium cultivation, out-of-work, landless sharecroppers were forced into the former desert areas of Helmand to eke out a living. However, once in the ungoverned territory, farmers undertook wide-scale opium cultivation, turning the desert into fertile agricultural land. Before long, the expansion of opium cultivation in the former desert area outstripped the 'reductions that had been achieved in the HFZ'.[97] Importantly, this transformation significantly increased Helmand's capacity to produce opium – leading to record amounts of opium cultivation in future years. The situation in Helmand again demonstrated that well-intentioned, but poorly designed and implemented, opium bans were counterproductive to the welfare of rural communities. In the process, they also failed to achieve the key aim of any counter-narcotics intervention: sustainably reducing opium cultivation. Opium bans could only be achieved when interventions were designed to spread economic development, and improved security and governance throughout all sections of the rural population. Unless the structural drivers of opium cultivation were addressed, bans that were underpinned by coercion, negotiation and quid pro quo arrangements would only be transitory.

With resources and troops being steadily decreased – 33,000 surge troops were withdrawn between July 2011 and September 2012[98] – the state's ability to enforce the ban diminished significantly. This, unfortunately, was to be expected: Obama made an error by setting an unrealistically short timeframe to make sustainable improvements. This error, amongst others, reinforced the point that sustainable policies were not given the time to succeed because of domestic political pressures. In November 2012, the UNODC announced that cultivation across Afghanistan had surged to 154,000 ha – an 18 per cent increase compared to 2011.[99] As the state retreated to Kabul, the provinces that had been considered as 'model' over the previous three years – Helmand, Nangarhar and Balkh[100] – returned to cultivation. Equally, as the international community increased the speed of transition, counter-narcotics was gradually downgraded across all actors and institutions. Transition was guiding all aspects of the allies' approach to Afghanistan and this was reflected in the 2012 US Counter-Narcotics Strategy, which stressed the need for the Afghan government and regional players to take greater responsibility for combating the narcotics industry.[101] Moreover, many counter-narcotics resources, including interdiction capabilities, were transferred to security and terrorism-related missions. This was followed by USAID dropping counter-narcotics as a strategic priority.[102]

By this time, Britain had also managed to withdraw from counter-narcotics, concluding the HFZ and scaling back its efforts to a limited number 'of law enforcement and rule of law activities'.[103] Against this backdrop, opium cultivation skyrocketed to record levels: reaching 209,000 ha in 2013, then 224,000 ha in 2014. Compounding matters, the new Afghan government, led by President Ashraf Ghani, demonstrated scant desire to engage with counter-narcotics, all of which, coupled to a weak economy and rising insecurity, resulted in opium cultivation rising unabated.[104] By 2017, cultivation reached an unprecedented 328,000 ha, a 63 per cent increase on the previous year. Responding to this record crop, the US and Afghan militaries launched bombing raids against '"Taliban narcotics production" facilities in Helmand Province'. Although the raids have thrust counter-narcotics back into focus, they were designed to disrupt the Taliban's funding structure as opposed to specific counter-narcotics interventions.[105]

There is little evidence to suggest that the international community or Afghan government are willing to re-engage with counter-narcotics beyond this limited form of intervention. Unfortunately, with Afghanistan slipping further into political and economic instability, there appears little hope that farmers will transition out of opium cultivation anytime soon. This current malaise underscores the transient and conditional nature of the opium bans introduced on the special relationship allies' watch.

14 Conclusion

There are three overriding important issues which arise from this narrative account. First, it has provided the most definitive account of Anglo-American counter-narcotics policies in Afghanistan between 2001 and 2011. Second, it has enriched the literature by detailing the development of policies from a British perspective throughout each phase of the counter-narcotics campaign. In particular, the discussions that underpinned: compensated eradication (2002); Britain assuming G8 lead nation on counter-narcotics (2002); Britain setting a ten-year timeframe to eliminate opium cultivation (2002–3); Anglo-American discord over aerial eradication (2004–7); and Britain ending its large-scale commitment to counter-narcotics (2009–12). Detailed analysis of these discussions has, until now, been absent from the literature, and this deficiency is notable given that Britain was the lead international nation on counter-narcotics. Moreover, the unfolding story revealed that the British government was not a unitary actor over counter-narcotics policy. Third, this work has provided the first book length treatment of an under-researched aspect of the special relationship: cooperation and competition when crafting counter-narcotics strategies.

Several lessons can be drawn from Anglo-American counter-narcotics policies in Afghanistan. However, before the specific lessons are discussed below, three broad themes need emphasis. First, the counter-narcotics policy process was constrained by domestic political pressures. That is to say, strategies that would have taken decades to come to fruition were not adopted because of the political imperative to demonstrate instant progress. Furthermore, even when the right policies were adopted, they were expected to produce results in an unrealistic timeframe. As cultivation rose, US actors led calls to abandon existing policies as they were not delivering results fast enough. This was particularly pronounced when opium cultivation rose to record levels in 2004 and 2007 and many actors called for more extreme measures. During these years, rampant opium cultivation was used as an indicator of broader state failure,[1] leading Afghanistan to be branded as a 'narco-state'. Counter-narcotics policies were also constrained by how success or failure was measured, in the annual UNODC statistics for poppy cultivation. It was against these findings that subsequent policies were maintained, adapted or abandoned. However, using this approach led to superficial assessments. If annual cultivation was reduced, observers concluded that the existing counter-narcotics policies were a success; an increase in cultivation led to the opposite reaction. These measures, however, failed to address complex external factors which contributed to reasons for cultivating opium, such as food insecurity, high wheat prices, levels of insecurity, levels of agricultural development and access to markets.[2] In short, repeatedly, analyses were flawed.

Second, the counter-narcotics agenda serves as a vivid example of a fractured policymaking process where a bureaucratic battleground of inter-governmental and intra-governmental conflict was prevalent, as both British and US governments were divided along departmental lines. Ironically, in some instances, actors were more aligned with their transatlantic partners than they were with their own governmental colleagues. At times, policymaking was less than collegial, and the Anglo-American counter-narcotics relationship was frayed to its core.

Third, the counter-narcotics landscape was heavily shaped by individual agency. On both sides of the Atlantic, individual actors were able to influence the policymaking process to suit their own agenda despite the absence of governmental consensus. The counter-narcotics campaign unfolded in three distinct phases, and throughout each phase individual agency was prevalent.

The three phases of the counter-narcotics campaign and the specific lessons learned

In 2001, the Anglo-American partners conceived their respective roles in Afghanistan through different prisms; this not only impacted the way both viewed the conflict but also the way they viewed the challenges posed by the narcotics industry. During the first phase of the counter-narcotics campaign, 2001–3, Britain exclusively formulated and implemented policies. Stemming the flow of Afghan heroin to British streets was an important topic before and after 9/11, but Whitehall was always divided over involvement in such a complex task. Several important lessons stand out regarding policymaking during this phase. Counter-narcotics decision-making was centralised in Number 10 with Blair relying on a small group of advisors to make key policy decisions. It was in this environment that Blair committed to Operation Drown and lead nation on counter-narcotics. In doing so, he ignored the sober warnings of FCO officials who argued that successful counter-narcotics policies would take a generation to succeed. In many respects, this period of policymaking was inextricably tied to Blair's desire to fulfil his international and domestic ambitions. This was one of the starkest examples of the dominance of individual agency over counter-narcotics policymaking.

It is worth noting, however, that while Blair was (mis)guided by an overly optimistic assessment of the situation, there was in fact, a bona fide political imperative to act. If Britain had failed to act against wide-scale opium cultivation it would have resulted in a public relations disaster and, of course, undermined the legitimacy of the new state. In the event, Britain *did* fail to prevent rampant opium cultivation and the ensuing public relations disaster. The real problem lay not with Blair's desire to curb opium cultivation but his lack of realism about what could be achieved against such an intractable narcotics trade. There was also a lack of understanding, at the top of government at least, about what could be achieved in Afghanistan – a country that was economically dependent on opium cultivation and devastated by twenty years of war. Notwithstanding FCO warnings, Number 10's assessment of the situation was severely lacking. Additionally, Britain failed to commit enough resources to counter-narcotics, which was further constrained by the failure of the lead nation approach. All in all, the policies implemented during this period were constrained by political realities and were doomed to fail.

On the other side of the Atlantic, the counter-narcotics debate was also heavily shaped by individual agency and, for a long time, by the dominance of the Pentagon over the policymaking process. Inhibited by dogmatic Pentagon opposition to state-building, the

US operated a light-footprint approach which had disastrous implications for the development of the state. As a result, counter-narcotics work was viewed as an unhelpful distraction to the primary mission of killing terrorists. Crucially, the US's hands-off approach and its focus on Iraq further constrained Britain's chances of success against the narcotics trade.

During the second phase of the counter-narcotics campaign, 2004–8, the policy landscape altered when the US was forced to confront the opium problem and formulate a strategy. However, the development of this strategy was highly contentious both within the Bush administration and wider Anglo-American alliance as INL championed a Colombian-style eradication policy, with aerial spraying at its core. Its possible introduction dismayed the Pentagon who feared the policy would drive insecurity and violence in rural Afghanistan. The policy process was fraught as the State Department struggled to defeat the Pentagon's opposition. In the end, Ambassador Khalilzad's intervention was decisive, convincing Bush – despite the president supporting the policy – that aerial eradication was not compatible with Afghanistan's political realities. Whilst the policy was defeated, the battle over aerial eradication dominated the counter-narcotics agenda for the subsequent years. The episode revealed that the US policy landscape was fragmented and dominated by individual agency. The Bush administration proved, in fact, to be more divided than the British government over aerial eradication and was more prone to institutional and individual agency. Furthermore, Bush was unable to exert the same level of influence over the policymaking agenda as Blair. The prime minister – at least in the first eighteen months of the conflict – had a firm grip on the levers of foreign policy, whereas the president proved incapable of decisively intervening in favour of aerial eradication.

This period also marked a seminal juncture in the Anglo-American counter-narcotics relationship as the US became highly influential in the policymaking process. The period also saw Anglo-American relations fray as the US, at several levels of officialdom, criticised Britain for failing to reduce opium cultivation. In direct response to this criticism, Britain reinvigorated its counter-narcotics approach.

The deployment to Helmand Province, more than any other event, shaped Britain's campaign in Afghanistan. Its deployment, however, was conceptually flawed and, much like its foray into counter-narcotics, built on inadequate intelligence. This failure left Britain unprepared to deal with the insurgency and prevented it from executing its original strategy. The move into Helmand had parallels with Britain assuming G8 lead nation on counter-narcotics. In both cases, a substantial factor was Blair's desire for Britain to fulfil a role that was commensurate with its international standing – irrespective if it had the resources or capability to succeed. Both were intractable problems, and Britain's under-resourced effort proved wholly insufficient. Moreover, by originally highlighting that both missions were compatible, the government demonstrated a woeful lack of understanding of the complexity of both problems. But again, the move into Helmand was conditioned as much by politics as it was by strategy. It also opened new disagreement in Whitehall over Britain's military and counter-narcotics mission, whilst at the same time, aggravating already tense relations with the State Department and White House over where and when to conduct eradication.

With the US wedded to the notion that widespread eradication equalled counter-narcotics success, the US Embassy in Kabul – responding to domestic political anxieties – ramped up pressure on Britain. This again illustrated how policy in Afghanistan was shaped by domestic political pressures to show success. Inevitably, this resulted in calls for stronger measures. By 2006, another record opium crop made it increasingly difficult for ADIDU to avoid the introduction of aerial spraying. In an effort to prevent its introduction, Britain reluctantly agreed to implement GBS. The policy, however, was never adopted due to Afghan concerns over the safety of glyphosate use. The following year tension exploded in the Anglo-American counter-narcotics relationship as the State Department, supported by the White House, demanded the introduction of aerial eradication.

This issue, above all, had been the most controversial aspect of the counter-narcotics campaign and also the bitterest source of friction between the Anglo-American partners from 2004 to 2007. British officials came under intense pressure to accede to the State Department and White House demands, but along with the Afghan government fought an embattled position. After objecting to aerial eradication for three years, the Pentagon naysayers could no longer oppose the policy in the NSC. With consensus reached across the Bush administration, the NSC approved aerial eradication. The policy was also approved because, by that stage, many in the US administration felt that all other options had been exhausted. But despite remaining passive during the policy discussions, the Pentagon was determined to kill off aerial eradication by back channels, enlisting British help to derail the plan. The British, who had opposed the policy from the start, pledged their support to Karzai to prevent its introduction. The plan worked. When US officials pressured Karzai to agree to aerial eradication, he refused, in part, by pointing to the disunity in the alliance. Bush was wise enough to realise it would have been political folly to force Karzai into this – although, this was unlikely given Bush's respect for Karzai and the office that he held.

In general, US perceptions of the narcotics problem and solutions required were more stringent than that of its British counterpart. There was something of a cultural divide between the partners, with some US officials being evangelical in their pursuit of aerial eradication, often in the face of widespread domestic and international opposition. The debate surrounding aerial eradication highlighted that individual agency dominated the policy process. The policy landscape was fractured along inter-governmental and intra-governmental lines, with the Pentagon preferring to aid the British than let its State Department colleagues win the policy debate.

Under the Obama administration, the third, and final, phase of the counter-narcotics campaign, 2009–11, commenced. The most fundamental difference between Obama and Bush was the former's increase of focus, manpower and financial resources dedicated to Afghanistan. The Obama administration sought to deliver key components of the previous strategy with more competence than the Bush administration. Unfortunately, throwing large sums of money at the problem was not the answer. The most notable difference in US policy was a rather ironic shift away from eradication. This episode serves as another example of the dominance of individual agency over the policymaking process, as Holbrooke sidestepped INL opposition to enact this change. Like his predecessors, Holbrooke's position was driven by personal belief – in this circumstance, however, the desire for less eradication was preferable to the push for blanket eradication. The policy change brought the Anglo-American counter-narcotics partners closer together. On the one hand, the removal of this friction meant there was greater harmony in the relationship; on the other hand, it demonstrated Britain's diminished influence as this harmonisation occurred more through happenstance than design.

With the security situation in Helmand deteriorating, the British government re-evaluated its goals and priorities in Afghanistan. Britain lacked the resources to focus on stabilising Helmand and counter-narcotics. Aside from the lack of resources, opium cultivation represented a symptom of the broader problem, thus for counter-narcotics strategies to succeed, improvements in security, governance and economic development would have also been required. Britain did not have the time, resources or political will to sustain this effort. Most in Whitehall accepted this reality, and subsequently agreed to end Britain's large-scale commitment to counter-narcotics.

Anglo-American counter-narcotics policies in Afghanistan: lessons for broader Anglo-American relations

The counter-narcotics partnership provides a useful model on which to evaluate the broader Anglo-American relationship. The counter-narcotics relationship in Afghanistan was, in its broadest sense, complex and fraught but nevertheless was characterised by cooperation and coordination. From 2004 to 2011, the allies were at the heart of policy formulation, funding and implementation. The partnership followed the unique conditions of the special relationship: extraordinary close diplomatic coordination and full disclosure of strategy and intelligence, buttressed by large formal decision-making meetings and regular informal contact. In short, it was a genuine partnership – although not equal – that had an unparalleled decision-making structure.

The first phase of the campaign demonstrated three salient characteristics of the special relationship: power asymmetry, Britain's symbolic value to the US in its time of need, and the special relationship being at the core of British foreign policy. First, the asymmetry between the partners meant that Britain did not have the resources or capacity to run a strategy that was independent of the US. This was confirmed when Afghanistan was engulfed by opium cultivation in 2004. That said, given the intractable nature of the narcotics industry, it would be remiss to suggest that, even if the US was fully engaged in counter-narcotics work, progress would have been achieved. But the fact that the US was not engaged certainly hindered Britain's chance of success. Second, although the US did not consider counter-narcotics a strategic priority, it was nevertheless content that Britain took on lead nation on counter-narcotics. By taking on a lead role, Britain demonstrated not only its commitment to the conflict but also to the special relationship. Similarly, when Britain ended its commitment to counter-narcotics, the US was concerned that Britain was withdrawing all support, thus leaving the US to shoulder the burden alone. Third, even when the US was not actively involved in counter-narcotics, FCO officials were cautious not to engage in any policy that might bring them into conflict with their special relationship ally, demonstrating that the maintenance of the alliance was still at the core of foreign policy decision-making.

The second phase of the campaign provides a valuable insight into the conflict resolution process between the partners. This phase experienced bitter diplomatic exchanges over the introduction of aerial eradication. Two points stand out during this phase. First, the lack of consideration that some US officials gave to the time-honoured tradition of avoiding, where possible, public criticism of Britain. This was best exemplified by Charles's congressional testimony in 2004, although this fact was not lost on all within the Bush administration, as NSC officials complained about the negative impact of the criticism on alliance unity. Equally, after subsequent critical US cable leaks, US officials bemoaned the damaging effect this had on the health of the overall relationship, especially when the allies were fighting in two wars. Second, on one hand, the debate regarding aerial eradication demonstrated that Britain was implementing a long-held diplomatic tradition of tempering American policy and, as far as aerial eradication was concerned, that was true. By supporting GBS, Britain hoped that it would jettison aerial eradication from the agenda. On the other, however, the episode shows that despite Britain having the lead position on counter-narcotics, the US held considerable, though not total, influence over policymaking, forcing Britain to bend to its will. Britain did adopt a stronger eradication policy, but this was partly to deflect calls for the introduction of aerial spraying. Britain's role within the partnership was complex and, while it bowed to pressure and accepted a stronger eradication policy than it thought wise because of US demands, at no point was it willing to acquiesce in aerial eradication. If the US had totally dominated the policy landscape, it would have been able to push through aerial eradication; in the event it was unable to do so, not only with Britain but also with the Afghan government.

The third phase of the counter-narcotics campaign provides an interesting parallel with the broader relationship. As Obama came into office, relations cooled at all levels of the partnership: Obama and Brown drifted from the special relationship, and British officials, particularly Cowper-Coles, struggled to make an impact on the US policymaking process. At the strategic level, not only was symbolism missing from the relationship there was far less consultation between the partners over the direction of travel. Whilst the ties between the counter-narcotics partners were still, institutionally at least, strong, the level of British influence over policy was minimal. This was best demonstrated by the US's decision to defund eradication.

In sum, the Anglo-American counter-narcotics relationship in Afghanistan exhibited many of the same hallmarks as the wider special relationship. The allies cooperated extremely closely on policymaking, but the relationship was also characterised by intense disagreement, with Britain often having to bend to the will of its special relationship ally. It also reinforced the power asymmetry between the two partners and revealed that British policies were, to a large extent, dependent on the US. Despite all the failings and friction, the conflict in Afghanistan still marked one of the closest periods of Anglo-American cooperation in a generation. A State Department official concludes: 'for all the friction – who doesn't have disagreement during war – there was a lot more coordination and mutual respect. This has been lost in the books so far, even though opposing views were expressed.'[3]

Appendix

Methodology

The study has adopted a historical approach in which to evaluate the empirical evidence. This is a traditional qualitative historical reconstruction of policymaking and implementation with critical appraisals. It is based on primary sources of an oral documentary kind, which are in the public domain, autobiographical and biographical studies, diaries and interviews, supplemented by a wealth of secondary published sources.

As a contemporary history study, the gold standard of documentary evidence would have been government generated evidence produced at the time, for example a government memorandum, a Cabinet Office paper or memorandum of conversation that was produced in a policy meeting. That is not to say that this evidence is without bias, but it is difficult to challenge its accuracy. Unfortunately, the methodological limitation of this contemporary history study includes restrictive access to contemporary government documents. Therefore, in a sense, the study has been conducted utilising limited research tools. That said, where possible, Freedom of Information requests and diplomatic cables released from WikiLeaks have been used to provide contemporary evidence. The next best available evidence was oral evidence from central actors involved in the counter-narcotics policy formulation and implementation process within Afghanistan. Whilst oral testimony is not the gold standard of historical evidence, expert opinion is of great value to any research and provides a first-hand account of the events from those involved.

Key actors within this field were identified through systemically searching numerous sources, such as: House of Commons

Parliamentary Debates, House of Commons Select Committee Reports, State Department and INL reports, US Congressional Committee Reports, UNODC reports, ISAF reports, WikiLeaks cables, political biographies, notable monographs, politics and international relations and history journal articles, quality newspaper articles, internet searches and referrals from other interviewees.

The primary research is centred on seventy-four interviews; eight separate email correspondences; and several personal communications with policy practitioners who were directly involved in the counter-narcotics policymaking or implementation process. Additional interviews were conducted with two academic experts. Because most of these sources were former senior government, inter-governmental, military and diplomatic officials it has not been possible to assign explicit authorship of the citations in this study. The interviewees came from a range of backgrounds including: British Cabinet ministers, junior ministers, senior diplomats in London, Washington and Kabul and high-ranking military officers based in Kabul. In Britain, the officials belonged to: the FCO; the embassy in Kabul; ADIDU; the Cabinet Office; the DFID; HMCE; SOCA; the Security Service; the MOD; the Department of Health; the military; and the Helmand PRT. In the US, the officials belonged to: the Department of State; the DOD; the embassy in Kabul; INL; DEA; the Office of National Drug Control Policy; NSC; and the military. Interviews were also conducted with officials from the ISAF and the UNODC. All interviewees are categorised by organisation/affiliation and represented by a reference code.

However, this method of evidence gathering presented several difficulties. Testimony elicited from interviews, by its very nature, is retrospective and that can present key methodological challenges. Recall bias can be introduced as interviewees may recollect events inaccurately or may be misleading with a view to justifying their own motives and actions. Therefore, it was vital to attain corroboration from at least two sources to verify the information as accurate. As such, all interview material garnered from key actors has been cross-referenced for corroboration with at least two other interview materials or documentary sources. Where direct corroboration was not possible then best judgment has been used based on levels of compatibility, with the major lines of interpretation based on other sources.

Another substantial methodological challenge was access to key actors due to a lack of contact details or actors being unresponsive after initial contact. This lack of access was particularly pronounced with Afghan governmental figures. Numerous Afghan actors were contacted over a three-year period through a variety of methods, but most did not respond. This lack of access to Afghan actors (and more generally to all actors identified) was detrimental to the research, in as much as primary evidence could not be collected from the Afghan perspective to provide a unique interpretation of the complex British, American and Afghan policymaking triangle. This was important because – even though the main thrust of the study is an examination of Anglo-American counter-narcotics policies – the Afghans were not passive actors within the policymaking process and held sway over key decisions. Thus, with an absence of primary evidence from Afghan actors, a full appreciation of the decision-making process was problematic. To circumvent this lack of primary evidence, information was gathered from WikiLeaks cables and secondary sources.

Notes

Chapter 1: Introduction

1 Chouvy, *Opium*; Felbab-Brown, *Shooting Up*; Mercille, *Cruel Harvest*; Morgan Edwards, *The Afghan Solution*; Paoli et al., *The World Heroin Market*; Rubin, Road to Ruin.

2 Special Inspector General for Afghanistan Reconstruction (SIGAR), Quarterly Report to the United States Congress, p. 127. There is no complete data on Britain's counter-narcotics spend from 2001 to 2014. However, using data from parliamentary sources, it is estimated that Britain spent approximately £500 million ($702 million) from 2001 to 2014. It is probable that the actual spend was higher.

3 There are two sources of opium poppy cultivation data in Afghanistan: the UNODC and US. Until 2005, both surveys produced significantly different results. The UNODC relied on a combination of satellite imagery and ground-based verification – a data collection method that was limited and produced unverifiable results. The US, by contrast, used satellite imagery and significantly more images producing a more accurate result. Despite the UNODC and US's estimates moving closer together at the national level, there are still differences at the provincial level. This is due to 'the different methodological approaches adopted by the two surveys and how they calculate the full extent of the agricultural areas – the agricultural "mask", how samples are selected, and the number of images collected' (Byrd and Mansfield, Afghanistan's Opium Economy). For a detailed discussion see ibid., pp. 101–2.

4 UNODC/Government of Afghanistan Ministry of Counter-narcotics (MCN), Afghanistan Opium Survey 2017, p. 5.

5 Mansfield, *A State Built on Sand*, pp. 149, 158.

6 Reynolds, *The Creation of the Anglo-American Alliance*.

7 Mansfield, *A State Built on Sand*, p. 149.

8 Berry, 'Allies at War in Afghanistan'.
9 Mansfield, *A State Built on Sand*, p. 80.

Chapter 2: Anglo-American relations and 9/11

1 Dimbleby and Reynolds, *An Ocean Apart*, p. 139.
2 Ibid., p. 140.
3 Ibid., pp. 142–4.
4 Churchill, *The Second World War*, vol. II, p. 22, in Ibid., p. 139.
5 Dimbleby and Reynolds, *An Ocean Apart*, pp. 152–3.
6 Reynolds, 'Re-thinking Anglo-American Relations', p. 92.
7 Quoted in Saville, *The Politics of Continuity*, p. 67.
8 Renwick, *Fighting with Allies*, pp. 123–4.
9 Reynolds, 'Re-thinking Anglo-American Relations', p. 95.
10 Marsh, The Anglo-American Defence Relationship, p. 179.
11 Dumbrell, *A Special Relationship*, p. 14.
12 Baylis, Britain, the United States and Europe, p. 77.
13 Yasamee and Hamilton, *Documents on British Policy Overseas, Series* II, p. 257.
14 Horne, *MacMillan 1894–1956*, p. 347, cited in Dumbrell, *A Special Relationship*, p. 52.
15 Dumbrell, *A Special Relationship*, pp. 53–4.
16 Dobson and Marsh, 'Anglo-American Relations', p. 677.
17 Reynolds, 'A "Special Relationship"?', p. 2.
18 Dumbrell, *A Special Relationship*, p. 162.
19 Ibid., pp. 172–5.
20 Lyndon Johnson Library, UK memos.
21 Dumbrell, *A Special Relationship*, p. 94.
22 Ibid., p. 106.
23 Dimbleby and Reynolds, *An Ocean Apart*, pp. 310–11.
24 Ibid., pp. 313–15.
25 Dumbrell, *A Special Relationship*, p. 135.
26 Seitz, 'Britain and America', cited in Dumbrell, *A Special Relationship*, p. 136.
27 Dobson and Marsh, 'Anglo-American Relations', pp. 679–80.
28 Phythian, From Asset to Liability, p. 193.
29 Quoted in Phythian, From Asset to Liability, p. 194
30 Dumbrell, Personal Diplomacy, p. 88.
31 Dobson and Marsh, 'Anglo-American Relations', p. 680.
32 Dumbrell, Personal Diplomacy, p. 88.
33 Hemmings, 'The UK-US Alliance Under the Microscope'.
34 Burke, *Al-Qaeda*, p. 22.
35 Bergen, *The Longest War*, p. 52.

36 Halper and Clarke, *America Alone*, p. 110.
37 Bird and Marshall, *Afghanistan*, pp. 48–9.
38 Bergen, *The Longest War*, p. 179.
39 Woodward, *Bush at War*, p. 14.
40 Author interview with former Department of State official (1), 7 March 2014.
41 Risen, *State of War*, pp. 161–2.
42 Seldon et al., *Blair Unbound*, p. 87.
43 Ibid.
44 *The Guardian*, 'Full text of Tony Blair's speech'.
45 Blair, 'Doctrine of the International Community'.
46 Bush, *Decision Points*, p. 230.
47 Campbell, *The Alastair Campbell Diaries*, p. 9.
48 Ibid., p. 6.
49 Bush, *Decision Points*, p. 140.
50 Campbell, *The Alastair Campbell Diaries*, pp. 12–13.
51 Ibid., pp. 9–10.
52 Woodward, *Bush at War*, pp. 74–92.
53 Ibid., pp. 96–101.
54 Seldon et al., *Blair Unbound*, p. 55.
55 Ibid., p. 53.
56 Cheney, *In My Time*, p. 331.
57 Seldon et al., *Blair Unbound*, p. 56.
58 Bush, Transcript of President Bush's address.
59 Blair, 'Labour Conference', 2001.
60 Dumbrell, Personal Diplomacy, p. 88.
61 Bergen, *The Longest War*, p. 59.
62 Kampfner, *Blair's Wars*, p. 117.
63 Bird and Marshall, *Afghanistan*, p. 73.
64 Ibid., pp. 78–9.
65 Clarke, Foreign Policy, p. 605.
66 Campbell, *The Alastair Campbell Diaries*, pp. 91–3.
67 Ibid., p. 93.
68 Bird and Marshall, *Afghanistan*, pp. 89–92.
69 Dyson, *The Blair Identity*, pp. 77–8.
70 Bird and Marshall, *Afghanistan*, p. 93.
71 Seldon et al., *Blair Unbound*, p. 67.
72 Author interview with former UK minister (1), 23 April 2013.
73 The AIA was mandated to govern for two years until a representative government was elected through democratic elections.
74 Dobbins, *After the Taliban*, quoted in Bird and Marshall, *Afghanistan*, p. 97.
75 Ibid., pp. 83–4.
76 Ibid., pp. 83–4, 97.

77 Ibid., pp. 98–9.
78 Dobbins, *After the Taliban*, pp. 16–17.
79 Steele, *Ghosts of Afghanistan*, pp. 261–2.
80 Seldon et al., *Blair Unbound*, p. 67.
81 Maloney, 'The International Security Assistance Force', p. 6.
82 Bergen, *The Longest War*, p. 181.
83 Ibid.
84 Seldon et al., *Blair Unbound*, p. 68
85 Kampfner, *Blair's Wars*, p. 149.
86 Bird and Marshall, *Afghanistan*, pp. 9–10.

Chapter 3: The legacy of drugs and a weak state

1 Saikal, *Modern Afghanistan*, p. 19.
2 Ibid., p. 20.
3 Yapp, 'The Legend of the Great Game'.
4 Bird and Marshall, *Afghanistan*, p. 13.
5 Saikal, *Modern Afghanistan*, p. 28.
6 Bird and Marshall, *Afghanistan*, pp. 14–15.
7 Chouvy, *Opium*, p. 21.
8 Bird and Marshall, *Afghanistan*, p. 15.
9 Ibid., p. 16.
10 Ibid., pp. 16–17.
11 Young, 'Overcoming the Obstacles to Establishing a Democratic State in Afghanistan', p. 8.
12 Saikal, *Modern Afghanistan*, p. 133.
13 Bird and Marshall, *Afghanistan*, p. 19.
14 For example, the United States funded the Helmand Valley Project in the late 1940s and early 1950s – an unsuccessful scheme designed to modernise Helmand Province's agricultural sector. The Soviet Union funded improvements in the army, education and transport systems.
15 Saikal, *Modern Afghanistan*, pp. 172–3.
16 Ibid. p. 165; Hafvenstein, *Opium Season*, pp. 17–18.
17 Saikal, *Modern Afghanistan*, p. 184.
18 BBC News, 'Afghanistan's Turbulent History'.
19 Ibid.
20 Bird and Marshall, *Afghanistan*, p. 21.
21 Hafvenstein, *Opium Season*, p. 19.
22 Saikal, *Modern Afghanistan*, p. 191.
23 Mujahideen means fighters engaged in jihad or sacred struggle.
24 Bird and Marshall, *Afghanistan*, pp. 21–2.
25 Ibid., p. 22.

26 Wahab and Youngerman, *Afghanistan*, pp. 184–5.
27 Saudi Arabia also played a substantial role in funding the Afghan resistance.
28 Bird and Marshall, *Afghanistan*, p. 23.
29 Wahab and Youngerman, *Afghanistan*, p. 199.
30 Ibid., p. 208.
31 Cornell, 'The Narcotics Threat in Greater Central Asia', p. 51.
32 Bird and Marshall, *Afghanistan*, pp. 34–5.
33 Rashid, *Taliban*, p. 121.
34 Rubin, *The Fragmentation of Afghanistan*, p. xxiii.
35 Wahab and Youngerman, *Afghanistan*, pp. 211–12.
36 Ibid., p. 212.
37 Zaeef, *My Life with the Taliban* quoted in Bird and Marshall, *Afghanistan*, p. 39.
38 Rashid, *Taliban*, pp. 190–1.
39 Wahab and Youngerman, *Afghanistan*, p. 212–13.
40 Saikal, *Modern Afghanistan*, p. 222.
41 Mansfield, *A State Built on Sand*, p. 133.
42 Ibid., p. 135.
43 Saikal, *Modern Afghanistan*, p. 222.
44 Steele, *Ghosts of Afghanistan*, p. 206.
45 Ibid., p. 208.
46 Ibid., pp. 208–13.
47 Macdonald, *Drugs in Afghanistan*, pp. 59–60.
48 UNODC, The Opium Economy in Afghanistan, p. 88.
49 Macdonald, *Drugs in Afghanistan*, p. 60.
50 Ibid.
51 UNODC, The Opium Economy in Afghanistan, p. 88.
52 Bradford, *Opium in a Time of Uncertainty*, pp. 12, 77.
53 UNODC, The Opium Economy in Afghanistan, p. 88.
54 Chouvy, *Opium*, p. 31.
55 Ibid., p. 20.
56 UNODC, The Opium Economy in Afghanistan, p. 90.
57 Khan, 'Opium Brides'; and *The Economist*, 'The Gardens of Eden'.
58 *The Economist*, 'The Gardens of Eden'.
59 Chouvy, *Opium*, p. 31.
60 Cooley, *Unholy Wars*, p. 110.
61 Chouvy, *Opium*, p. 32.
62 Myanmar was the leading opium cultivator until 2003. Since 1990, Myanmar had more land under cultivation than Afghanistan but due to poor soil and climatic conditions, the opium yield was less (Macdonald, *Drugs in Afghanistan*, p. 61).
63 Chouvy, *Opium*, pp. 33–4.
64 UNODC, The Opium Economy in Afghanistan, p. 90.

65 Ibid.
66 Koehler and Zuercher, 'Statebuilding, Conflict and Narcotics in Afghanistan', p. 63.
67 Hafvenstein, *Opium Season*, p. 10.
68 Mansfield et al., Time to Move on, p. 47.
69 Byrd and Mansfield, Drugs in Afghanistan, p. 2.
70 Maletta, 'The Grain and the Chaff' cited in LSE Ideas, After the Drugs Wars, p. 133.
71 SIGAR, Counternarcotics, p. 5.
72 Mansfield, *A State Built on Sand*, p. 105
73 Assistant Secretary of State for INL Robert B. Charles, 'Afghanistan: Are the British Counternarcotics Efforts Going Wobbly?', testimony before the House of Representatives Subcommittee on Criminal Justice, Drug Policy and Human Resources of the Committee on Government Reform, hearing on 'British Counternarcotics Efforts in Afghanistan', p. 11.
74 United Nations Drug Control Programme (UNDCP), Afghanistan Annual Opium Poppy Survey 2000, p. 23.
75 Mansfield, *A State Built on Sand*, p. 107.
76 Ibid., p. 108.
77 Ibid.
78 Ibid.
79 McCoy, *The Politics of Heroin*, p. 508 and Rashid, *Taliban*, p. 124.
80 Chouvy, *Opium*, pp. 51–2.
81 Mansfield, *A State Built on Sand*, pp. 130–2.
82 Rashid, *Taliban*, p. 124.
83 Ibid., p. 118.
84 Ibid.
85 McCoy, *The Politics of Heroin*, p. 508.
86 Steele, *Ghosts of Afghanistan*, p. 219.
87 Crossette, 'Taliban Open a Campaign to Gain Status at the U.N.'.
88 Rashid, *Taliban*, p. 126.
89 Ibid., p. 127.
90 Mansfield, *A State Built on Sand*, p. 123.
91 Transnational Institute, Afghanistan, Drugs and Terrorism Merging Wars, p. 9.
92 Ibid., p. 11.
93 Steele, *Ghosts of Afghanistan*, p. 197.
94 Farrell and Thorne, 'Where Have All the Flowers Gone?', p. 85.
95 Ibid., p. 84.
96 Cornell, Taliban Afghanistan, p. 284.
97 McCoy, *The Politics of Heroin*, p. 510.
98 UNDCP, Afghanistan Annual Opium Poppy Survey 2000, p. 37.

99   Farrell and Thorne, 'Where Have All the Flowers Gone?', p. 85.

100 Mansfield, *A State Built on Sand*, pp. 123–5.

101 Ibid., p. 133.

102 Whilst considered effective in reducing the amount of land under cultivation, the ban cannot be considered *successful*. The lack of economic alternatives made available to farmers rendered the ban counterproductive and unsustainable.

103 Mansfield, *A State Built on Sand*, pp. 121–2.

104 UNDCP, Afghanistan Opium Survey 2001, p. ii.

105 Cornell, 'The Narcotics Threat in Greater Central Asia?', p. 44.

106 Rashid, *Descent into Chaos*, p. 19.

107 Mansfield, *A State Built on Sand*, p. 129.

108 United Nations Security Council, Report of the Committee of Experts appointed pursuant to Security Council resolution 1333 (2000), p. 11, para. 58.

109 Author interview with former UNODC official (1), 27 February 2014.

110 Byrd and Jonglez, Prices and Market Interactions in the Opium Economy, p. 132.

111 Author interview with former UNODC official (1), 27 February 2014.

112 McCoy, *The Politics of Heroin*, p. 518.

113 Cornell, Taliban Afghanistan, p. 285.

114 McCoy, *The Politics of Heroin*, p. 518.

115 Steele, *Ghosts of Afghanistan*, p. 211.

116 Executive Order 13129.

117 Mansfield, *A State Built on Sand*, p. 134.

118 McCoy, *The Politics of Heroin*, p. 520.

Chapter 4: Taliban drugs on British streets, 2001–2002

1   Berry, 'From London to Lashkar Gah'.

2   Blair, 'Labour Conference', 2001.

3   House of Commons Home Affairs Committee, The Government's Drug Policy, Q 708.

4   Intelligence and Security Committee of Parliament, Annual Report 2001–2002, p. 19.

5   Barnett, *Britain Unwrapped*, pp. 366–7.

6   National Crime Intelligence Service, United Kingdom Threat Assessment of Serious and Organised Crime, p. 7. CIDA comprised representatives from HMCE, the National Crime Squad, the National Criminal Intelligence Service, the Scottish Drug Enforcement Agency, the Metropolitan Police, the Association

of Chief Police Officers, the UK Anti-Drug Co-ordinator's Unit, Home Office, Cabinet Office, FCO and the SIS.

7 Author interview with former Cabinet Office official (1), 21 October 2014.

8 Author interview with former FCO official (9), 16 July 2015.

9 Author interview with former HMCE official (1), 13 July 2017.

10 House of Commons Home Affairs Committee, The Government's Drug Policy, Q 720.

11 Campbell, *The Alastair Campbell Diaries*, p. 16.

12 Author email communication with MOD official, 29 January 2017 and Security Service official, 3 February 2017.

13 Author interview with former Cabinet Office official (3), 22 June 2017.

14 Campbell, *The Alastair Campbell Diaries*, p. 21.

15 Author interview with former UK minister (3), 16 January 2017.

16 Ibid.; author interview with former FCO official (9), 16 July 2015.

17 Author interview with former Department of Health official, 21 October 2014.

18 HC Deb, 14 November 2001, c872.

19 Author interview with former UK official (1), 6 June 2017.

20 Campbell, *The Alastair Campbell Diaries*, p. 43.

21 Author interview with former UK minister (3), 16 January 2017.

22 HC Deb, 14 November 2001, c872.

23 Blair, 'Labour Conference', 2002.

24 Author interview with former Department of Defense official (3), 3 July 2017.

25 US Department of State cable, State 176819.

26 Author interview with former Department of State official (8), 16 October 2017.

27 Risen, *State of War*, p. 154.

28 Representative Mark Souder, Opening Statement, House of Representatives Subcommittee on Criminal Justice, Drug Policy and Human Resources for the Committee on Government Reform, hearing on 'Afghanistan: Law Enforcement Interdiction Efforts in Transshipment Countries to Stem the Flow of Heroin', p. 2.

29 Risen, 'An Afghan's Path from U.S. Ally to Drug Suspect'.

30 Author interview with former Department of Defense official (3), 3 July 2017.

31 McGirk, 'Terrorism's Harvest'.

32 Ibid.

33 Bonn Agreement, 5 December 2001.

34 Author interview with former Department of State official (4), 24 October 2016.

35 Transnational Institute, Afghanistan, Drugs and Terrorism Merging Wars, p. 9.
36 There was also a smaller intervening conference in Brussels in December 2001, where counter-narcotics policies in Afghanistan were discussed. Personal communication with former FCO official, 22 May 2017.
37 Freedom of Information Request 0103-17.
38 Author interview with former Department of State official (4), 24 October 2016.
39 Freedom of Information Request 0909-16.
40 Author interview with former Department of State official (4), 24 October 2016.
41 Ibid.
42 Freedom of Information Request 0103-17.
43 Blair and Karzai, Rebuilding Afghanistan.
44 Dyson, *The Blair Identity,* pp. 80–1; Seldon et al., *Blair Unbound,* p. 57.
45 Seldon et al., *Blair Unbound,* p. 57.
46 Author interview with former UK minister (3), 16 January 2017.
47 Author interview with former FCO official (9), 16 July 2015.
48 Chilcot, The Report of the Iraq Inquiry, pp. 279–81.
49 Author interview with former FCO official (9), 16 July 2015.
50 Morgan Edwards, *The Afghan Solution*, p. 118.
51 UNDCP, Afghanistan Opium Survey 2001, p. ii.
52 Freedom of Information Request 0525-06.
53 Rashid, *Descent into Chaos*, p. 321; Integrated Regional Information Network, 'Afghanistan: Donor-Supported Approaches to Eradication'.
54 Integrated Regional Information Network, 'Afghanistan: Donor-Supported Approaches to Eradication'.
55 HC Deb, 28 January 2002, c34.
56 Author interviews with former FCO official (4), 23 and 24 September 2014.
57 Author interview with former FCO official (9), 16 July 2015.
58 Freedom of Information Request 0525-06.
59 Author interview with former FCO official (9), 16 July 2015.
60 Author interview with former Department of Health official, 21 October 2014.
61 Author interview with former HMCE official (2), 19 June 2018.
62 Author interview with former HMCE official (1), 13 July 2017.
63 Author interview with former UK minister (3), 16 January 2017; author interview with former Cabinet Office official (2), 6 June 2017; author interview with former FCO official (9), 16 July 2015.
64 Fairweather, *The Good War*, p. 93.

65 McCoy, *The Politics of Heroin*, p. 510.
66 Mansfield, *A State Built on Sand*, p. 127.
67 Author interview with former FCO official (9), 16 July 2015.
68 Author interview with former Cabinet Office official (2), 6 June 2017.
69 Author interview with former FCO official (9), 16 July 2015.
70 Author interview with former UK minister (2), 19 December 2016.
71 Seldon et al., *Blair Unbound*, p. 83.
72 Author interview with former FCO official (9), 16 July 2015.
73 Ibid.
74 Author interview with former FCO official (4), 23 and 24 September 2014.
75 Author interview with former UK official (1), 6 June 2017.
76 Author interview with former UK minister (3), 16 January 2017.
77 Author interview with former FCO official (4), 23 and 24 September 2014.
78 Ibid.
79 Ibid.
80 Morgan Edwards, *The Afghan Solution,* pp. 185–6.
81 Author interview with former FCO official (9), 16 July 2015.
82 Freedom of Information Request 0525-06.
83 Author interview with former UNODC official (1), 27 February 2014.
84 SIGAR, Counternarcotics, p. 39.
85 Author interview with former UNODC official (2), 13 March 2014.
86 Ibid.
87 UNODC/Government of Afghanisatn Counter-Narcotics Directorate, Afghanistan Opium Survey 2003: Executive Summary, p. 3.
88 Author interview with former UNODC official (2), 13 March 2014.

Chapter 5: Lead nation on counter-narcotics, 2002

1 Author interview with former FCO official (9), 16 July 2015.
2 Ibid.
3 Ibid.
4 Personal communication with former FCO official, 22 May 2017.
5 Author interview with former FCO official (4), 23 and 24 September 2014.
6 Author interview with former UK minister (3), 16 January 2017.
7 Author interview with former Department of State official (4), 24 October 2016.

8 Freedom of Information Request 0909-16.
9 Author interview with former Department of State official (4), 24 October 2016.
10 Quoted in Oborne and Morgan Edwards, 'A Victory for Drug-Pushers', pp. 26–7.
11 Author interview with former Department of Health official, 21 October 2014.
12 Freedom of Information Request 0525-06.
13 Ibid.
14 Ibid.
15 Ibid.
16 Ibid.
17 Ibid.
18 HC Deb, 14 May 2002, c625.
19 Freedom of Information Request 0525-06.
20 Ibid.
21 Author interview with former FCO official (4), 23 and 24 September 2014.
22 Author interview with former HMCE official (1), 13 July 2017.
23 Author interview with former FCO official (9), 16 July 2015.
24 Ibid.
25 Author interview with former FCO official (4), 23 and 24 September 2014; HC Deb, 20 October 2003, vol. 411 c381W.
26 Author interview with former FCO official (9), 16 July 2015.
27 Ibid.
28 Ibid.
29 United Nations Office for Drug Control and Crime Prevention, Afghanistan Opium Survey 2002, p. 4.
30 Freedom of Information Request 0525-06.
31 Author interview with former HMCE official (2), 19 June 2018.
32 Freedom of Information Request 0525-06.
33 Author interview with former UNODC official (1), 27 February 2014.
34 Oborne and Morgan Edwards, 'A Victory for Drug-Pushers', pp. 26–7.
35 Philps, 'Britain Reopens Its Embassy as "Commitment to Better Future"'.
36 Morgan Edwards, *The Afghan Solution*, p. 117.
37 Freedom of Information Request 0525-06.
38 Ibid.
39 Wyatt, 'Afghan Farmers Die in Poppy Protest'.
40 Chouvy, 'The Ironies of Afghan Opium Production'.
41 Author interview with former HMCE official (1), 13 July 2017.
42 Author interview with former FCO official (9), 16 July 2015.

43 Personal communication with former FCO official, 26 September 2016.
44 Author interview with former UK official (1), 6 June 2017.
45 Ibid.
46 Author interview with former UNODC official (2), 13 March 2014.
47 Mansfield, *A State Built on Sand*, p. 113.
48 The National Archives, UK Strategy for Co-ordinating International Assistance to Afghanistan to Combat Drugs, pp. 2–3.
49 Ibid., p. 3.
50 Martin and Symansky, Macroeconomic Impact of the Drug Economy and Counter-Narcotics Efforts, p. 35.

Chapter 6: Counter-narcotics on the hoof, 2002–2004

1 Author interview with former FCO official (9), 16 July 2015.
2 Author interview with former US military officer (3), 3 October 2017.
3 Ibid.
4 HC Deb, 5 November 2002, vol. 392 c130.
5 Author interview with former FCO official (9), 16 July 2015.
6 Ibid.
7 Ibid.
8 Author interview with former Department of State official (3), 6 October 2014.
9 Author interview with former FCO official (9), 16 July 2015.
10 Ibid.
11 SIGAR, Counternarcotics, p. 90.
12 Ibid., p. 84.
13 Personal communication with former FCO official, 24 August 2016.
14 US Department of State cable, Kabul 1277.
15 SIGAR, Counternarcotics, pp. 84–5.
16 Author interview with former Cabinet Office official (2), 6 June 2017.
17 Author interview with former UK official (1), 6 June 2017.
18 Author interview with former Cabinet Office official (2), 6 June 2017.
19 Ibid.
20 Author interview with former HMCE official (2), 19 June 2018.
21 UNODC/Government of Afghanistan Ministry of Counternarcotics, Afghanistan: Mapping of Alternative Livelihood Projects, p. 38.
22 HC Deb, 19 November 2003, vol. 413 c1046W.
23 World Bank, Afghanistan, p. 125.

24 Ibid.
25 HC Deb, 17 November 2003, vol. 413 c649w; and House of Commons Defence Committee, UK Operations in Afghanistan, Written Evidence, Memorandum from the Afghan Drugs Inter-Departmental Unit, Ev 117.
26 HC Deb, 24 October 2005, c74W.
27 Personal communication with former UK military officer, 7 March 2014.
28 Personal communication with former FCO official, 12 October 2015.
29 SIGAR, Counternarcotics, p. 26.
30 HM Treasury, Budget Leaflet, p. 1.
31 Author interview with former UK official (1), 6 June 2017.
32 Ibid.
33 Personal communication with former FCO official, 12 October 2015.
34 Author interview with former UK minister (3), 16 January 2017.
35 Council on Foreign Relations, The U.S. War in Afghanistan Timeline 1999 – 2018.
36 Jones, *In the Graveyard of Empires*, pp. 139–40.
37 Khalilzad, *The Envoy*, p. 179.
38 Farrell, *Unwinnable*, p. 138.
39 DEA Administrator Karen Tandy, testimony before the House of Representatives Subcommittee on Criminal Justice, Drug Policy and Human Resources for the Committee on Government Reform, hearing on 'Afghanistan: Law Enforcement Interdiction Efforts in Transshipment Countries to Stem the Flow of Heroin', p. 26; and author interview with former US Embassy Kabul official (6), 24 July 2018.
40 Lt Gen. David W. Barno (US Army Ret.) quoted in Hughes, 'Planning and Directing a Campaign', p. 52.
41 Department of State, Robert B. Charles Biography.
42 SIGAR, Counternarcotics, p. 44.
43 Risen, *State of War*, pp. 152–3.
44 Author interview with former Department of State official (1), 7 March 2014.
45 Risen, *State of War*, p. 153.
46 Perito, Afghanistan's Police, p. 3.
47 The National Archives, 'UK Provides Counter-Narcotics Training for Afghans'.
48 Author interview with former HMCE official (1), 13 July 2017.
49 Ibid.
50 SIGAR, Counternarcotics, p. 41.
51 The National Archives, 'Recent Successes'.

52 Author interview with former HMCE official (1), 13 July 2017.
53 Ibid.
54 SIGAR, Counternarcotics, p. 41.
55 Author interview with former HMCE official (1), 13 July 2017.
56 Author interview with former British Military officer (1), 13 February 2014.
57 Ledwidge, *Losing Small Wars*, p. 73.
58 Author interview with former British Military officer (1), 13 February 2014.
59 Martin and Symansky, Macroeconomic Impact of the Drug Economy and Counter-Narcotics Efforts, p. 35.
60 Pain, Opium Trading Systems in Helmand and Ghor Provinces, pp. 91–3.
61 SIGAR, Counternarcotics, p. 6.
62 Rubin, 'Putting an End to Warlord Government'.
63 Bewley-Taylor, 'Drug Trafficking and Organised Crime in Afghanistan, p. 12.
64 Felbab-Brown, *Shooting Up*, p. 137.
65 SIGAR, Counternarcotics, p. 5.
66 DEA Administrator Karen P. Tandy, testimony before the House of Representatives Committee on International Relations, hearing on 'Afghanistan Drugs and Terrorism and U.S. Security Policy', p. 15.
67 Author interview with former UK minister (1), 23 April 2013.
68 Department of State, Zalmay Khalilzad Biography.
69 Ibid.
70 Author interview with former US Embassy Kabul official (6), 24 July 2018.
71 SIGAR, Counternarcotics, pp. 44, 47.
72 Assistant Secretary of State for INL Robert B. Charles, testimony before the House of Representatives Subcommittee on Criminal Justice, Drug Policy and Human Resources of the Committee on Government Reform, hearing on 'British Counternarcotics Efforts in Afghanistan', p. 11.
73 Author interview with former Department of State official (8), 16 October 2017.
74 Mansfield, *A State Built on Sand*, p. 122.
75 HC Deb, 9 June 2004, c125WH.
76 Khalilzad, *The Envoy*, p. 205.
77 Assistant Secretary of State for INL Robert B. Charles, testimony before the House of Representatives Subcommittee on Criminal Justice, Drug Policy and Human Resources for the Committee on Government Reform, hearing on 'Afghanistan: Law Enforcement Interdiction Efforts in Transshipment Countries to Stem the Flow of Heroin', pp. 17, 35.

78 SIGAR, Counternarcotics, p. 65.
79 Representative Henry Hyde, Opening Statement, the House of Representatives Committee on International Relations, hearing on 'Afghanistan Drugs and Terrorism and U.S. Security Policy', pp. 2–3.
80 Author interview with former US Embassy Kabul official (6), 24 July 2018.

Chapter 7: Plan Afghanistan, 2004–2005

1 Charles, 'Counternarcotics initiatives for Afghanistan'. After Charles's remarks, the policy was thereafter referred to as Plan Afghanistan; however, no official Department of State policy document was entitled 'Plan Afghanistan'. Author interview with former Department of State official (1), 7 March 2014.
2 'Plan Colombia was a comprehensive program launched in 1999 to reduce illicit drug production and improve security in Colombia. The program was a state-building, counterinsurgency, and counterdrug initiative that included increased interdiction activities, aerial eradication, and alternative livelihoods projects for farmers' (SIGAR, Counternarcotics, p. 27).
3 Author interview with former Department of State official (1), 7 March 2014.
4 Schweich, 'Is Afghanistan a Narco-State?'
5 Author interview with former Department of State official (1), 7 March 2014.
6 Ibid.
7 Risen, *State of War*, pp. 159–60.
8 SIGAR, Counternarcotics, p. 28.
9 Ibid.
10 Author interview with former FCO official (1), 13 June 2013.
11 Author interview with former UK Embassy Kabul official (3), 3 July 2013.
12 Author interview with former Department of State official (3), 6 October 2014.
13 Ibid.
14 Personal communication with former FCO official, 24 August 2016.
15 Author interview with former UK minister (1), 23 April 2013.
16 Ibid.
17 Author interview with former Department of State official (6), 25 July 2017.
18 In the coming years, discussions were confined to key moments in

the poppy planting cycle, for example in the pre-planting phase from August to October, when decisions were made regarding the method of eradication for the coming year, and from February to April, during the actual eradication campaign. Personal communication with former FCO official, 12 October 2015. The majority of poppy is planted between October and December and is harvested between April and May. In higher elevations, poppy is planted between February and June and there is also evidence of a summer crop planted in Helmand between July and August (SIGAR, Counternarcotics, pp. 8–10).

19 Rennie and La Guardia, 'America Accuses Britain of Failing in War on Drugs'.

20 Representative Mark Souder, Opening Statement, the House of Representatives Subcommittee on Criminal Justice, Drug Policy and Human Resources of the Committee on Government Reform, hearing on 'British Counternarcotics Efforts in Afghanistan', p. 1.

21 Ibid., p. 2.

22 Ibid., p.16.

23 SIGAR, Counternarcotics, p. 86.

24 Ibid., pp. 31–3, 86, 88.

25 Assistant Secretary of State for INL Robert B. Charles, testimony before the House of Representatives Subcommittee on Criminal Justice, Drug Policy and Human Resources of the Committee on Government Reform, hearing on 'British Counternarcotics Efforts in Afghanistan', p. 20.

26 Ibid., p. 25.

27 Personal communication with former FCO official, 12 October 2015.

28 Author interview with former Department of State official (1), 7 March 2014.

29 Author interview with former UK minister (1), 23 April 2013.

30 Wintour, 'Battle Begins to Stem Afghan Opium Harvest'.

31 Author interview with former UK minister (1), 23 April 2013.

32 Author interview with former Department of State official (2), 21 March 2014.

33 General Sir David Richards recounted a meeting between President Karzai and British Chargé d'Affaires Michael Ryder in which the former berated the latter over Helmand. To make matters worse, Karzai invited US Ambassador Ron Neumann to spectate and, in the words of Richards, '[act as] big brother umpiring as their major ally got a bollocking' (Richards, *Taking Command*, p. 265).

34 Kampfner, *Blair's Wars*, p. 117.

35 HC Deb, 19 April 2004, vol. 420 c21.

36 Personal communication with former FCO official, 12 October 2015.

37 Khalilzad, *The Envoy*, p. 205.
38 Author interview with former UK official (2), 20 July 2018.
39 UNODC/Government of Afghanistan Counter-Narcotics Directorate, Afghanistan Opium Survey 2004, p. 1
40 Ibid., p. 3
41 Author interview with former Department of State official (6), 25 July 2017.
42 Ibid.
43 Inspectors General for Department of State and Department of Defense, Interagency Assessment of the Counternarcotics Program in Afghanistan, p. 22.
44 The group consisted of representatives of DOD, State, Treasury, USAID, the NSC and Office of Management and Budget (Government Accountability Office, Afghanistan Reconstruction, p. 31).
45 Department of Defense, Progress toward Security and Stability in Afghanistan, p. 62.
46 Waltz, *Warrior Diplomat*, pp. 36–7.
47 Risen, *State of War*, p. 159.
48 US Department of State cable, Bogota 11995.
49 Author interview with former Department of State official (2), 21 March 2014.
50 Ibid.
51 Khalilzad, *The Envoy*, pp. 207–8.
52 Author interview with former US military commander (4), 18 December 2017.
53 Author interview with former British Military officer (1), 13 February 2014.
54 Author interview with former US NSC official, 26 March 2017.
55 Waltz, *Warrior Diplomat*, p. 38.
56 US Department of State cable, Kabul 1029.
57 Risen, *State of War*, pp. 160–1.
58 Ibid., p. 162.
59 Waltz, *Warrior Diplomat*, p. 38.
60 Khalilzad, *The Envoy*, p. 206.
61 Author interview with former US Embassy Kabul official (4), 20 June 2018.
62 Author interview with former Department of State official (6), 25 July 2017.
63 Khalilzad, *The Envoy*, p. 208.
64 Author interview with former US Embassy Kabul official (4), 20 June 2018.
65 Author interview with former US Embassy Kabul official (2), 21 October 2014.

66 Author interview with former Department of State official (2), 21 March 2014.

67 SIGAR, Counternarcotics, p. 45.

68 The three most common methods of forced eradication are: manually, which typically consists of striking poppy stalks with sticks or by hand; mechanically, driving tractors or other vehicles through opium fields; and chemically, spraying chemicals such as glyphosate over poppy fields either by air or by using ground-based spraying techniques (Chouvy, *Opium*, p. 157).

69 Risen, *State of War*, p. 162.

70 Charles, Counternarcotics initiatives for Afghanistan.

71 Author interview with former Department of State official (6), 25 July 2017.

72 Mansfield, *A State Built on Sand*, p. 150.

73 HC Deb, 24 October 2005, c73W.

74 Lancaster, 'Karzai Urges War on Opium'.

75 Mansfield, *A State Built on Sand*, p. 150.

76 SIGAR, Counternarcotics, p. 130.

77 HC Deb, 10 March 2005, c121WS.

78 Author interview with former British Military officer (1), 13 February 2014.

79 Personal communication with former FCO official, 12 October 2015.

80 Berry, 'Allies at War in Afghanistan', p. 283.

81 Personal communication with former FCO official, 12 October 2015.

82 The unit contained staff from the FCO, DFID, HMCE, the Home Office and MOD (and later SOCA) (HC Deb, 24 October 2005, c74W).

83 Personal communication with former FCO official, 12 October 2015.

84 HC Deb, 24 October 2005, c74W.

85 In either 2006 or 2007, the BEDT was divided into two: a Counter-Narcotics Team and a Rule of Law Team (House of Commons Defence Committee, UK Operations in Afghanistan, Ev 117).

86 The National Archives, 'Country Profiles: Afghanistan'.

87 Inspectors General for Department of State and Department of Defense, Interagency Assessment of the Counternarcotics Program in Afghanistan, p. 47.

88 SIGAR, Counternarcotics, p. 68.

89 Author interview with former British military officer (1), 13 February 2014.

90 Inspectors General for Department of State and Department of

Defense, Interagency Assessment of the Counternarcotics Program in Afghanistan, p. 48.

91 United States Drug Enforcement Administration, History 2003–2008, pp. 122–3.

92 SIGAR, Counternarcotics, p. 69.

93 Ibid.

94 *The Economist*, 'After the Taliban'. The centrally led eradication force was known as the Central Poppy Eradication Force (2004–5); the Afghan Eradication Force (2005–7); and Poppy Eradication Force (2007–9).

95 HC Deb, 10 March 2005, c122WS.

96 House of Commons Defence Committee, The UK Deployment to Afghanistan, Ev 33, Q 192.

97 Mansfield, *A State Built on Sand*, p. 114.

98 The National Archives, 'Country Profile: Afghanistan'.

99 Cloud and Gall, 'U.S. Memo Faults Afghan Leader on Heroin Fight'.

100 SIGAR, Counternarcotics, p. 87.

101 Ibid., p. 91.

102 Author interview with former Department of State official (6), 25 July 2017.

103 The National Archives, 'UK Announces Increased Funding for Afghanistan Counter-Narcotics Work'. Of the £270 million committed, DFID contributed £130 million, with other Government Departments, including the FCO and MOD contributing the remaining £140 million (HC Deb, 24 October 2005, c73W).

104 Author interview with former UK official (2), 20 July 2018.

105 SIGAR, Counternarcotics, p. 130.

106 HC Deb, 10 March 2005, c123WS.

107 SIGAR, Counternarcotics, pp. 130–1.

108 Mansfield, *A State Built on Sand*, p. 151.

109 Meyerle et al., *On the Ground in Afghanistan*, p. 82.

110 McNerney, 'Stabilization and Reconstruction in Afghanistan', p. 32.

111 Mansfield, *A State Built on Sand*, pp. 151–3.

112 Ibid., p. 152.

113 Ibid., p. 153.

114 Ibid., p. 152.

115 Ibid., p. 153.

116 Ibid., p. 152.

117 SIGAR, Counternarcotics, p. 110.

118 Ibid., pp. 111–12.

119 Mansfield, *A State Built on Sand*, p. 154.

120 Ibid.

121 UNODC/MCN, Afghanistan Opium Survey 2005, p. 9.
122 Ibid., p. 25.
123 UNODC/Government of Afghanistan Counter-Narcotics Director-
    ate, Afghanistan Opium Survey 2004, p. 3.
124 HC Deb, 10 March 2005, cc121–2WS.
125 *Panorama*, 'Britain's Heroin Fix'.
126 United States Agency for International Development, Afghanistan.
    Fact Sheet.
127 UNODC/MCN, Afghanistan Opium Survey 2005, p. iv.
128 Ibid., p. 32.
129 Ibid., p. 4.
130 Ibid., p. iii.
131 Agence France-Presse, 'Afghanistan aims to cut opium fields by 40
    percent in 2006'.

Chapter 8: Afghanistan's poppy capital, 2005–2006

1 Thruelsen, 'Counterinsurgency and a Comprehensive Approach'.
2 Seldon et al., *Blair Unbound*, pp. 391–2.
3 Cavanagh, 'Ministerial Decision-Making in the Run-Up to the
   Helmand Deployment', p. 50.
4 Neumann et al., The United States Army in Afghanistan, p. 52.
5 Author interview with former British military officer (1), 13
   February 2014.
6 Mansfield, A *State Built on Sand*, p. 215.
7 House of Commons Defence Committee, Operations in Afghanistan, 17 July 2011, Ev 143, Q 670; Farrell, *Unwinnable*, pp. 141–2.
8 Clarke, 'The Helmand Decision', p. 16.
9 Farrell, *Unwinnable*, p. 142.
10 Cavanagh, 'Ministerial Decision-Making in the Run-Up to the
    Helmand Deployment', pp. 50–1.
11 Ibid.
12 Farrell, *Unwinnable*, p. 134.
13 Author interview with former British military officer (1), 13
    February 2014.
14 Cavanagh, 'Ministerial Decision-Making in the Run-Up to the
    Helmand Deployment', pp. 51–2.
15 Author interview with former UK minister (6), 9 October 2018.
16 DEA Administrator, Karen P. Tandy, testimony before the House
    of Representatives Committee on Armed Services, hearing on the
    'Status of Security and Stability in Afghanistan', p. 6.
17 Chandrasekaran, *Little America*, pp. 42–3.
18 Ibid., p. 46.

19 US Department of State cable, Kabul 116.
20 Ledwidge, *Losing Small Wars*, p. 72.
21 Fergusson, *A Million Bullets*, pp. 153–4.
22 Ledwidge, *Losing Small Wars*, pp. 70–1.
23 Quoted in Fergusson, *A Million Bullets*, p. 154.
24 Ledwidge, *Losing Small Wars*, p. 71.
25 HC Deb, 26 January 2006, c1531.
26 NATO/ISAF, The Afghanistan Compact, p. 2.
27 HL Deb, 13 February 2006, cWS49.
28 US Department of State cable, Kabul 329.
29 US Department of State cable, Kabul 5024.
30 Ibid.
31 US Department of State cable, Kabul 5256.
32 Government of the Islamic Republic of Afghanistan, Ministry of Counter-Narcotics, National Drug Control Strategy, pp. 6, 21.
33 Byrd, Responding to Afghanistan's Opium Economy, p. 15.
34 Ibid.
35 Jelsma et al., 'Losing Ground', p. 15.
36 Author interview with academic (2), 19 March 2013.
37 Human Rights Watch, 'Lessons in Terror', p. 14.
38 Schweich, 'Is Afghanistan a Narco-State?'
39 Ibid.
40 US Department of State cable, Kabul 5050.
41 US Department of State cable, Kabul 1267.
42 Author interview with former US Embassy Kabul official (2), 21 October 2014.
43 Ibid.
44 Neumann, *The Other War*, p. 61.
45 Author interview with former UK Embassy Kabul official (7), 17 July 2015.
46 Previously the Central Poppy Eradication Force.
47 US Department of State cable, Kabul 1267.
48 Ibid.
49 US Department of State cable, Kabul 962.
50 US Department of State cable, Kabul 5223.
51 House of Commons Defence Committee, Operations in Afghanistan, Ev 144, Q 674.
52 Quoted in Maloney, *Fighting for Afghanistan*, p. 71.
53 House of Commons Defence Committee, Operations in Afghanistan, Ev 144–5, Q 674.
54 US Department of State cable, Kabul 2021.
55 Pamela Constable, 'In Afghan Poppy Heartland, New Crops, Growing Danger U.S. Pushes Eggplants and Tomatoes, but Farmers Risk Reprisals', *The Washington Post*, 6 May 2006.

56 US Department of State cable, Kabul 2008.

57 Ibid.

58 Ibid.

59 Ibid.

60 SIGAR, Counternarcotics, p. 92.

61 Inspector General for United States Agency for International Development, Audit of USAID/Afghanistan's Alternative Livelihoods Program-Eastern Region, pp. 5–8.

62 UNODC/MCN, Afghanistan Opium Survey 2006, p. iii.

63 House of Commons Defence Committee, Operations in Afghanistan, p. 21.

64 HC Deb, 17 June 2008, cc176–7WH.

65 House of Commons Defence Committee, The UK Deployment to Afghanistan, p. 16.

66 House of Commons Defence Committee, Operations in Afghanistan, p. 26.

67 Ware, 'UK's Original Helmand Deployment Plan Examined'.

68 House of Commons Defence Committee, Operations in Afghanistan, p. 28.

69 Fergusson, *Taliban*, p. 132.

70 House of Commons Defence Committee, Operations in Afghanistan, Ev 91, Q 415.

71 BBC News, 'UK Troops "to target Terrorists"'.

72 House of Commons Defence Committee, The UK Deployment to Afghanistan, p. 16.

73 Norton-Taylor, 'Full interview: General David Richards'.

74 Gordon, Winning Hearts and Minds?, p. 34.

75 Author interview with former UK minister (6), 9 October 2018.

76 Author interview with former UK minister (5), 18 December 2017.

77 Author interview with former FCO official (13), 19 December 2017.

78 Gordon, Winning Hearts and Minds?, p. 39.

79 House of Commons Defence Committee, UK Operations in Afghanistan, Written Evidence, Memorandum from the Ministry of Defence, Ev 84.

80 Ibid., Ev 53, Q 252.

81 US Department of State cable, Kabul 5584.

82 House of Commons Defence Committee, UK Operations in Afghanistan, Ev 53, Q 252; author interview with former British military officer (1), 13 February 2014.

83 Author interview with former US NSC official, 26 March 2017.

84 House of Commons Defence Committee, UK Operations in Afghanistan, Written Evidence, Memorandum from the Ministry of Defence, Ev 84.

Chapter 9: The lesser of two evils, 2006–2007

1 SOCA was an amalgamation of the National Crime Squad, the National Criminal Intelligence Service, HM Customs & Excise investigation unit, and Immigration and Nationality Department.
2 BBC News, 'FBI-style unit'.
3 Author interview with former SOCA official (2), 23 March 2017.
4 Ibid.
5 Author interview with former SOCA official (1), 17 March 2017.
6 Author interview with former SOCA official (2), 23 March 2017.
7 Author interview with former SOCA official (1), 17 March 2017.
8 SIGAR, Counternarcotics, p. 47.
9 Blanchard, Afghanistan, 24 January 2008, pp. 35–6.
10 Karen P. Tandy, testimony before the House of Representatives Committee on Armed Services, hearing on the 'Status of Security and Stability in Afghanistan', pp. 4–5.
11 Author interview with former US Embassy Kabul official (2), 21 October 2014.
12 Schweich, 'Is Afghanistan a Narco-State?'
13 Author interview with former Department of State official (7), 12 October 2017.
14 Author interview with former US Embassy Kabul official (6), 24 July 2018.
15 Eligon and Yokley, 'Police Say Thomas Schweich, Candidate for Missouri Governor, Killed Himself'.
16 Author interview with former FCO officials (1), (4) and (7), 3 November 2014. Author interview with former UK Embassy Kabul official (7), 17 July 2015 and (6), 29 October 2014. Author interview with former British military officer (1), 13 February 2014.
17 Author interview with former UK Embassy Kabul official (7), 17 July 2015.
18 Author interview with former US Embassy Kabul official (6), 24 July 2018.
19 Author interview with former UK Embassy Kabul official (7), 17 July 2015.
20 Author interview with former UK minister (5), 18 December 2017.
21 Author interview with former US Embassy Kabul official (6), 24 July 2018.

22 Whilst some promoted aerial eradication as a 'silver bullet' against the narcotics trade, others championed the legalisation of opium cultivation for medical purposes. Between 2005 and 2007, the most vocal proponent of this viewpoint was the Senlis Council, later renamed the International Council on Security and Development. Whilst the idea gained some limited support, it was widely rejected by the Afghan, British and American governments. Among the proposal's many flaws was the basic fact that the Afghan government did not have the capacity or resources to administer such a scheme. Furthermore, if the scheme was sanctioned, it would ultimately lead to more, not less, opium finding its way onto the illegal market.

23 Author interview with former FCO official (6), 22 October 2014.

24 Author interview with former UK Embassy Kabul official (5), 4 August 2014.

25 Ibid.

26 US Department of State cable, Kabul 4005.

27 Rice, *No Higher Honor*, p. 446.

28 Author interview with former US Embassy Kabul official (2), 21 October 2014.

29 US Department of State cable, Kabul 5277.

30 Ibid.

31 SIGAR, Counternarcotics, p. 95.

32 US Department of State cable, Kabul 5446.

33 US Department of State cable, London 8039.

34 Ibid.

35 SIGAR, Counternarcotics, p. 95.

36 Author interview with former FCO official (7), 3 November 2014.

37 Author interview with former FCO official (13), 19 December 2017.

38 Author interview with former FCO official (6), 22 October 2014.

39 Author interview with former FCO official (13), 19 December 2017.

40 Author interview with former FCO official (4), 23 and 24 September 2014.

41 Author interview with former FCO official (7), 3 November 2014.

42 SIGAR, Counternarcotics, p. 96.

43 Personal communication with former FCO official, 12 October 2015.

44 US Department of State cable, Kabul 184.

45 US Department of State cable, Kabul 185.

46 US Department of State cable, Kabul 184.

47 Neumann, *The Other War*, p. 148.

48 UNC Global, 'Afghan Minister Visits UNC to Discuss Global Health Issues'.

49 Author interview with former US Embassy Kabul official (6), 24 July 2018.

50 Semple and Golden, 'Afghans Pressed by US on Plan to Spray Poppies'.

51 Author interview with former US Embassy Kabul official (2), 21 October 2014.

52 Ibid.

53 Gordon, Winning Hearts and Minds?, p. 20.

54 Richards, *Taking Command*, pp. 265–6.

55 Neumann, *The Other War*, p. 190.

56 Ibid., p. 106.

57 US Department of State cable, Kabul 1045.

58 Author interview with former US Embassy Kabul official (2), 21 October 2014.

59 Ibid.

Chapter 10: The showdown over aerial eradication, 2007

1 The committee comprised officials from the Departments of State, Defense, Justice and Agriculture, DEA, Office of National Drug Control Policy and USAID. Ambassador Thomas Schweich, testimony before the House of Representatives Subcommittee on the Middle East and South Asia of the Committee on Foreign Affairs, hearing on 'Counternarcotics Strategy and Police Training in Afghanistan', p. 6.

2 Schweich, 'Is Afghanistan a Narco-State?'

3 Author interview with former Department of State official (7), 12 October 2017.

4 Department of Defense, Robert M. Gates Biography.

5 Stolberg and Rutenberg, 'Rumsfeld Resigns as Defense Secretary after Big Election Gains for Democrats'.

6 Letter to Secretary of State Condoleezza Rice and Secretary of Defense Robert Gates from Various Members of Congress, 7 February 2007 the House of Representatives Committee on Foreign Affairs, hearing on 'Afghanistan on the Brink: Where Do We Go from Here?', p. 61 (underlining in original).

7 House of Commons Defence Committee, UK Operations in Afghanistan, p. 40.

8 US Department of State cable, Kabul 1420.

9 Ibid.

10 Schweich, 'Is Afghanistan a Narco-State?'

11 Author interview with former FCO official (13), 19 December 2017.

12 Author interview with former FCO official (1), 13 June 2013.

13 US Department of State cable, Kabul 1132.

14 Author interview with former US military officer (3), 3 October 2017.

15 US Department of State cable, Kabul 1132.

16 Rice, *No Higher Honor*, p. 446.

17 US Department of State cable, Kabul 1014.

18 International Monetary Fund, IMF Country Report No. 05/33, p. 17.

19 Schweich, 'Is Afghanistan a Narco-State?'

20 Author interview with former UK Embassy Kabul official (7), 17 July 2015.

21 Cowper-Coles, *Cables from Kabul*, p. 3.

22 Prior to 2006, the consensus dictated Afghanistan was not a full-scale war. Ibid., p. 4.

23 Author interview with former UK Embassy Kabul official (6), 29 October 2014.

24 Cowper-Coles, *Cables from Kabul*, p. 19.

25 Schweich, 'Is Afghanistan a Narco-State?'

26 Coghlan, 'US Officials Push to Spray Afghan Drug Crops'.

27 Author interview with former US military officer (3), 3 October 2017.

28 Cowper-Coles, *Cables from Kabul*, p. 19.

29 Author interview with former UK Embassy Kabul official (7), 17 July 2015.

30 Author interview with former US Embassy Kabul official (6), 24 July 2018.

31 Seldon et al., *Blair Unbound*, p. 562.

32 Cowper-Coles, *Cables from Kabul*, p. 84.

33 Ibid.

34 Schweich, 'Is Afghanistan a Narco-State?'

35 Author interview with former British military officer (1), 13 February 2014.

36 Author interview with former FCO official (13), 19 December 2017.

37 Cowper-Coles, *Cables from Kabul*, p. 51.

38 Semple and Golden, 'Afghans Pressed by US on Plan to Spray Poppies'.

39 Wilson and Harnden, 'Gordon Brown Plots own Course in Iraq'.

40 Hennessy and Alderson, 'How Bush and Blair Plotted in Secret to Stop Brown'.

41 Wilson, 'Gordon Brown and George Bush are Distant'.
42 Dumbrell, Personal Diplomacy, p. 94.
43 Schweich, US Counternarcotics Strategy for Afghanistan, pp. 17–18.
44 Ibid., p. 2.
45 Ibid., pp. 3–4.
46 Ibid., p. 6.
47 Weitz, 'Ambassador: Washington Will Change its Afghan Counternarcotics Programs'.
48 Weitz, 'Afghanistan: US and EU Anti-Drugs Strategies are Diverging'.
49 Mohammed, 'U.S. Unveils Carrot and Stick Afghan Drug Strategy'.
50 Embassy of the United States, Press Release, 'U.S. Embassy Deputy Director for International Narcotics and Law Enforcement, Lee "Rusty" Brown's Remarks at the Paris Pact Conference in Kabul'.
51 Mansfield, *A State Built on Sand*, p. 158.
52 UNODC/MCN, Afghanistan Opium Survey 2007, p. iii.
53 US Coordinator for Counternarcotics and Justice Reform in Afghanistan Thomas Schweich, testimony before the House of Representatives Subcommittee on the Middle East and South Asia of the Committee on Foreign Affairs, hearing on 'Counternarcotics Strategy and Police Training in Afghanistan', 4 October 2007, p. 11.
54 US Department of State cable, Kabul 2968.
55 Ibid.
56 UNODC/MCN, Afghanistan Opium Survey 2007, p. iii.
57 US Coordinator for Counternarcotics and Justice Reform in Afghanistan Thomas Schweich, testimony before the House of Representatives Subcommittee on the Middle East and South Asia of the Committee on Foreign Affairs, hearing on 'Counternarcotics Strategy and Police Training in Afghanistan', 4 October 2007, pp. 7–8.
58 Author interview with former Department of State official (1), 7 March 2014.
59 Author interview with former Department of State official (7), 12 October 2017.
60 Kilcullen, *The Accidental Guerrilla*, p. 63.
61 Author interview with former FCO official (1), 13 June 2013.
62 Author interview with former SOCA official (1), 17 March 2017.
63 Mansfield, Understanding Control and Influence, p. 37.
64 While there is little concrete evidence, it is reported that the Taliban could earn between $70 and $500 million annually from the narcotics trade. The disparity in amount demonstrates the difficulty in producing accurate data. Senate Committee on Foreign

Relations, hearing on 'Afghanistan's Narco War: Breaking the Link between Drug Traffickers and Insurgents', p. 10.

65 Mansfield and Pain, Counter-Narcotics in Afghanistan, p. 17.

66 Author interview with former FCO official (1), 13 June 2013.

67 Author interview with former UK Embassy Kabul official (6), 29 October 2014.

68 Author interview with former British military officer (1), 13 February 2014.

69 Author interview with former FCO official (8), 27 April 2015.

70 Author interview with former UK Embassy Kabul official (6), 29 October 2014.

71 Mansfield, *A State Built on Sand*, p. 158.

72 US Department of State cable, Brussels 3037.

73 Author interview with former UK Embassy Kabul official (6), 29 October 2014.

74 Department of State Inspector General, Status of the Bureau of International Narcotics and Law Enforcement Affairs Counter-narcotics Programs in Afghanistan, p. 28. The timing of this research is unclear, but it is likely to have occurred between 2006 and 2007.

75 Author interview with former Department of State official (7), 12 October 2017.

76 Author interview with former Department of State official (5), 8 June 2017.

77 US Department of State cable, Kabul 2998.

78 Ibid.; US Department of State cable, Kabul 3765.

79 Author interview with former Department of State official (5), 8 June 2017.

80 US Department of State cable, Hague 2048.

81 Author interview with former Department of State official (5), 8 June 2017.

82 US Department of State cable, Hague 2048.

83 Author interview with former US Embassy Kabul official (1), 25 June 2013.

84 US Department of State cable, Kabul 2470.

85 Author interview with former FCO official (13), 19 December 2017.

86 Author interview with former FCO official (1), 13 June 2013.

87 Adams, 'Colombia Sheds Messy Drug Spraying At Last'.

88 Author interview with former UK Embassy Kabul official (7), 17 July 2015.

89 Author interview with former FCO official (13), 19 December 2017.

90 Author interview with former US military officer (3), 3 October 2017.

91 Author interview with former FCO official (13), 19 December 2017.

92 Author interview with former FCO official (8), 27 April 2015.

93 Author interview with former FCO official (13), 19 December 2017.

94 Author interview with former Department of State official (5), 8 June 2017.

95 US Department of State cable, Kabul 409.

96 Author interview with former British military officer (1), 13 February 2014.

97 Ibid.

98 Author interview with former UK Embassy Kabul official (3), 3 July 2013.

99 Author interview with former Department of State official (5), 8 June 2017.

100 Author interview with former US military officer (3), 3 October 2017.

101 Author interview with former Department of State official (5), 8 June 2017.

102 Author interview with former British military officer (1), 13 February 2014.

103 Personal communication with former FCO official, 24 August 2016.

104 Author interview with former FCO official (1), 13 June 2013.

105 Ibid.

106 US Department of State cable, Kabul 409.

107 Blanchard, Afghanistan, 12 August 2009, p. 28.

Chapter 11: Counter-narcotics in Transition, 2008

1 In 2007, Balkh was declared 'poppy free' and in Badakhshan opium cultivation reduced dramatically. Both reductions were attributed to, among other things, a strong governor-led counter-narcotics campaign (Bureau of International Narcotics and Law Enforcement Affairs, 'Fighting the Opium Trade in Afghanistan).

2 UNODC/MCN, Afghanistan Opium Survey 2007, p. 11.

3 Mansfield, A State Built on Sand, p. 160.

4 Ibid., pp. 160–1.

5 Jones, 'Getting Back on Track in Afghanistan', p. 1.

6 Mansfield, A State Built on Sand, p. 163.

7 Ibid., pp. 161–2.

8 UNODC/MCN, Afghanistan Opium Survey 2008, p. 7.

9   Ibid., p. 5.

10   Ibid., p. 12.

11   Farrell, *Unwinnable*, p. 233.

12   Mansfield, *A State Built on Sand*, p. 226.

13   Ibid.

14   Mansfield, Truly Unprecedented, p. 5.

15   Mansfield, *A State Built on Sand*, p. 226.

16   Mansfield et al., Managing Concurrent and Repeated Risks, p. 19.

17   Mansfield, Truly Unprecedented, p. 6.

18   Ibid.

19   Byrd and Mansfield, Afghanistan's Opium Economy, p. 129 cited in SIGAR, Counternarcotics, p. 116.

20   Mansfield, Truly Unprecedented, p. 10.

21   Ibid., p. 5.

22   Cowper-Coles, *Cables from Kabul*, p. 191; Mansfield, *A State Built on Sand*, p. 228.

23   US Department of State cable, London 2821.

24   Farrell, Back from the Brink, p. 121.

25   Ibid.; Farrell, *Unwinnable*, pp. 145–7, 248–9.

26   BBC News, 'Britain Suffered Defeat in Iraq'.

27   Mansfield, *A State Built on Sand*, p. 217.

28   US Department of State cable, Kabul 3030.

29   US Department of State cable, Kabul 3237.

30   US Department of State cable, Kabul 3176.

31   Author interview with former FCO official (1), 13 June 2013.

32   Author interview with former FCO official (8), 27 April 2015.

33   Author interview with former FCO official (6), 22 October 2014.

34   Author interview with former FCO official (13), 19 December 2017.

35   Ibid.

36   Author interview with former FCO official (6), 22 October 2014.

37   Author interview with former FCO official (13), 19 December 2017.

38   Author interview with former FCO official (6), 22 October 2014.

39   Author interview with former FCO official (13), 19 December 2017.

40   Ibid.

41   Ibid.

42   Author interview with former UK minister (6), 9 October 2018.

43   Author interview with former UK minister (5), 18 December 2017.

44   Author interview with former UK Embassy Kabul official (5), 4 August 2014.

45 Mansfield, *A State Built on Sand*, p. 216.

46 Author interview with former UK Embassy Kabul official (3), 3 July 2013.

47 There is little available evidence to indicate whether Britain's ten-year timeline to eliminate opium cultivation entirely by 2013 was still active in 2008 (or later years). It is possible that, given the improbability of Britain achieving the target, it was quietly dropped.

48 US Department of State cable, London 1991.

49 US Department of State cable, London 639.

50 US Department of State cable, London 4472.

51 US Department of State cable, London 930.

52 Author interview with former FCO official (13), 19 December 2017.

53 US Department of State cable, State 97395.

54 Department of State Inspector General, Status of the Bureau of International Narcotics and Law Enforcement Affairs Counternarcotics Programs in Afghanistan, p. 12.

55 UNODC/MCN, Afghanistan Opium Survey 2008: Executive Summary, p. vii.

56 US Department of State cable, State 97395.

57 US Department of State cable, NATO 200.

58 US Department of State cable, State 97395.

59 US Department of State cable, NATO 317.

60 Ibid.

61 US Department of State cable, State 97395.

62 Author interview with former FCO official (10), 27 July 2015.

63 US Department of State cable, State 97395.

64 Author interview with former FCO official (10), 27 July 2015.

65 US Department of State cable, Paris 1715; US Department of State cable, Hague 754.

66 US Department of State cable, Berlin 1255.

67 US Department of State cable, NATO 375.

68 Dempsey, 'NATO Allows Strikes on Afghan Drug Sites'.

69 SIGAR, Counternarcotics, p. 70.

70 Blanchard, Afghanistan: Narcotics and U.S. Policy, 2009, p. 15.

71 Senate Committee on Foreign Relations, hearing on 'Afghanistan's Narco War: Breaking the Link between Drug Traffickers and Insurgents', p. 1.

Chapter 12: Obama and shifting Anglo-American relations, 2009

1 US Department of State cable, Kabul 3677.

2 Woodward, *Obama's Wars*, pp. 41–2.

3 Cowper-Coles, *Cables from Kabul*, p. 206.
4 McFadden, 'Strong American Voice in Diplomacy and Crisis'.
5 Cowper-Coles, *Cables from Kabul*, p. 204.
6 Woodward, *Obama's Wars*, p. 80.
7 Ibid., p. 88.
8 Author interview with former Cabinet Office official (4), 11 January 2018.
9 Cowper-Coles, *Cables from Kabul*, p. 217.
10 Ibid., p. 219.
11 Author interview with former Cabinet Office official (4), 11 January 2018.
12 Obama had made negative remarks about Brown's conduct with his underlings at the G20 London summit in April 2009. In September 2009, Brown had 'virtually stalked' Obama in the UN building in New York, eventually accosting him in the kitchen (Dumbrell, 'David Cameron, Barack Obama, and the "US-UK Special Relationship"').
13 Obama, 'Statement by the President'.
14 The officials came from the State Department, USAID, DOJ, FBI, the Departments of Agriculture, Treasury, Homeland Security, Transportation, and Health and Human Services, as well as the Federal Aviation Administration and DEA (US Department of State cable, Kabul 1321).
15 UNODC/MCN, Afghanistan Opium Survey 2008: Executive Summary, p. 3.
16 Holbrooke, 'Afghanistan'.
17 Holbrooke, 'Afghanistan and Pakistan', p. 22.
18 Obama, 'Remarks by the President'.
19 Woodward, *Obama's Wars*, p. 99.
20 Obama, 'Remarks by the President'.
21 Woodward, *Obama's Wars*, pp. 123-4.
22 Author interview with former Cabinet Office official (4), 11 January 2018.
23 Brown, *My Life, Our Time*, pp. 279–80.
24 Government Accountability Office, *Afghanistan Drug Control*, p. 10.
25 Felbab-Brown, Afghanistan Trip Report VI, p. 1.
26 US Special Representative for Afghanistan and Pakistan, Ambassador Richard C. Holbrooke, testimony before the House of Representatives Committee on Oversight and Government Reform and Subcommittee on National Security and Foreign Affairs of the Committee on Oversight and Government Reform, joint hearing on 'Afghanistan and Pakistan: Oversight of a New Interagency Strategy', p. 126.

27 Personal communication with former FCO official, 12 October 2015.

28 Holbrooke, 'Afghanistan and Pakistan', p. 22.

29 Department of State Inspector General, Status of the Bureau of International Narcotics and Law Enforcement Affairs Counternarcotics Programs in Afghanistan, p. 17.

30 UNODC/MCN, Afghanistan Opium Survey 2010, p. 42.

31 Senate Committee on Foreign Relations, hearing on 'Afghanistan's Narco War: Breaking the Link between Drug Traffickers and Insurgents', p. 8.

32 Author interview with former Department of State official (3), 6 October 2014.

33 Author interview with former Department of Defense official (2), 23 March 2017.

34 Ibid.

35 Author interview with former FCO official (8), 27 April 2015.

36 Author interview with former FCO official (4), 23 and 24 September 2014.

37 Author interview with former UK Embassy Kabul official (3), 3 July 2013.

38 Personal communication with former FCO official, 12 October 2015.

39 Author interview with former FCO official (3), 11 August 2014.

40 Ibid.

41 Cowper-Coles, *Cables from Kabul*, p. 87.

42 US Department of State cable, Kabul 2346.

43 Cowper-Coles, *Cables from Kabul*, p. 87.

44 US Department of State cable, Kabul 1321.

45 US Special Representative for Afghanistan and Pakistan, Ambassador Richard C. Holbrooke, testimony before the House of Representatives Committee on Oversight and Government Reform and Subcommittee on National Security and Foreign Affairs of the Committee on Oversight and Government Reform, joint hearing on 'Afghanistan and Pakistan: Oversight of a New Interagency Strategy', p. 171.

46 Senate Committee on Foreign Relations, hearing on 'Afghanistan's Narco War: Breaking the Link between Drug Traffickers and Insurgents', p. 1.

47 Ibid.

48 Blanchard, Afghanistan: Narcotics and U.S. Policy, 2009, p. 16.

49 White House, 'White Paper'.

50 Cowper-Coles, *Cables from Kabul*, p. 230.

51 Author interview with former Department of State official (3), 6 October 2014.

52 600 Afghan National Security Forces and 1,480 coalition forces were also deployed.
53 Chandrasekaran, *Little America*, p. 208.
54 UK Government, 'The UK's work in Afghanistan: timeline'.
55 Chandrasekaran, *Little America*, p. 209.
56 Author email communication with former Department of State official, 10 June 2013.
57 Author interview with former PRT official (2), 15 February 2017.
58 Farrell, *Unwinnable*, pp. 254–6, 262–3.
59 BBC News, 'Ambassador backs Afghan mission'.
60 Chandrasekaran, *Little America*, p. 70.
61 Mansfield et al., Managing Concurrent and Repeated Risks, p. 3.
62 Chandrasekaran, *Little America*, p. 71.
63 Mansfield, *A State Built on Sand*, pp. 217–18.
64 Mansfield et al., Managing Concurrent and Repeated Risks, pp. 6, 23.
65 UNODC/MCN, Afghanistan Opium Survey 2009: Summary Findings, Commentary by the Executive Director.
66 Ibid.
67 Hafvenstein, *Opium Season*, p. 193.
68 Mansfield, Truly Unprecedented, p. 14.
69 Mansfield, *A State Built on Sand*, pp. 211–12.
70 Mansfield, Truly Unprecedented, p. 14.
71 Ibid., p.15.
72 Mansfield et al., Managing Concurrent and Repeated Risks, pp. 2–3.
73 Author interview with former UK Embassy Kabul official (6), 29 October 2014.
74 Mansfield, *A State Built on Sand*, p. 231.
75 Ibid., p. 232.
76 Ibid., p. 236.
77 Mansfield, Between a Rock and a Hard Place, p. 32.
78 MacKenzie, 'Could Helmand be the Dubai of Afghanistan?'
79 Mansfield, Truly Unprecedented, pp. 14, 16–17.
80 Farrell, *Unwinnable*, p. 269.
81 Ibid., pp. 269–70.

Chapter 13: A poisoned chalice, 2009–2011

1 Cowling, 'Poll Watch'.
2 BBC News, 'UK Afghan Mission Support "Rises"'.
3 Author interview with former FCO official (14), 20 December 2017.

4 House of Commons Foreign Affairs Committee, Global Security, Ev 66–7, Q 217.

5 Author interview with former FCO official (14), 20 December 2017.

6 Author interview with former FCO official (8), 27 April 2015.

7 BBC News, 'Afghan timeline'.

8 Martin, *An Intimate War*, p. 189.

9 Author interview with former FCO official (14), 20 December 2017.

10 Author interview with former FCO official (8), 27 April 2015.

11 Author interview with former FCO official (14), 20 December 2017.

12 House of Commons Foreign Affairs Committee, Global Security, p. 52.

13 Author interview with former FCO official (14), 20 December 2017.

14 Author interview with former FCO official (8), 27 April 2015.

15 Freedom of Information Request 1164-17.

16 Author interview with former FCO official (3), 11 August 2014.

17 Author interview with former FCO official (14), 20 December 2017.

18 Mansfield, 'The Rise of Opium Poppy Cultivation in Afghanistan'.

19 Author interview with former FCO official (8), 27 April 2015.

20 Author interview with former UK Embassy Kabul official (10), 5 October 2017.

21 Personal communication with former FCO official, 12 October 2015.

22 The meeting was attended by Department of State, DOD, INL and USAID officials. Author interview with former FCO official (8), 27 April 2015.

23 Author interview with former FCO official (8), 27 April 2015.

24 House of Commons Defence Committee, Ministry of Defence Annual Report and Accounts 2011–12, Ev 28, Figure 6.

25 HC Deb, 1 February 2011, c716.

26 McChrystal, 'COMISAF Initial Assessment'.

27 Chandrasekaran, *Little America*, p. 128.

28 Cowper-Coles, *Cables from Kabul*, p. 288.

29 Chandrasekaran, *Little America*, p. 128.

30 SIGAR, Counternarcotics, pp. 50–1.

31 Ibid.

32 Mansfield, *A State Built on Sand*, p. 319.

33 Norland, 'U.S. Turns a Blind Eye to Opium in Afghan Town'.

34 Ibid.

35 Ibid.

36 Author interview with former UK Embassy Kabul official (10), 5 October 2017.

37 Author email communication with former Department of State official, 9 June 2013. Author interviews with former FCO officials (3), 11 August 2014; and (4), 23 and 24 September 2014.

38 Author interview with former PRT official (2), 15 February 2017.

39 Ibid.

40 Author email communication with former Department of State official, 9 June 2013.

41 Mansfield et al., Managing Concurrent and Repeated Risks, p. 72.

42 NATO-ISAF, 'Marjah - 1 Year On'.

43 Mansfield, *A State Built on Sand*, p. 238.

44 SIGAR, Counternarcotics, p. 52.

45 Personal communication with former FCO official, 12 October 2015.

46 Author interview with former UK Embassy Kabul official (10), 5 October 2017.

47 Author interview with former FCO official (14), 20 December 2017.

48 Author interview with former UK Embassy Kabul official (10), 5 October 2017.

49 Ibid.

50 Author interview with former Department of Defense official (3), 3 July 2017.

51 Author interview with former UK Embassy Kabul official (10), 5 October 2017.

52 Wintour, 'Afghanistan Withdrawal before 2015, Says David Cameron'.

53 Farrell, *Unwinnable*, p. 373.

54 Woodward, *Obama's Wars*, pp. 371–3.

55 Manea, 'Reflections on the "Counterinsurgency Decade"'.

56 Commander of U.S. Central Command General David Petraeus, testimony before the Senate Armed Services Committee, 16 March 2010, quoted in Senate Caucus on International Narcotics Control, 'U.S. Counternarcotics Strategy in Afghanistan', July 2010, p. 24.

57 Author interview with former Department of Defense official (2), 23 March 2017.

58 Ibid.

59 SIGAR, Counternarcotics, p. 53.

60 Felbab-Brown, 'War and Drugs in Afghanistan'.

61 SIGAR, Counternarcotics, p. 74.

62 Independent Consultant and Fellow at Carr Center, Kennedy School, Harvard University, David Mansfield, 'Challenging the Rhetoric: Supporting an Evidence Based Counter-Narcotics Policy

in Afghanistan', testimony before the House of Representatives Subcommittee on National Security and Foreign Affairs of the Committee on Oversight and Government Reform, 1 October 2009, p. 10.
63 SIGAR, Counternarcotics, p. 119.
64 Ibid., p. 118.
65 SIGAR, Stabilisation, pp. 37–43.
66 Chandrasekaran, *Little America*, p. 107.
67 Ibid., pp. 108–9.
68 Ibid. The project focused on Helmand and Kandahar but was later expanded to thirty-two provinces with the expenditure increasing to $450 million.
69 SIGAR, Stabilisation, p. 57.
70 Inspector General for United States Agency for International Development, Audit of USAID/Afghanistan's Afghanistan Vouchers for Increased Productive Agriculture (AVIPA) Program, p. 9.
71 SIGAR, Stabilisation, p. 45.
72 Chandrasekaran, *Little America*, p. 191.
73 Ibid., p. 194.
74 Ibid., p. 192.
75 SIGAR, Stabilisation, p. 56.
76 Chandrasekaran, *Little America*, p. 198.
77 Ibid., p.194.
78 Ibid.
79 Senate Committee on Foreign Relations, 'Evaluating U.S. Foreign Assistance to Afghanistan', p. 12.
80 Ibid.
81 Ibid., p.13.
82 Author interview with former Department of State official (8), 16 October 2017.
83 Author interview with former UK Embassy Kabul official (10), 5 October 2017.
84 Ibid.
85 Principal Deputy Assistant Secretary of State for International Narcotics and Law Enforcement Affairs, Brian A. Nichols, testimony before the Senate Caucus on International Narcotics Control, hearing on 'Counternarcotics Efforts in Afghanistan', p. 6.
86 Author interview with former UK Embassy Kabul official (10), 5 October 2017.
87 Ibid.
88 Author interview with former Department of Defense official (3), 3 July 2017.

89 Ibid.
90 Author interview with former UK Embassy Kabul official (10), 5 October 2017.
91 UNODC/MCN, Afghanistan Opium Survey 2011, p. 1
92 Mansfield et al., Managing Concurrent and Repeated Risks, pp. 53, 55, 57–8.
93 Mansfield and Fishstein, Eyes Wide Shut, p. 6.
94 Mansfield et al., Managing Concurrent and Repeated Risks, pp. 53, 55.
95 Ibid., p. 3.
96 Mansfield, 'The Rise of Opium Poppy Cultivation in Afghanistan'.
97 Mansfield, Truly Unprecedented, p. 17.
98 BBC News, 'Afghanistan: Obama orders withdrawal of 33,000 troops'.
99 UNODC/MCN, Afghanistan Opium Survey 2012, p. 9.
100 Mansfield and Fishstein, Eyes Wide Shut, p. 6.
101 SIGAR, Counternarcotics, p. 73.
102 Ibid., p. 54.
103 Ibid.
104 Ibid., p.55.
105 Ibid., pp. 55–7.

Conclusion

1 Mansfield, A State Built on Sand, pp. 149, 158.
2 Mansfield and Pain, Counter-Narcotics in Afghanistan, pp. 1–3.
3 Author email communication with former Department of State official, 10 June 2013.

Bibliography

Books, book chapters, PhD theses

Barnett, Hilaire. *Britain Unwrapped: Government and Constitution Explained* (London: Penguin, 2002)

Baylis, John. Britain, the United States and Europe: To Choose Or Not To Choose? in John Baylis and Jon Roper (eds), *The United States and Europe: Beyond the Neo-Conservative Divide?* (London and New York: Routledge, 2006)

Bergen, Peter. *The Longest War: The Enduring Conflict between America and Al-Qaeda* (New York: Free Press, 2011)

Bird, Tim and Marshall, Alex. *Afghanistan: How the West Lost its Way* (New Haven, CT: Yale University Press, 2011)

Bradford, James. *Opium in a Time of Uncertainty: State Formation, Diplomacy, and Drug Control in Afghanistan during the Musahiban Dynasty, 1929-1978* (PhD thesis, Northeastern University, April 2013)

Brown, Gordon. *My Life, Our Time* (London: Penguin, 2017)

Burke, Jason. *Al-Qaeda: The True Story of Radical Islam, Third Edition* (London: Penguin, 2007)

Bush, George W. *Decision Points* (New York: Virgin, 2010)

Campbell, Alastair. *The Alastair Campbell Diaries: The Burden of Power Countdown to Iraq*, Volume 4 (London: Hutchinson, 2012)

Chandrasekaran, Rajiv. *Little America: The War within the War for Afghanistan* (London: Bloomsbury, 2012)

Cheney, Dick. *In My Time: A Personal and Political Memoir* (New York: Threshold, 2011)

Chouvy, Pierre-Arnaud. *Opium: Uncovering the Politics of the Poppy* (London: I. B. Tauris, 2009)

Churchill, Winston S. *The Second World War* (6 vols, London: Cassell, 1948–54)

Clarke, Michael. Foreign Policy, in Anthony Seldon (ed.), *Blair's Britain 1997-2007* (Cambridge: Cambridge University Press, 2007)

Cooley, John, K. *Unholy Wars: Afghanistan, America and International Terrorism, Third Edition* (London: Pluto Press, 2002)

Cornell, Svante E. Taliban Afghanistan: A True Islamic State? in Brenda Shaffer (ed.), *The Limits of Culture: Islam and Foreign Policy* (Cambridge, MA: MIT Press, 2006)

Cowper-Coles, Sherard. *Cables from Kabul: The Inside Story of the West's Afghanistan Campaign* (London: Harper Press, 2011)

Dimbleby, David and Reynolds, David. *An Ocean Apart: The Relationship between Britain and America in the Twentieth Century* (New York: Random House, 1988)

Dobbins, James. *After the Taliban: Nation-Building in Afghanistan* (Washington: Potomac Books, 2008)

Dobson, Alan and Marsh, Steve (eds). *Anglo-American Relations: Contemporary Perspectives* (London and New York: Routledge, 2013)

Dumbrell, John. *A Special Relationship: Anglo-American Relations from the Cold War to Iraq* (Basingstoke: Palgrave, 2006)

Dumbrell, John. Personal Diplomacy: Relations between Prime Ministers and Presidents, in Alan Dobson and Steve Marsh (eds), *Anglo-American Relations: Contemporary Perspectives* (London and New York: Routledge, 2013)

Dyson, Stephen B. *The Blair Identity: Leadership and Foreign Policy* (Manchester: Manchester University Press, 2009)

Fairweather, Jack. *The Good War: Why We Couldn't Win the War or the Peace in Afghanistan* (London: Jonathan Cape, 2015)

Farrell, Theo. Back from the Brink: British Military Adaptation and the Struggle for Helmand, 2006-2011, in Theo Farrell, Frans Osinga and James A. Russell (eds), *Military Adaptation in Afghanistan* (Stanford, CA: Stanford University Press, 2013)

Farrell, Theo. *Unwinnable: Britain's War in Afghanistan, 2001–2014* (London: The Bodley Head, 2017)

Felbab-Brown, Vanda. *Shooting Up: Counterinsurgency and the War on Drugs* (Washington, DC: Brookings Institution Press, 2010)

Fergusson, James. *A Million Bullets: The Real Story of the British Army in Afghanistan* (London: Bantam Press, 2008)

Fergusson, James. *Taliban: The True Story of the World's Most Feared Guerrilla Fighters* (London: Bantam Press, 2010)

Hafvenstein, Joel. *Opium Season: A Year on the Afghan Frontier* (Guilford, CT: Lyons Press, 2007)

Halper, Stefan and Clarke, Jonathan. *America Alone: The Neo-Conservatives and the Global Order* (Cambridge: Cambridge University Press, 2004)

Horne, Alistair. *MacMillan 1894-1956* (London: MacMillan, 1988)

Hughes, J. Patrick. Planning and Directing a Campaign: General Barno in Afghanistan, in Christopher N. Koontz (ed.), *Enduring Voices: Oral Histories of the U.S. Army Experience in Afghanistan, 2003–2005* (Washington, DC: Centre of Military History, US Army, 2008)

Jones, Seth. *In the Graveyard of Empires: America's War in Afghanistan* (New York: W. W. Norton, 2010)

Kampfner, John. *Blair's Wars* (London: The Free Press, 2004)

Khalilzad, Zalmay. *The Envoy: From Kabul to the White House, My Journey through a Turbulent World* (New York: St. Martin's Press, 2016)

Kilcullen, David. *The Accidental Guerrilla: Fighting Small Wars in the Midst of a Big One* (London: Hurst, 2009)

Koontz, Christopher N. (ed.). *Enduring Voices: Oral Histories of the U.S. Army Experience in Afghanistan, 2003-2005* (Washington, DC: Centre of Military History, US Army 2008)

Ledwidge, Frank. *Losing Small Wars: British Military Failure in Iraq and Afghanistan, Second Edition* (New Haven, CT: Yale University Press, 2017)

McCoy, Alfred. *The Politics of Heroin: CIA Complicity in the Global Drug Trade*, Revised edn (Chicago: Lawrence Hill Books, 2003)

Macdonald, David. *Drugs in Afghanistan: Opium, Outlaws and Scorpion Tales* (London: Pluto Press, 2007)

Maloney, Sean. *Fighting for Afghanistan: A Rogue Historian at War* (Annapolis: Naval Institute Press, 2011)

Mansfield, David. *A State Built on Sand: How Opium Undermined Afghanistan* (London: Hurst, 2016)

Marsh, Steve. The Anglo-American Defence Relationship, in Alan Dobson and Steve Marsh (eds), *Anglo-American Relations: Contemporary Perspectives* (London and New York: Routledge, 2013)

Martin, Mike. *An Intimate War: An Oral History of the Helmand Conflict, 1978-2012* (London: Hurst, 2014)

Mercille, Julien. *Cruel Harvest: US Intervention in the Afghan Drugs Trade* (London: Pluto Press, 2013)

Meyerle, Jerry, Katt, Megan and Gavrilis, Jim. *On the Ground in Afghanistan: Counterinsurgency in Practice* (Quantico, VA: Marine Corps University Press, 2012)

Morgan Edwards, Lucy. *The Afghan Solution: The Inside Story of Abdul Haq, the CIA and How Western Hubris Lost Afghanistan* (London: Pluto Press, 2011)

Neumann, Ronald, E. *The Other War: Winning and Losing in Afghanistan* (Dulles: Potomac Books, 2009)

Paoli, Letizia, Greenfield, Victoria A. and Reuter, Peter. *The World*

Heroin Market: Can Policy Reduce Supply? (New York: Oxford University Press, 2009)

Phythian, Mark. From Asset to Liability: Blair, Brown and the 'Special Relationship', in Oliver Daddow and Jamie Gaskarth (eds), *British Foreign Policy: The New Labour Years* (Basingstoke: Palgrave MacMillan, 2011)

Rashid, Ahmed. *Descent into Chaos: The United States and the Failure of Nation Building in Pakistan, Afghanistan, and Central Asia* (New York: Viking Penguin, 2008)

Rashid, Ahmed. *Taliban: The Power of Militant Islam in Afghanistan and Beyond* (London: I. B. Tauris, 2010)

Renwick, Robin. *Fighting with Allies: America and Britain in Peace and War* (London: Biteback, 2016)

Reynolds, David. *The Creation of the Anglo-American Alliance, 1937-41: A Study in Competitive Co-Operation* (London: Europa, 1981)

Rice, Condoleezza. *No Higher Honor: A Memoir of My Years in Washington* (New York: Crown, 2011)

Richards, David. *Taking Command: The Autobiography* (London: Headline, 2014)

Risen, James. *State of War: The Secret History of the CIA and the Bush Administration* (New York: Free Press, 2006)

Rubin, Barnett, R. *The Fragmentation of Afghanistan: State Formation and Collapse in the International System, Second Edition* (New Haven, CT: Yale University Press, 2002)

Saikal, Amin. *Modern Afghanistan: A History of Struggle and Survival* (London: I. B. Tauris, 2004)

Saville, John. *The Politics of Continuity: British Foreign Policy and the Labour Government 1945-46* (London: Verso, 1993)

Seldon, Anthony with Snowdon, Peter and Collings, Daniel. *Blair Unbound* (London: Simon and Schuster, 2007)

Steele, Jonathan. *Ghosts of Afghanistan: The Haunted Battleground* (London: Portobello, 2011)

Wahab, Shaista and Youngerman, Barry. *Afghanistan: A Brief History, Second Edition* (New York: Checkmark Books, 2010)

Waltz, Michael, G. *Warrior Diplomat: A Green Beret's Battles from Washington to Afghanistan* (Lincoln, NE: Potomac Books, 2014)

Woodward, Bob. *Bush at War* (London: Pocket, 2003)

Woodward, Bob. *Obama's Wars: The Inside Story* (London: Simon & Schuster, 2010)

Yasamee, H. J. and Hamilton, K. A (eds). *Documents on British Policy Overseas, Series II: Volume IV, Korea June 1950-April 1951* (London: HMSO, 1991)

Zaeef, Abdul Salam. *My Life with the Taliban* (London: Hurst & Company, 2010)

Journals

Berry, Philip, A. 'Allies at War in Afghanistan: Anglo-American Friction Over Poppy Aerial Eradication 2004-08', *Diplomacy and Statecraft*, Vol. 29, No. 2, 2018, 274–97

Berry, Philip, A. 'From London to Lashkar Gah: British Counter Narcotics Policies in Afghanistan 2001-03', *The International History Review*, Vol. 40, No. 4, 2018, 713–31

Bewley-Taylor, David. 'Drug Trafficking and Organised Crime in Afghanistan: Corruption, Insecurity and the Challenges of Transition', *RUSI Journal*, Vol. 158, No. 6, 2013, 6–17

Cavanagh, Matt. 'Ministerial Decision-Making in the Run-Up to the Helmand Deployment', *RUSI Journal*, Vol. 157, No. 2, 2012, 48–54

Clarke, Michael. 'The Helmand Decision', *Whitehall Papers*, Vol. 77, No. 1, 2011, 5–29

Cornell, Svante, E. 'The Narcotics Threat in Greater Central Asia: From Crime-Terror Nexus to State Infiltration?' *The China and Eurasia Forum Quarterly*, Vol. 4, No. 1, 2006, 37–67

Dobson, Alan and Marsh, Steve. 'Anglo-American Relations: End of a Special Relationship?' *The International History Review*, Vol. 36, No. 4, 2014, 673–97

Farrell, Graham and Thorne, John. 'Where Have All the Flowers Gone?: Evaluation of the Taliban Crackdown against Opium Poppy Cultivation in Afghanistan', *International Journal of Drug Policy*, Vol. 16, No. 2, 2005, 81–91

Koehler, Jan and Zuercher, Christoph. 'Statebuilding, Conflict and Narcotics in Afghanistan: The View from Below', *International Peacekeeping*, Vol. 14, No. 1, 2007, 62–74

McNerney, Michael, J. 'Stabilization and Reconstruction in Afghanistan: Are PRTs a Model or a Muddle? *Parameters*, Vol. 35, No. 4, 2005–6, 32–46

Maloney, Sean, M. 'The International Security Assistance Force: Origins of a Stabilization Force', *Canadian Military Journal*, Vol. 4, No. 2, 2003, 3–11

Manea, Octavian. 'Reflections on the "Counterinsurgency Decade": Small Wars Journal Interview with General David H. Petraeus', *Small Wars Journal*, 1 September 2013

Reynolds, David. 'A "Special Relationship"? America, Britain and the International Order Since the Second World War', *International Affairs*, Vol. 62, No.1, Winter 1985–6, 1–20

Reynolds, David. 'Re-Thinking Anglo-American Relations', *International Affairs*, Vol. 65, No. 1, Winter 1988–9, 89–111

Thruelsen, Peter Dahl. 'Counterinsurgency and a Comprehensive

Approach: Helmand Province, Afghanistan', *Small Wars Journal*, Vol. 4, No. 9, September 2008

Reports, statements, policy documents

Blair, Tony and Karzai, Hamid. Rebuilding Afghanistan, 31 January 2002 <https://www.c-span.org/video/?168469-1/rebuilding-afghanistan> (last accessed 25 February 2019)

Blanchard, Christopher, M. Afghanistan: Narcotics and U.S. Policy, Congressional Research Service, Report RL32686, 24 January 2008

Blanchard, Christopher, M. Afghanistan: Narcotics and U.S. Policy, Congressional Research Service, Report RL32686, 12 August 2009

Bureau of International Narcotics and Law Enforcement Affairs. 'Fighting the Opium Trade in Afghanistan: Myth, Facts and Sound Policy', 11 March 2008

Byrd, William, A. Responding to Afghanistan's Opium Economy Challenge: Lessons and Policy Implications from a Development Perspective, Policy Research Working Paper 4545 (Washington, DC: World Bank, 2008)

Byrd, William, A. and Jonglez, Oliver. Prices and Market Interactions in the opium economy, in Doris Buddenberg and William A. Byrd (eds), *Afghanistan's Drug Industry: Structure, Functioning, Dynamics & Implications for Counter-Narcotics Policy* (Kabul: UNODC/World Bank, 2006)

Byrd, William, and Mansfield, David. Drugs in Afghanistan – A Forgotten Issue? United States Institute of Peace, Brief 126, 18 May 2012

Byrd, William, A. and Mansfield, David. Afghanistan's Opium Economy: An Agriculture, Livelihoods and Governance Perspective, prepared for the World Bank Afghanistan Agriculture Sector Review (revised), 23 June 2014

Charles, Robert, B. Counternarcotics initiatives for Afghanistan, Department of State, On-the-Record Briefing, 17 November 2004

Chilcot, John. The Report of the Iraq Inquiry, Volume I (London: HMSO) 6 July 2016

Department of Defense. Progress toward Security and Stability in Afghanistan: Report to Congress in accordance with the 2008 National Defence Authorisation Act (Section 1230, Public Law 110-181), January 2009

Department of State Inspector General. Status of the Bureau of International Narcotics and Law Enforcement Affairs Counternarcotics Programs in Afghanistan: Performance Audit, Report Number MERO-A-10-02, December 2009

Embassy of the United States. Press Release. 'U.S. Embassy Deputy Director for International Narcotics and Law Enforcement, Lee "Rusty" Brown's Remarks at the Paris Pact Conference in Kabul', 20 November 2007

Executive Order 13129 – Continuation of Emergency with Respect to the Taliban, 30 June 2000

Felbab-Brown, Vanda. Afghanistan Trip Report VI: Counternarcotics Policy in Afghanistan: A Good Strategy Poorly Implemented, Brookings Institution, 10 May 2012

Gordon, Stuart. Winning Hearts and Minds? Examining the Relationship between Aid and Security in Afghanistan's Helmand Province, Feinstein International Center, Tufts University, April 2011

Government Accountability Office. Afghanistan Reconstruction: Deteriorating Security and Limited Resources Have Impeded Progress; Improvements in U.S. Strategy Needed, GAO-04-403, 2 June 2004

Government Accountability Office. Afghanistan Drug Control: Strategy Evolving and Progress Reported, but Interim Performance Targets and Evaluation of Justice Reform Efforts Needed, GAO-10-291, March 2010

Government of the Islamic Republic of Afghanistan, Ministry of Counter-Narcotics. National Drug Control Strategy: An updated Five-Year Strategy for Tackling the Illicit Drug Problem, January 2006

HM Treasury. Budget Leaflet, March 2001

Holbrooke, Richard C. 'Afghanistan and Pakistan: What Will it Take to Get it Right?' The German Marshall Fund of the United States Conference, Brussels Form, 21 March 2009, <http://www.gmfus.org/sites/default/files/BFDay2_AfghanistanPakistan.pdf> (last accessed 25 February 2019)

House of Commons Defence Committee, The UK Deployment to Afghanistan, HC 558 2005-06, 6 April 2006

House of Commons Defence Committee, UK Operations in Afghanistan, HC 408 2006-07, 18 July 2007

House of Commons Defence Committee, Operations in Afghanistan, HC 554 2010-12, 17 July 2011

House of Commons Defence Committee, Ministry of Defence Annual Report and Accounts 2011–12, HC 828 2012–13, 7 March 2013

House of Commons Foreign Affairs Committee, Global Security: Afghanistan and Pakistan, HC 302 2008-09, 2 August 2009

House of Commons Home Affairs Committee, The Government's Drug Policy: Is It working? HC 318 2001-02, 22 May 2002

House of Representatives Committee on Armed Services, hearing on the 'Status of Security and Stability in Afghanistan', 28 June 2006

House of Representatives Committee on Foreign Affairs, hearing on 'Afghanistan on the Brink: Where Do We Go from Here?', 15 February 2007

House of Representatives Committee on International Relations, hearing on 'Afghanistan Drugs and Terrorism and U.S. Security Policy', 12 February 2004

House of Representatives Committee on Oversight and Government Reform and Subcommittee on National Security and Foreign Affairs of the Committee on Oversight and Government Reform, joint hearing on 'Afghanistan and Pakistan: oversight of A New Interagency Strategy', 24 June 2009

House of Representatives Subcommittee on Criminal Justice, Drug Policy and Human Resources for the Committee on Government Reform, hearing on 'Afghanistan: Law Enforcement Interdiction Efforts in Transshipment Countries to Stem the Flow of Heroin', 26 February 2004

House of Representatives Subcommittee on Criminal Justice, Drug Policy and Human Resources of the Committee on Government Reform, hearing on 'British Counternarcotics Efforts in Afghanistan', 1 April 2004

House of Representatives Subcommittee on the Middle East and South Asia of the Committee on Foreign Affairs, hearing on 'Counternarcotics Strategy and Police Training in Afghanistan', 4 October 2007

Human Rights Watch. 'Lessons in Terror: Attacks on Education in Afghanistan', Vol. 18, No. 6 (C), July 2006

Inspector General for United States Agency for International Development. Audit of USAID/Afghanistan's Alternative Livelihoods Program-Eastern Region, Audit Report No. 5-306-07-002-P, 13 February 2007

Inspector General for United States Agency for International Development. Audit of USAID/Afghanistan's Afghanistan Vouchers for Increased Productive Agriculture (AVIPA) Program, Audit Report No. 5-306-10-008-p, 20 April 2010

Inspectors General for Department of State and Department of Defense. Interagency Assessment of the Counternarcotics Program in Afghanistan, State Report No. ISP-I-07-34, DOD Report No. IE-2007-005, July 2007

Intelligence and Security Committee of Parliament. Annual Report 2001-2002, HC CM 5542, 7 June 2002

International Monetary Fund, IMF Country Report No. 05/33 – Islamic State of Afghanistan: 2004 Article IV Consultation and Second Review, February 2005.

Jelsma, Martin, Kramer, Tom and Rivier, Cristian. 'Losing Ground: Drug Control and War in Afghanistan', TNI Briefing Series No. 15 2006/5, December 2006

Jones, Seth, G. 'Getting Back on Track in Afghanistan', testimony before the House Subcommittee on the Middle East and South Asia of the Committee on Foreign Affairs, 2 April 2008, Reproduced as RAND Corporation Testimony series, 2008

LSE Ideas. After the Drugs Wars: Report of the LSE Expert Group on the Economics of Drug Policy (LSE: London, 2016)

Maletta, Hector. 'The Grain and the Chaff: Crop Residues and the Cost of Production of Wheat in Afghanistan in a Farming-system Perspective', unpublished paper, 2004

Mansfield, David. 'Challenging the Rhetoric: Supporting an Evidence Based Counter-Narcotics Policy in Afghanistan', testimony before the House of Representatives Subcommittee on National Security and Foreign Affairs of the Committee on Oversight and Government Reform, 1 October 2009

Mansfield, David. Between a Rock and a Hard Place: Counter-Narcotics Efforts and Their Effects in Nangarhar and Helmand in the 2010-11 Growing Season, Afghanistan Research and Evaluation Unit (AREU), October 2011

Mansfield, David. Understanding Control and Influence: What Opium Poppy and Tax Reveal about the Writ of the Afghan State, AREU, August 2017

Mansfield, David. Truly Unprecedented: How the Helmand Food Zone Supported an Increase in the Province's Capacity to Produce Opium, AREU, 31 October 2017

Mansfield, David and Fishstein, Paul. Eyes Wide Shut: Counter-Narcotics in Transition, AREU, September 2013

Mansfield, David and Pain, Adam. Counter-Narcotics in Afghanistan: The Failure of Success? AREU, December 2008

Mansfield, David, Alcis Ltd. and OSDR. Managing Concurrent and Repeated Risks: Explaining the Reductions in Opium Production in Central Helmand between 2008 and 2011, AREU, August 2011

Mansfield, David, Fishstein, Paul and OSDR. Time to Move on: Developing an Informed Development Response to Opium Poppy Cultivation, AREU, October 2016

Martin, Edouard and Symansky, Steven. Macroeconomic Impact of the Drug Economy and Counter-Narcotics Efforts, in Doris Buddenberg and William A. Byrd (eds), *Afghanistan's Drug Industry: Structure, Functioning, Dynamics & Implications for Counter-Narcotics Policy* (Kabul: UNODC/World Bank, 2006)

National Crime Intelligence Service. United Kingdom Threat Assessment of Serious and Organised Crime, August 2003

NATO/ISAF. The Afghanistan Compact: Building on Success, The London Conference on Afghanistan, 31 January – 1 February 2006

<https://www.nato.int/isaf/docu/epub/pdf/afghanistan_compact.pdf> (last accessed 8 April 2019)

NATO-ISAF. 'Marjah - 1 Year On', Media Backgrounder, 9 March 2011 <https://www.nato.int/nato_static/assets/pdf/pdf_2011_03/20110309 _110309-ISAF-backgrounder-Marjah.pdf> (last accessed 25 February 2019)

Neumann, Brian, Mundey, Lisa and Mikolashek, Jon. The United States Army in Afghanistan: Operation Enduring Freedom March 2002– April 2005 (Washington, DC: Center of Military History, US Army, 2013)

Obama, Barack. 'Statement by the President on Afghanistan', White House Press Release, 17 February 2009

Obama, Barack. 'Remarks by the President on a New Strategy for Afghanistan and Pakistan', White House Press Release, 27 March 2009

Pain, Adam. Opium Trading Systems in Helmand and Ghor Provinces, in Doris Buddenberg and William A. Byrd (eds), *Afghanistan's Drug Industry: Structure, Functioning, Dynamics & Implications for Counter-Narcotics Policy* (Kabul: UNODC/World Bank, 2006)

Perito, Robert, M. Afghanistan's Police: The Weak Link in Security Sector Reform, United States Institute of Peace, Special Report 227, August 2009

Rubin, Barnett, R. Road to Ruin: Afghanistan's Booming Opium Industry, Centre on International Cooperation, 7 October 2004

Schweich, Thomas A. US Counternarcotics Strategy for Afghanistan, compiled by the Coordinator for Counternarcotics and Justice Reform in Afghanistan, Ambassador Thomas A. Schweich, August 2007

Senate Caucus on International Narcotics Control. U.S. Counternarcotics Strategy in Afghanistan, July 2010

Senate Caucus on International Narcotics Control, hearing on 'Counternarcotics Efforts in Afghanistan', 20 July 2011

Senate Committee on Foreign Relations, hearing on 'Afghanistan's Narco War: Breaking the Link between Drug Traffickers and Insurgents', 10 August 2009

Senate Committee on Foreign Relations. Evaluating U.S. Foreign Assistance to Afghanistan, 8 June 2011

SIGAR. Quarterly Report to the United States Congress, 30 April 2016

SIGAR. Stabilisation: Lessons from the US Experience in Afghanistan, May 2018

SIGAR. Counternarcotics: Lessons from the US Experience in Afghanistan, June 2018

Transnational Institute. Afghanistan, Drugs and Terrorism Merging Wars, Drugs & Conflict Debate Papers, No. 3, TNI Briefing Series, December 2001

UNDCP. Afghanistan Annual Opium Poppy Survey 2000 (Islamabad: UNDCP, 2000)

UNDCP. Afghanistan Opium Survey 2001 (Vienna: UNDCP, 2001)

United Nations Office for Drug Control and Crime Prevention. Afghanistan Opium Survey 2002 (Kabul: UNODCCP, October 2002)

United Nations Security Council. Report of the Committee of Experts appointed pursuant to Security Council resolution 1333 (2000), paragraph 15 (a), regarding monitoring of the arms embargo against the Taliban and the closure of terrorist training camps in the Taliban-held areas of Afghanistan, S/2001/511, 22 May 2001

United States Agency for International Development. Afghanistan. Fact Sheet, Kabul, 15 September 2005 <http://2001-2009.state.gov/p/sca/rls/fs/2005/53382.htm> (last accessed 25 February 2019)

United States Drug Enforcement Administration. History 2003–2008 <https://www.dea.gov/history> (last accessed 25 February 2019)

UNODC. The Opium Economy in Afghanistan: An International Problem (New York: United Nations 2003)

UNODC/Government of Afghanistan Counter-Narcotics Directorate. Afghanistan Opium Survey 2003: Executive Summary (Kabul: UNODC/CND, October 2003)

UNODC/Government of Afghanistan Ministry of Counternarcotics. Afghanistan Opium Survey 2004 (Kabul: UNODC/CND, November 2004)

UNODC/MCN. Afghanistan: Mapping of Alternative Livelihood Projects (Kabul: UNODC/MCN September 2005)

UNODC/MCN. Afghanistan Opium Survey 2005 (Kabul: UNODC/MCN, November 2005)

UNODC/MCN. Afghanistan Opium Survey 2006 (Kabul: UNODC/MCN, October 2006)

UNODC/MCN. Afghanistan Opium Survey 2007 (Kabul: UNODC/MCN, October 2007)

UNODC/MCN. Afghanistan Opium Survey 2008 (Kabul: UNODC/MCN, November 2008)

UNODC/MCN. Afghanistan Opium Survey 2008: Executive Summary (Kabul: UNODC/MCN, August 2008)

UNODC/MCN. Afghanistan Opium Survey 2009: Summary Findings (Kabul: UNODC/MCN, September 2009)

UNODC/MCN. Afghanistan Opium Survey 2010 (Kabul: UNODC/MCN, December 2010)

UNODC/MCN. Afghanistan Opium Survey 2011 (Kabul: UNODC/MCN, December 2011)

UNODC/MCN. Afghanistan Opium Survey 2012 (Kabul: UNODC/MCN, May 2013)

UNODC/MCN. Afghanistan Opium Survey 2017 (Kabul: UNODC/
MCN, November 2017)
World Bank. Afghanistan: State Building, Sustaining Growth, and
Reducing Poverty. World Bank Country Study (Washington, DC:
World Bank, 2005)
Young, Dennis, O. 'Overcoming the Obstacles to Establishing a
Democratic State in Afghanistan', Carlisle Papers in Security
Strategy, Strategic Studies Institute, US Army War College, October
2007

Newspaper and magazine articles, blog posts, lectures

Adams, David. 'Colombia Sheds Messy Drug Spraying At Last', *Tampa
Bay Times*, 19 August 2007
Agence France-Presse. 'Afghanistan Aims to Cut Opium Fields by 40
Percent in 2006', Agence France-Presse, 2 January 2006
BBC News. 'FBI-Style Unit "Will Be Ruthless"', *BBC News*, 9 February
2004
BBC News. 'UK Troops "to Target Terrorists"', *BBC News*, 24 April
2006
BBC News. 'Afghanistan's Turbulent History', *BBC News*, 21 November
2008
BBC News. 'UK Afghan Mission Support "Rises"', *BBC News*, 13 July
2009
BBC News. 'Ambassador Backs Afghan Mission', *BBC News*, 27 August
2009
BBC News. 'Britain Suffered Defeat in Iraq, Says US General', *BBC
News*, 29 September 2010
BBC News. 'Afghanistan: Obama Orders Withdrawal of 33,000
Troops', *BBC News*, 23 June 2011
BBC News. 'Afghan timeline (factbox)', *BBC News*, 4 October 2011
Blair, Tony. 'Labour Conference: Full Text: Tony Blair's Speech (Part
One)', *The Guardian*, 2 October 2001
Blair, Tony. 'Labour Conference: Full Text: Tony Blair's Speech (Part
One)', *The Guardian*, 1 October 2002
Bush, George W. Transcript of President Bush's address, CNN, 21
September 2001
Chouvy, Pierre-Arnaud. 'The Ironies of Afghan Opium Production',
Asia Times, 17 September 2003
Cloud, David, S. and Gall, Carlotta. 'U.S. Memo Faults Afghan Leader
on Heroin Fight', *The New York Times*, 22 May 2005
Coghlan, Tom. 'US Officials Push to Spray Afghan Drug Crops', *The
Telegraph*, 10 October 2007

Constable, Pamela. 'In Afghan Poppy Heartland, New Crops, Growing Danger U.S. Pushes Eggplants and Tomatoes, but Farmers Risk Reprisals', *The Washington Post*, 6 May 2006

Council on Foreign Relations. The U.S. War in Afghanistan Timeline 1999 – 2018, Council on Foreign Relations <https://www.cfr.org/timeline/us-war-afghanistan> (last accessed 25 February 2019)

Cowling, David. 'Poll watch: British in Afghanistan', *BBC News*, 4 September 2009

Crossette, Barbara. 'Taliban Open a Campaign to Gain Status at the U.N.', *The New York Times*, 21 September 2000

Dempsey, Judy. 'NATO Allows Strikes on Afghan Drug Sites', *The New York Times*, 10 October 2008

Dumbrell, John. 'David Cameron, Barack Obama, and the "US-UK Special Relationship"', LSE Blog, 14 March 2012, <http://blogs.lse.ac.uk/politicsandpolicy/special-relationship-dumbrell/> (last accessed 25 February 2019)

Eligon, John and Yokley, Eli. 'Police Say Thomas Schweich, Candidate for Missouri Governor, Killed Himself', *The New York Times*, 26 February 2015

Felbab-Brown, Vanda. 'War and Drugs in Afghanistan, *World Politics Review*, 25 October 2011

Hemmings, John. 'The UK-US Alliance Under the Microscope', RUSI Commentary, 27 April 2010

Hennessy, Patrick and Alderson, Andrew. 'How Bush and Blair Plotted in Secret to Stop Brown', *The Telegraph*, 28 August 2010

Holbrooke, Richard. 'Afghanistan: The Long Road Ahead', *The Washington Post*, 2 April 2006

Integrated Regional Information Network. 'Afghanistan: Donor-Supported Approaches to Eradication', Integrated Regional Information Network, 24 August 2004

Khan, Azmat. 'Opium Brides: Why Eradication Won't Solve Afghanistan's Poppy Problem', *Frontline*, 3 January 2012

Lancaster, John. 'Karzai Urges War on Opium Trade', *Washington Post*, 10 December 2004

McChrystal, Stanley. 'COMISAF Initial Assessment (Unclassified) – Searchable Document', *Washington Post*, 21 September 2009

McFadden, Robert, D. 'Strong American Voice in Diplomacy and Crisis', *The New York Times*, 13 December 2010

McGirk, Tim. 'Terrorism's Harvest', *Time*, 2 August 2004

MacKenzie, Jean. 'Could Helmand Be the Dubai of Afghanistan?' *Foreign Policy*, 19 March 2010

Mansfield, David. 'The Rise of Opium Poppy Cultivation in Afghanistan: When Will Too Much Be Enough? Hurst Publishers website, 15 November 2017

Mohammed, Arshad. 'U.S. Unveils Carrot and Stick Afghan Drug Strategy', Reuters, 9 August 2007

Norland, Rod. 'U.S. Turns a Blind Eye to Opium in Afghan Town', *The New York Times*, 20 March 2010

Norton-Taylor, Richard. 'Full Interview: General David Richards', *The Guardian*, 22 January 2007

Oborne, Peter and Morgan Edwards, Lucy. 'A Victory for Drug-Pushers', *Spectator*, 31 May 2003, pp. 26–30

Panorama. 'Britain's Heroin Fix', BBC programme transcript, *Panorama*, 24 July 2005

Philps, Alan. 'Britain Reopens Its Embassy as "Commitment to Better Future"', *The Telegraph*, 20 November 2001

Rennie, David and La Guardia, Anton. 'America Accuses Britain of Failing in War on Drugs', *The Telegraph*, 2 April 2004

Risen, James. 'An Afghan's Path from U.S. Ally to Drug Suspect', *The New York Times*, 2 February 2007

Rubin, Barnett, R. 'Putting an End to Warlord Government', *The New York Times*, 15 January 2002

Schweich, Thomas. 'Is Afghanistan a Narco-State?' *The New York Times*, 27 July 2008

Seitz, Raymond. 'Britain and America: Towards Strategic Coincidence', *The World Today*, May 1993, 85–7

Semple, Kirk and Golden, Tim. 'Afghans Pressed by US on Plan to Spray Poppies', *The New York Times*, 8 October 2007

Stolberg, Sheryl Gay and Rutenberg, Jim. 'Rumsfeld Resigns as Defense Secretary after Big Election Gains for Democrats', *The New York Times*, 8 November 2006

The Economist. 'The Gardens of Eden', *The Economist*, 19 September 2002

The Economist. 'After the Taliban', *The Economist*, 18 November 2004

The Guardian, 'Full Text of Tony Blair's Speech', *The Guardian*, 11 September 2001.

Ware, John. 'UK's Original Helmand Deployment Plan Examined', BBC News, 22 June 2011

Weitz, Richard. 'Afghanistan: US and EU Anti-Drugs Strategies are Diverging', EurasiaNet, 3 April 2007

Weitz, Richard. 'Ambassador: Washington Will Change its Afghan Counternarcotics Programs', EurasiaNet, 30 July 2007

White House. 'White Paper of the Interagency Policy Group's Report on U.S. Policy toward Afghanistan and Pakistan', *The New York Times*, 27 March 2009

Wilkinson, Isambard. 'Blow to British as New Helmand Governor Vetoes Local Peace Deals', *The Telegraph*, 19 December 2006

Wilson, Graeme. 'Gordon Brown and George Bush are Distant', *The Telegraph*, 13 September 2007

Wilson, Graeme and Harnden, Toby. 'Gordon Brown Plots own Course in Iraq', *The Telegraph*, 31 July 2007

Wintour, Patrick. 'Battle Begins to Stem Afghan Opium Harvest', *The Guardian*, 3 May 2004

Wintour, Patrick. 'Afghanistan Withdrawal before 2015, Says David Cameron', *The Guardian*, 26 June 2010

Wyatt, Caroline. 'Afghan Farmers Die in Poppy Protest', BBC News, 8 April 2002

Yapp, Malcolm. 'The Legend of the Great Game', Elie Kedourie Memorial Lecture, Proceedings of the British Academy, 111, 2001, 179–98

House of Commons and House of Lords Debates

HC Deb, 14 November 2001, c872

HC Deb, 28 January 2002, c34

HC Deb, 14 May 2002, c625

HC Deb, 5 November 2002, vol. 392 c130

HC Deb, 20 October 2003, vol. 411 c381W

HC Deb, 17 November 2003, vol. 413 c649W

HC Deb, 19 November 2003, vol. 413 c1046W

HC Deb, 19 April 2004, vol. 420 c21

HC Deb, 9 June 2004, c125WH

HC Deb, 10 March 2005, c121WS

HC Deb, 10 March 2005, c122WS

HC Deb, 10 March 2005, c123WS

HC Deb, 24 October 2005, c73W

HC Deb, 24 October 2005, c74W

HC Deb, 26 January 2006, c1531

HL Deb, 13 February 2006, cWS49

HC Deb, 17 June 2008, cc176–7WH

HC Deb, 1 February 2011, c716

US Department of State cables

US Department of State cable, Berlin 1255, 'Germans Remain Wary about Expanding ISAF Authority on Counternarcotics', 12 September 2008

US Department of State cable, Bogota 11995, 'Multilateral Strategy on Aerial Eradication near Colombia-Ecuador Border', 29 December 2005

US Department of State cable, Brussels 3037, 'Amb Wood Discusses EU's Work in Afghanistan', 1 October 2007

US Department of State cable, Hague 754, 'Netherlands/Afghanistan: Dutch Support Amendment of ISAF OPLAN', 12 September 2008

US Department of State cable, Hague 2048, 'Netherlands/Afghanistan: Dutch Positive on Counternarcotics Message', 10 December 2007

US Department of State cable, Kabul 116, 'Karzai Dissatisfied; Worries about Newsweek; Plans More War Against Narcotics', 10 January 2006

US Department of State cable, Kabul 184, 'A/S Boucher Meeting with Afghan NSA Rassoul', 20 January 2007

US Department of State cable, Kabul 185, 'Boucher, Mosbacher and Karzai Talk Energy, Investment, Pakistan and Comprehensive Strategy', 20 January 2007

US Department of State cable, Kabul 329, 'London Conference Scenesetter for Secretary Rice', 24 January 2006

US Department of State cable, Kabul 409, 'Scenesetter for Visit of Codel Biden to Afghanistan', 19 February 2008

US Department of State cable, Kabul 962, 'PRT/Lashkar Gah – Significant Challenges to Upcoming Eradication Campaign', 6 March 2006

US Department of State cable, Kabul 1014, 'Karzai Supports Continued Eradication with Reservations', 27 March 2007

US Department of State cable, Kabul 1029, 'Congressman Rohrabacher's April 16 Meeting with President Karzai', 21 April 2003

US Department of State cable, Kabul 1045, 'Brokering Eradication Consensus in Helmand', 29 March 2007

US Department of State cable, Kabul 1132, 'ONDCP Director Walters' March 17-20 visit to Afghanistan', 6 April 2007

US Department of State cable, Kabul 1267, 'Ambassador's Visit to Helmand; Poppy Eradication Efforts', 22 March 2006

US Department of State cable, Kabul 1277, 'Codel Hoekstra Sees Poppy Problem First Hand', 23 March 2006

US Department of State cable, Kabul 1321, 'Scenesetter for Codel Langevin', 26 May 2009

US Department of State cable, Kabul 1420, 'GOA Tells ISAF That Its IO Campaign Undermines Counter-Narcotics Activities', 25 April 2007

US Department of State cable, Kabul 2008, 'PRT/Helmand – Helmand Eradication Wrap Up', 3 May 2006

US Department of State cable, Kabul 2021, 'PRT/Helmand from the Stars and Stripes to the Union Jack the UK Assumes Control of Lashkar Gah PRT', 5 May 2006

US Department of State cable, Kabul 2346, 'Afghans to Continue Poppy Eradication', 13 August 2009

US Department of State cable, Kabul 2470, 'Ambassador Discusses Security, Counternarcotics and IROA Support in Nangarhar', 31 July 2007

US Department of State cable, Kabul 2968, 'Scene-Setter for Deputy Secretary Negroponte's Visit to Kabul', 5 September 2007

US Department of State cable, Kabul 2998, 'Boucher and Karzai, Spanta on Jirgas, Drugs, Econ Cooperation, Governance, Iran', 8 September 2007

US Department of State cable, Kabul 3030, 'Political and Security Situation in Helmand: Spanta and Spenzada Views', 22 November 2008

US Department of State cable, Kabul 3176, 'Scenesetter for December 10-11, 2008 Visit to Afghanistan by SecDef Robert M. Gates', 9 December 2008

US Department of State cable, Kabul 3237, 'Karzai Urges Codel McCain to Support Zardari and Welcomes Increase in U.S. Forces', 21 December 2008

US Department of State cable, Kabul 3677, 'Welcome to Afghanistan', 16 November 2009

US Department of State cable, Kabul 3765, 'Scenesetter for Undersecretary Edelman's November 7-8 Visit to Afghanistan', 6 November 2007

US Department of State cable, Kabul 3973, 'Scenesetter for SecDef Gates' December 3-5 Visit to Afghanistan', 2 December 2007

US Department of State cable, Kabul 4005, 'Karzai Comments on Counter-Narcotics Policy', 6 September 2006

US Department of State cable, Kabul 5024, 'Revised Afghanistan Compact for Washington Review', 13 December 2005

US Department of State cable, Kabul 5050, 'Karzai Promises Results on CN, Asks for Greater Commitment to AL', 14 December 2005

US Department of State cable, Kabul 5223, 'Update on CN Activities 11/20-12/20', 9 January 2006

US Department of State cable, Kabul 5256, 'Revised Afghanistan Compact', 27 December 2005

US Department of State cable, Kabul 5277, 'Scenesetter for NSA Hadley visit to Afghanistan', 30 October 2006

US Department of State cable, Kabul 5446, 'Boucher's Conversation with Key Donors on What's Needed in Afghanistan', 13 November 2006

US Department of State cable, Kabul 5584, 'Musa Qala Agreement: Opposing Interests and Opposing Views, But One Way Forward', 27 November 2006

US Department of State cable, London 639, 'UK Labour Spring Conference: Good Intentions but Few Good Vibrations', 3 March 2008

US Department of State cable, London 930, 'William Hague Says "Near Death Experience" Has Improved Tory Chances', 1 April 2008

US Department of State cable, London 1991, '(C/NF) Who Would Replace Gordon Brown as UK Prime Minister – If he Goes?', 31 July 2008

US Department of State cable, London 2821, 'FCO Pleased with U.S./ UK Alignment on Afghanistan CN; Wants Robust Role for ISAF in CN', 7 November 2008

US Department of State cable, London 4472, 'Scenesetter for Secretary Peters' December 7 Visit to London', 5 December 2007

US Department of State cable, London 8039, 'Afghanistan: DAS Gastright's Meeting with FCO November 14', 21 November 2006

US Department of State cable, NATO 200, 'ISAF Commander McNeill Praises Allied Unity, Highlights Remaining Challenges in his Farewell Address', 6 June 2008

US Department of State cable, NATO 317, 'Readout: September 3 North Atlantic Council Meeting', 4 September 2008

US Department of State cable, NATO 375, 'Decisions by NATO Defense Ministers Regarding Counter-Narcotics Efforts in Afghanistan', 16 October 2008

US Department of State cable, Paris 1715, 'France Cautiously Supportive of Expanding on ISAF Counter-Narcotics Authorities', 12 September 2008

US Department of State cable, State 97395, 'Corrected Copy: Supporting Amendment of the ISAF OPLAN to Expand CN Authorities', 11 September 2008

US Department of State cable, State 176819, 'Afghanistan's Political Future (Corrected Copy)', 11 October 2001

Archival sources

Lyndon Johnson Library, Austin Texas, NSF Country File, box 210-12, folder: UK memos. Vol. XI 4/67–6/67 Bruce to Rusk

Freedom of Information requests

Freedom of Information Request 0103-17, Conference on Afghanistan aid in Tokyo January 2002, 22 February 2017

Freedom of Information Request 0525-06, D Spivack – Extract of documents held by the FCO regarding opium poppy eradication in Afghanistan in 2002 (with information formerly withheld from FOI

0525-06) and Extracts of new documents held by FCO regarding opium poppy eradication in Afghanistan in 2002, Deposited Papers, House of Lords Library, Deposited 29 November 2006

Freedom of Information Request 0909-16, G8 donors conference, Geneva, April 2002, 18 October 2016

Freedom of Information Request 1164-17, 6 March 2018

Websites

Blair, Tony. 'Doctrine of the International Community' Speech, Chicago, 22 April 1999 <http://www.britishpoliticalspeech.org/speech-archive. htm?speech=279> (last accessed 25 February 2019)

Department of Defense. Robert M. Gates Biography, <https://dod.d efense.gov/About/Biographies/Biography-View/article/602797/> (last accessed 25 February 2019)

Department of State. Robert B. Charles Biography, <https://2001-2009. state.gov/outofdate/bios/c/25156.htm> (last accessed 25 February 2019)

Department of State. Zalmay Khalilzad Biography, <https://2001-2009. state.gov/outofdate/bios/k/26933.htm> (last accessed 25 February 2019)

The National Archives. 'UK Strategy for Co-ordinating International Assistance to Afghanistan to Combat Drugs', September 2002 <http:// webarchive.nationalarchives.gov.uk/20031124132559/http://www.fc o.gov.uk:80/Files/kfile/Afghanistan%20drugs%20strategy%208.pdf> (last accessed 25 February 2019)

The National Archives. 'UK Provides Counter Narcotics Training for Afghans', 5 December 2003 <http://webarchive.nationalarchives.go v.uk/20031223134845/http://www.fco.gov.uk:80/servlet/Front?pagen ame=OpenMarket/Xcelerate/ShowPage&c=Page&cid=10070293916 29&print=true&a=KArticle&aid=1070639032957> (last accessed 25 February 2019)

The National Archives. Statement to Parliament on the PM's Visit to America, 20 April 2004 <http://webarchive.nationalarchives.gov. uk/20080909020556/http://www.number10.gov.uk/Page5668> (last accessed 25 February 2019)

The National Archives. 'UK Announces Increased Funding for Afghanistan Counter-Narcotics Work', 5 September 2005. <http://web archive.nationalarchives.gov.uk/20060620192342/http://www.fco.go v.uk/servlet/Front/TextOnly?pagename=OpenMarket/Xcelerate/Show Page&c=Page&cid=1050509860482&to=true&a=KArticle&aid=112 5559465083> (last accessed 25 February 2019)

The National Archives. 'Country Profile: Afghanistan: Counter-Narcotics', 16 September 2005, <http://webarchive.nationalarchives.gov.uk/20051004053952/http://www.fco.gov.uk/servlet/Front/TextOnly?pagename=OpenMarket/Xcelerate/ShowPage&c=Page&cid=1050510446431&to=true> (last accessed 25 February 2019)

The National Archives. Country Profiles: Afghanistan, 8 November 2006 <http://webarchive.nationalarchives.gov.uk/20070506130400/http://www.fco.gov.uk/servlet/Front?pagename=OpenMarket/Xcelerate/ShowPage&c=Page&cid=1050510446431> (last accessed 25 February 2019)

The National Archives. 'Recent Successes', n.d., <http://webarchive.nationalarchives.gov.uk/20040329080645/http://www.fco.gov.uk/servlet/Front/TextOnly?pagename=OpenMarket/Xcelerate/ShowPage&c=Page&cid=1044551747293&to=true> (last accessed 25 February 2019)

UK Government. 'The UK's Work in Afghanistan: Timeline', 14 January 2014 <https://www.gov.uk/government/publications/uks-work-in-afghanistan/the-uks-work-in-afghanistan-timeline#nato-troops-increase-in-helmand-province> (last accessed 25 February 2019)

UNC Global. 'Afghan Minister Visits UNC to Discuss Global Health Issues', 12 October 2011 <https://global.unc.edu/news/afghan-minister-visits-unc-to-discuss-global-health-issues/> (last accessed 25 February 2019)

Index

11 September attacks, 15, 16, 17, 18, 19, 44, 45, 46, 52, 55, 187
Abdullah, Abdullah, 60
Abdur Rahman Khan, Amir of Afghanistan, 25
Abizaid, John, 91
aerial eradication (spraying), 4, 58–9, 83, 85, 87–8, 89–94, 96, 106, 108, 115–22, 128–40, 141, 161, 185, 188–90, 192–3, 211n, 220n
Afghan Drugs Inter-Departmental Unit (ADIDU), 95, 97, 126, 145, 189, 195
Afghan Eradication Force (AEF), 109–10, 123–4, 159, 215n
Afghan National Army (ANA), 69, 109–10, 126, 157
Afghan National Drug Control Strategy (ANDCS), 73, 106–7, 119, 132, 161
Afghan National Security Forces, 172, 230n
Afghan Special Narcotics Force (ASNF), 77–8
Afghan state
  post-11 September 2001 – Afghan Interim Administration (AIA), 22, 23, 26, 46, 49, 50, 53, 56, 61, 62, 64, 65–6, 69, 74, 78–80, 90, 187–8, 199n
  post-2004 elections, Government of Islamic Republic of Afghanistan (GOIRA), 2, 3, 4, 26, 89, 95, 105–7, 108–9, 111, 126, 127–8, 130–2, 135, 137, 139–40, 158, 166, 172–4, 177–8, 181–4, 186, 189, 193, 196, 220n
  pre-Taliban, 25–9, 31–2, 33
  Taliban, 29–31, 35–40

Afghan Threat Finance Cell (ATFC), 150–1
Afghan Transit Trade Agreement, 29
Afghanistan Compact (2006), 104–5, 169
Afghanistan Interagency Operations Group (AIOG), 89
Afghanistan Voucher for Increased Production in Agriculture (AVIPA-Plus), 165, 178
Akhundzada, Amir Mohammed, 123
Akhundzada, Sher Mohammed, 102–4, 113, 123, 138, 143
al-Qaeda, 16, 19, 20, 21, 23, 40, 45, 49, 75, 113, 157, 162, 171
Alexander the Great, 31
alternative livelihoods/development, 37–8, 53, 67, 71, 72–3, 83–4, 86, 90, 94, 95, 96, 98–100, 101, 106–7, 110, 111–13, 119, 123, 132, 134, 138, 142–3, 146, 159, 162–3, 165–7, 177–80, 211n
Anglo-Afghan Wars, 25, 109
Arcadia Conference (1941–2), 9
Arlacchi, Pino, 37
Attlee, Clement, 12

Babaji, Helmand, 164
Badakhshan, Afghanistan, 61, 73, 99–100, 120, 225n
Bagram Air Base, 68
Balkh, Afghanistan, 102, 183, 225n
Basra, Iraq, 144
BBC Newsnight, 168
Beckett, Margaret, 146
Beers, Rand, 56, 75
Benn, Hilary, 97
Bewley-Taylor, David, 78

Bin Laden, Osama, 16, 19, 21, 23,
  31, 39–40, 49
Blair, Anthony 'Tony'
  11 September attacks, 15, 18–20
  Anglo-American relations, 15–16,
    18–20, 21, 85, 88, 131, 147,
    157
  Atlantic bridge, 15
  counter-narcotics, 2, 3–4, 43–7,
    51–5, 59–64, 66, 69–70, 72,
    73, 88, 95, 97, 102, 112, 116,
    129–30, 145–7, 187–9
  decision-making, 45, 51–5, 72,
    187–8
  doctrine of the international
    community, 19, 45
  ethical foreign policy, 45
  influence on American policy, 20,
    21, 23, 157
  sofa cabinet, 52
  state-building, 17, 21–3
Bolton, John, 17
Bonn Agreement, 22, 50, 105, 170
Bosnia, 155
Boucher, Richard, 119, 122, 135
Boyce, Michael, 45
Brahimi, Lakhdar, 22, 60
Brandenburg, Ulrich, 149
Brexit, 146
Britain
  11 September attacks, 15, 18–20
  Afghanistan Senior Officials Group,
    145, 170
  Afghanistan Strategy Group,
    146
  American criticism of, 79–80,
    86–8, 95, 96–7, 113, 116, 127,
    144, 147, 164, 188
  Cabinet meetings, 52, 55, 60, 69,
    72, 102, 170
  Cold War, 9, 11–15
  Commonwealth, 11, 14
  counter-narcotics, 1–5, 21, 40,
    43–7, 48, 50–6, 58–67, 68–71,
    72–5, 76–9, 80, 84–8, 89, 91–3,
    94, 95–8, 99–100, 102–4, 105,
    108–10, 111–13, 114–24, 125–6,
    128–32, 134–5, 137–40, 142–7,
    148–50, 160–1, 164, 165–7,
    168–71, 172–6, 180–4, 185–93,
    227n
  Helmand, 4, 61, 65–6, 73, 86,
    101–4, 109, 111–13, 117–18,

  120, 122–4, 126–7, 129, 138–9,
    142–4, 146, 157, 163–7, 168–9,
    172–4, 182, 188–9, 191
  Obama review of strategy, 155–8
  post-Cold War, 15–16
  post-intervention policy, 21–3,
    43–7, 50–6, 58–67, 68–71, 72–5,
    76–9, 80
  Whitehall, 1, 21, 45, 46, 54,
    55, 56, 63, 64, 66, 69, 72, 74,
    75, 145, 167, 169, 187, 189, 191
  World War II, 9–10
British Embassy (Afghanistan), 65,
  73, 85, 110, 116, 118, 122,
  126, 128, 129, 137, 138, 147,
  166, 173, 175, 176, 181, 195
British Embassy Drugs Team (BEDT),
  73, 95, 110, 129, 214n
British military, 14, 21, 22, 23, 66–7,
  68–70, 73, 77–8, 91, 95, 102–4,
  109, 111–12, 113, 117–18,
  123–4, 126–7, 129, 130, 134,
  139, 144, 146, 158, 163–4, 166,
  167, 168–9, 172, 176
British Special Forces, 21, 67, 77
Brown, Gordon, 131, 137, 143, 145,
  147, 156, 157, 158, 167, 193,
  228n
Bruce, David, 13–14
Brzezinski, Zbigniew, 28
Bucharest, Romania, 150
Bureau of International Narcotics
  and Law Enforcement Affairs
  (INL), 4, 56, 58–9, 69, 71, 75,
  83, 84–90, 92–3, 96, 107, 108,
  116–21, 125, 130–5, 138–40,
  160–1, 173, 180–1, 188, 190,
  195, 231n
Burma, 32, 59; see also Myanmar
Bush, George H. W., 15, 76, 86
Bush, George W.
  11 September attacks, 15, 16–20
  Anglo-American relations, 15–16,
    18–20, 21, 23, 45, 85, 88, 137,
    147, 157, 167
  Cabinet meetings, 19–20, 76, 91,
    93, 125
  counter-narcotics, 45, 69–70, 85,
    88, 91–4, 116–18, 130–1, 137–9,
    188, 190
  post-intervention policy, 21–4
  pre-11 September relationship with
    Taliban, 39–40

presidential style, 17–18, 93, 137–9
state-building, 17, 21–3, 48, 75
Butler, Ed, 111

Cabinet Office, 44, 54, 69, 72, 119,
    145, 156, 158, 194, 195
Callaghan, James, 14
Cambridge University, 52, 54, 95
Cameron, David, 147–8, 176
Campbell, Alastair, 46, 52
Canada, 63, 101–2
capacity building, 63, 72–3, 76, 94–5,
    175, 181
Caribbean, 58
Carter, Jimmy, 28
Central Eradication Planning Cell, 96
Central Intelligence Agency (CIA), 16,
    19, 21, 28, 155
Central Narcotics Tribunal, 96
Central Poppy Eradication Force
    (CPEF), 96–7, 215n, 217n
Chamberlain, Neville, 25
Charles, Robert B., 75–6, 83–4,
    86–8, 89–91, 93–4, 96, 116,
    192, 211n
Cheney, Richard 'Dick', 17, 20, 79
China, 31
Churchill, Winston, 10–11, 18
civil war (Afghanistan), 29–30
Clinton, Hillary, 155, 160
Clinton, William 'Bill', 15, 17
Cold War, 9, 11–15, 27
Colombia, 4, 48, 58, 76, 83–4, 89,
    90, 92, 96, 116, 128–9, 131,
    133, 137, 140, 180, 188, 211n
    coca, 84
    Revolutionary Armed Forces
    Colombia (FARC), 84, 133–4
Columbia Law School, 76
Combined Forces Command-
    Afghanistan, 91
Combined Joint Task Force, 180
    (CJTF-180), 68
Commanders Emergency Response
    Programme, 165
communism, 12, 27, 28–9
compensated eradication (Operation
    Drown, 2002), 1, 51–6, 58–9,
    60–2, 63, 64–6, 71, 72, 185, 187
    compensated eradication (2010),
    172–4
Concerted Inter-Agency Drugs Action
    Group (CIDA), 44, 203n

Conservative Party, 147–8, 176
Conservative–Liberal Democrat
    Coalition Government, 176
corruption, 50, 65, 71, 74, 78, 79,
    86, 97, 101, 103, 107, 110, 128,
    136, 147, 149, 158, 162, 166–7,
    174–6
Costa, Antonio Maria, 133, 149
counterinsurgency, 142, 150, 158,
    159, 163, 165, 169, 171, 172,
    176, 211n
Counter-Narcotics Directorate
    (CND), 67, 94
Counter-Narcotics Implementation
    Plan, 95
Counter-Narcotics Police of
    Afghanistan (CNPA), 76
Counter-Narcotics Trust Fund
    (CNTF), 97–8
Cowper-Coles, Sherard, 129–30,
    155–6, 161–2, 163, 174–6, 193
Craddock, Bantz J., 149
Criminal Justice Task Force, 96

Daoud, Mohammed, 103, 109, 111,
    113, 123
Daoud Khan, Sardar Mohammed, 27
Daud, Mohammed, 100, 126
Daykundi, Afghanistan, 148
Dearlove, Richard, 52–5, 61, 64, 66
demand reduction, 95, 106–7
Department for International
    Development (DFID), 45, 54,
    72–3, 99–100, 112–13, 146,
    165, 195, 214n, 215n
Department of Defense (DOD), 3,
    4, 14, 16–18, 21, 47–9, 59,
    68–70, 71, 79, 80, 84, 90–4,
    115, 125–6, 130–1, 136, 138–9,
    148, 150–1, 162, 171, 177, 187,
    188–90, 195, 213n, 221n, 231n
Department of Health, 53, 195
Department of State, 4, 48, 76, 79,
    83–5, 87–8, 89–90, 92–4, 97,
    106, 190, 116, 118–20, 133–9,
    148, 155, 160–1, 163–4, 173,
    180, 188–90, 193, 195, 211n,
    221n, 228n, 231n
destroyers for bases deal, 9
Din Mohammed, Haji, 98–9
disarmament, demobilisation and
    reintegration, 51, 60
Dobbins, James, 22

Dobson, Alan, 12
Dostum, Abdul Rashid, 29
drought, 32, 34, 37, 38
Drug Enforcement Administration
    (DEA), 75, 77, 79, 84, 90, 96,
    103, 114–15, 177, 195, 221n,
    228n
Drugs and International Crime
    Department, 54, 63
Dumbrell, John, 11, 15
Durand Line, 25–6, 30
Durand, Mortimer, 25
Durrani Empire, 25
DynCorp, 96, 109, 159

Ecuador, 90
Eden, Anthony, 12
Eggers, Jeffery, 172
Egypt, 12
Eikenberry, Karl, 69
elections (Afghanistan), 89, 157, 164,
    199n
eradication, 1, 4, 51, 53–7, 58–9,
    60–2, 63, 64–6, 68–71, 72–3,
    78, 83–94, 95, 96–7, 99–100,
    105–7, 108–10, 115–24, 125–6,
    128–40, 141–3, 149, 159–62,
    163, 166, 172–4, 180–1, 182,
    185, 188–90, 192–3, 211–12n,
    214n, 215n, 217n, 220n
European Community, 14
European Single Market, 15
Evans, Stephen, 119

Falklands (Malvinas) War, 14
Farah, Afghanistan, 148
Faryab, Afghanistan, 102
Federally Administered Tribal Areas
    (Pakistan), 26
Feith, Douglas J., 17, 47
Ford, Gerald, 17
Foreign and Commonwealth Office
    (FCO), 10, 44, 45, 52–6, 58–60,
    61–2, 63–6, 68–70, 71, 72–3, 80,
    87, 95–6, 112–13, 115, 116–21,
    126, 129–30, 134, 137–8, 140,
    144–7, 148–50, 156, 161,
    168–71, 174–5, 187, 192, 195,
    204n, 214n, 215n
Foreign-deployed Advisory and
    Support Teams, 96
France, 12, 149, 150
Freakley, Benjamin, 115

Garmser, Helmand, 164–5
Gastright, John, 119–20
Gates, Robert, 125, 148, 150
Gereshk, Helmand, 111, 164
Germany, 22, 50, 51, 58, 59, 60, 79,
    112, 148–50
Ghani, Ashraf, 56, 183
Gilchrist, Peter, 130, 138
glyphosate, 90, 120, 122, 129, 189,
    214n; see also aerial eradication
    spraying; ground-based spraying
Good Performers Initiative, 132
Gorbachev, Mikhail, 28
Government Communications
    Headquarters, 44
governor-led eradication (GLE),
    70–1, 97, 160, 162, 166–7, 174,
    180, 225n
Great Game (Britain–Russia), 25
Grenada, 14
Grossman, Marc, 180
ground-based spraying (GBS),
    118–23, 136, 139, 189, 192
Group of Eight (G8) lead and partner
    nations, 1–2, 50–1, 58–60, 63–4,
    74, 79–80, 84, 94, 98, 105, 109,
    117, 121, 139, 144–6, 168–71,
    175–6, 181, 185, 187, 189, 192
  Geneva meeting (2002), 60
  Kananaskis Summit (2002), 63–4,
    73

Hadley, Stephen J., 17, 119, 135, 156
Hague, William, 147
Harriman, Anthony, 130
Harvard Law School, 116
Hassan, Mullah Mohammed, 37
Heath, Edward, 14
Hekmatyar, Gulbuddin, 29
Helmand, Afghanistan, 4, 61, 65–6,
    73, 86, 99, 101–4, 108–13,
    117–18, 120, 122–4, 126–7,
    129, 133, 138–9, 141–4, 146,
    148, 157, 163–7, 168–9, 172–4,
    178–9, 181–2, 183, 188–9, 191,
    195, 200n, 212n, 233n
Helmand Food Zone (HFZ), 142–3,
    165–7, 174, 182, 183
Helmand Valley Project, 200n
Hemmings, John, 16
HM Customs & Excise (HMCE), 44,
    54, 58, 62, 64, 72, 76–7, 114,
    195, 203n

HM Treasury, 64
Holbrooke, Richard, 155–7, 159–63, 178–9, 180, 190
Holland, Peter, 95
Home Office, 114, 204n, 214n
Hoon, Geoff, 68–9, 71
Houghton, Nicholas, 109
House of Commons Foreign Affairs Committee (FAC), 168, 170
House of Commons Home Affairs Committee, 44
House of Representatives Committee of International Relations, 80
House of Representatives Committee on Foreign Affairs, 132
House of Representatives Committee on Oversight and Government Reform, 159
Hussein, Saddam, 16
Hyde, Henry J., 80

Indiana University, 122
insurgency, 78, 84, 90, 102, 109–10, 111, 115, 126, 127, 128, 133–4, 137, 141, 144, 148–51, 155, 158, 159, 162–3, 164–5, 171, 172, 176–7, 179, 189; *see also* Taliban
Interagency Operation Coordination Centre, 95–6
inter-cropping, 85
interdiction, 44, 58, 61, 66, 67, 72, 76–8, 84, 94, 95, 96, 114–15, 132, 135, 142, 148–50, 159, 162–3, 166, 171, 176–7, 183, 211n
International Monetary Fund (IMF), 34, 128
International Relief and Development, 179
International Security Assistance Force (ISAF), 22–3, 56, 98, 101, 104, 119, 126, 127, 158, 175, 195
interdiction policy, 148–50
Iran, 32, 33
Iraq
  First Gulf War, 15
  Second Gulf War, 16–17, 19, 23, 45, 70, 72, 75–6, 87, 89, 97, 101–2, 125, 131, 144, 150, 155, 172, 176, 188
Islamism, 18, 27–8

Israel, 10, 129
Italy, 79, 149

Jalalabad, Nangarhar, 21
Japan, 51, 59, 79
Jawad, Sayed, 91
jihad, 94, 200n
Joint Intelligence Committee, 44, 52
Joint Narcotics Analysis Centre (JNAC), 95–6, 176
judicial system, 51, 76, 78–9, 95, 96, 106, 132, 135
Juma Khan, Haji, 49

Kabul, Afghanistan, 21–2, 29, 30, 36, 56, 62, 65–6, 68, 69, 73, 75, 76, 79, 91–2, 94, 96, 98, 101, 103, 105, 106, 110, 113, 115, 116, 118–19, 120, 122, 123, 124, 126, 128, 129, 133, 134–5, 136, 137, 138, 143, 144, 146, 155, 173, 175, 176, 180, 181, 183, 189, 195
Kajaki, Helmand, 111
Kakar, Faizullah, 122
Kandahar, Afghanistan, 36, 101–2, 133, 148, 178, 233n
Karmal, Babrak, 27
Karzai, Hamid, 22, 26, 38, 50, 51, 56, 61, 65–7, 68, 79, 84, 89, 90–4, 98, 100, 101, 103, 105, 108, 111, 113, 118–20, 122–3, 126, 127–8, 131, 133, 135–6, 138–40, 142–3, 144, 190, 212n
Kennedy, John F., 13, 18
Khalilzad, Zalmay, 75, 79–80, 88, 90–4, 105, 118, 188
Khan Neshin, Helmand, 164
Khyber, Mir Akbar, 27
Kilcullen, David, 133
Killion, Michael, 173
Korea, 12
Kosovo, 19
Kunar, Afghanistan, 61, 123

Labour Party, 15, 20, 43, 46, 74, 131, 147
Labour Party Conference, 20, 43, 46
Laghman, Afghanistan, 61, 142
Lander, Stephen, 45, 52
Lantos, Tom, 132
Laos, 32

Lashkar Gah, Helmand, 102, 111,
  164
Latin America, 58, 59, 90, 160
Ledwidge, Frank, 104
legalisation of opium industry, 220n
Lend-Lease, 9–10
London Conference (2006), 104–7
London School of Economics, 95

McChrystal, Stanley, 158, 171, 172,
  174, 176
McDonald, Simon, 156
McMahon Act (1946), 13
Macmillan, Harold, 12–13, 18
McNeill, Dan, 69–70, 91, 127, 137,
  149
MacShane, Denis, 62, 64–5
Major, John, 15
Malgir, Helmand, 164
Malloch-Brown, Mark, 168
Mangal, Gulab, 142–3, 166
Manning, David, 52, 88
Mansfield, David, 34, 35, 38, 99,
  170, 174
Marjah, Helmand, 172, 174
Marsden, Rosalind, 92, 109
Marsh, Steve, 11, 12
Martin, Mike, 169
Massood, Ahmed Shah, 29
Maymaneh, Faryab, 102
Mazar-e-Sharif, Balkh, 79, 102
Mexico, 48
Middle East Peace Process (MEPP),
  19, 20,
Miliband, David, 137–8, 146, 174–5
Ministry of Counter-Narcotics
  (MCN), 94, 174–5, 181
Ministry of Defence (MOD), 68–9,
  119, 195, 214n, 215n
Ministry of Interior (MOI), 115, 126,
  174–6
mujahideen, 28–9, 33, 141, 200n
Musa Qala, Helmand, 111, 113,
  127
Myanmar, 33, 201n; see also Burma

Nad-e-Ali, Helmand, 169, 172, 174
Najibullah, Mohammed, 29, 30
Nangarhar, Afghanistan, 61, 65–6,
  86, 98–100, 115, 136, 141–3,
  183
Nasser, Abdul, 12
National Interdiction Unit, 96

National Security Council (Afghan),
  67
Nawa, Helmand, 164–5, 179
Negroponte, John, 125
Neo-conservatives (US), 17, 79
Netherlands, 101, 149–50
Neumann, Ronald, 105–6, 108–9,
  118–19, 122–4, 128, 212n
Nixon, Richard, 75
North Atlantic Treaty Organization
  (NATO), 2, 20, 75, 101, 117,
  122, 126, 127, 139, 148–50,
  176
Northern Alliance (NA), 19, 21–2,
  30, 38
Northern Ireland, 15
Now Zad, Helmand, 111
nuclear policy (Britain–United States),
  10, 13, 14, 16

O'Brien, Mike, 68
Obama, Barack
  Anglo-American relations, 156–7,
    167, 193, 228n
  counter-narcotics, 158, 163, 172
  McChrystal, Stanley, 176
  review of strategy, 4, 155–8
  surge, 171–2, 183
Office of National Drug Control
  Policy, 125, 195, 221n
Omar, Mullah Mohammed, 30, 31,
  37–8
Operation Achilles, 126
Operation Drown see compensated
  eradication
Operation Enduring Freedom, 21, 23
Operation Infinite Reach, 31
Operation Panther's Claw, 164
Operation Strike of the Sword, 164
opium poppy, 2–4, 29, 31–40,
  47–8, 50–4, 57, 58, 60–6, 67,
  68, 70–4, 76, 79–80, 83–4, 86,
  89, 91, 92, 95–100, 102–4,
  105–7, 108–10, 111–13, 115–16,
  119–20, 124, 125–9, 131–6,
  141–4, 147, 148–9, 159–60,
  163, 164–7, 169–70, 172–4,
  177–80, 180–4, 185–9, 191,
  197n, 201n, 211–12n, 214n,
  215n, 217n, 220n, 225n
opium poppy loan, 34, 54
opium poppy planting cycle,
  211–12n

Osborne, George, 147
Osmani, Zarar, 166, 174–6, 180
Oxford University, 75, 129

Pain, Adam, 78
Pakistan, 21, 25, 28–9, 30, 36, 45,
    98, 119, 155, 157, 158, 171
  Inter-Services Intelligence (ISI), 28,
    30, 33
  National Logistical Cell, 29
  opium ban, 32
Paktika, Afghanistan, 142
Palestine, 10
Pallett, Lesley, 87
Patey, William, 174–6
patronage, 22, 128, 176
Patterson, Anne, 116, 125
Pentagon see Department of Defense
People's Democratic Party of
    Afghanistan (PDPA), 27–8
Perle, Richard, 17
Petraeus, David, 176–7
Plan Afghanistan, 83, 91, 137, 211n
Plan Colombia, 83, 133, 211n
police (Afghan), 27, 51, 59, 66, 75,
    76, 78, 97, 109–10, 114
Poppy Eradication Force, 159, 160,
    215n
Powell, Colin, 17–18, 39, 76, 91, 93,
    105, 137
Powell, Jonathan, 52
prison, 79
Provincial Reconstruction Teams
    (PRTs), 98, 102–3, 143, 164,
    173, 195
public information campaigns, 73,
    94, 95, 106, 109, 132, 136, 142,
    166

Qaderi, Habibullah, 119

Rabbani, Burhanuddin, 22, 29
Rammell, Bill, 87, 96
Rassoul, Zalmai, 122
Reagan, Ronald, 14, 15, 18, 28
Reid, John, 104, 111
Reynolds, David, 11
Rice, Condoleezza, 17, 105, 118,
    119, 125, 127, 131, 135, 137,
    138
Richards, David, 88, 104, 112,
    123–4, 212n
Riedel, Bruce, 155, 157, 159, 162

Rohrabacher, Dana, 91
Roosevelt, Franklin, 10, 18
Ros-Lehtinen, Ileana, 132
Rubin, Barnett, 156, 159
Rumsfeld, Donald, 16–18, 20, 21, 48,
    68–9, 75, 79, 80, 91–3, 125, 148
Russia, 25; see also Soviet Union
Ryder, Michael, 54, 87, 212n

Sangin, Helmand, 111
Saudi Arabia, 36, 129, 201n
Saur Revolution, 27
Scarlett, John, 52
Schweich, Thomas, 107, 116–17,
    125–6, 129, 130, 132, 135, 137,
    140
Secret Intelligence Service (SIS),
    44, 52–4, 204n; see also
    compensated eradication
    (Operation Drown, 2002);
    Dearlove, Richard
Security Sector Reform (SSR), 50–1,
    60; see also Group of Eight (G8)
    lead and partner nations
Security Service, 45, 195
Senate Armed Services Committee,
    177
Senate Committee on Foreign
    Relations, 162, 179
Senlis Council (The International
    Council on Security and
    Development), 220n
Serious Organised Crime Agency
    (SOCA), 114–15, 134, 195,
    214n, 219n
Shah, Ahmad, 25
Shirzai, Gul Aga, 136, 141–2
Short, Clare, 53, 69, 71, 73, 97
Souder, Mark, 86
Soviet Union
  Cold War, 11, 13, 15, 27, 200n
  collapse, 29
  intervention in Afghanistan, 22, 24,
    26, 27, 28–9, 30, 31, 32–3, 94
  scorched earth policy, 32–3
  World War II, 10
  see also Russia
Spanta, Rangin Dadfar, 144
Special Air Service (SAS), 77, 103
Spin Masjid, Helmand, 164
state-building, 2–3, 17, 21–3, 48–9,
    75–6, 79, 98, 135, 171, 172,
    187, 211n

Stoletov, Nikolai, 25
Straw, Jack, 55, 66, 69, 71, 72, 97, 146
Strmecki, Marin, 75
Sudan, 15, 31
Suez Crisis, 12–13
Sunday Mirror, 60
Supreme Allied Commander Europe (SACEUR), 126, 149

Taliban, 2, 19–20, 21–3, 26, 29–31, 33, 35–40, 43–4, 46, 47, 49, 50, 53–4, 60, 69, 80, 99, 101–4, 109, 111–12, 113, 123, 126, 133–4, 135, 137, 141, 148–51, 157–8, 159, 162–3, 164–5, 166, 171–2, 177–8, 183, 223n; *see also* insurgency
Taraki, Nur Mohammed, 27
Tenet, George, 16, 19
Texas A&M University, 125
Thailand, 32, 59
Thatcher, Margaret, 14, 15, 18, 86, 147
The Guardian, 168
Thomson, Adam, 156
Tokyo donors' conference (2002), 50, 58
tribal structures, 25–6, 29, 32, 78, 102, 103, 109, 123, 141, 166
Truman, Harry, 11

United Arab Emirates, 36
United Nations (UN), 22, 23, 31, 36–9, 50, 56, 90, 97, 116, 170, 228n
United Nations Office on Drugs and Crime (UNODC), 2, 32, 37–8, 50, 56–7, 64, 65, 67, 86, 88, 89, 96, 97, 100, 110, 132–4, 142, 148–9, 165, 170–1, 175, 181, 183, 186, 195, 197n
United Nations Security Council, 20
United States (US)
    11 September attacks, 16–20
    Afghan Steering Group, 89
    African Embassy bombings, 31
    Camp David, 19–20, 131
    Cold War, 9, 11–15, 27–8
    counter-narcotics, 1–5, 18, 40, 47–9, 56, 58–9, 67, 68–70, 71, 75–6, 77, 79–80, 83–8, 89–94, 95–6, 98–100, 105–7, 108–11,
    114–24, 125–40, 141–2, 148–51, 156–7, 159–65, 171, 172–4, 175, 177–80, 181–4, 185–93
    Counter-Narcotics Task Force, 79
    criticism of Britain, 79–80, 86–8, 95, 96–7, 113, 116, 127, 144, 147, 164, 188
    Deputies Committee, 89, 130, 136
    National Security Council (NSC), 88, 89, 91, 113, 130, 136–7, 150, 189, 192, 195, 213n
    Obama review of strategy, 4, 155–8
    post-Cold War, 15–16
    post-intervention policy, 19–20, 21–4, 47–9, 51, 60, 63, 68–70, 74, 186–8
    pre-11 September relationship with Taliban, 30–1, 39–40
    Principals Committee, 89, 119
    surge, 171–2, 178–9, 182–3
    White House, 4, 18, 91, 106, 108, 118, 123–4, 125, 135, 138–9, 160, 189
    World War II, 9–10
United States Agency for International Development (USAID), 90, 99–100, 101, 110, 142, 162, 165, 177–9, 183, 213n, 221n, 228n, 231n
United States Central Command (CENTCOM), 47–8, 91, 173
United States Congress, 19, 59, 80, 86–7, 91, 93, 94, 108–9, 123–4, 125–6, 179, 192, 195
United States Embassy (Afghanistan), 75, 79, 85, 96–7, 105–6, 110, 113, 115, 117, 119, 122–4, 133, 136, 140, 144, 162, 172, 175, 180, 189, 195
United States Embassy (London), 119, 147–8
United States Marine Corps, 144, 157, 163–4, 172–4
United States military, 17, 21, 47–9, 56, 68–70, 75, 80, 84, 89, 91–2, 96, 98, 101–4, 113, 115, 127, 136, 138, 141–2, 144, 148–9, 151, 155, 163–5, 168, 171–4, 176, 177
United States Special Forces, 19
University of Chicago, 79
University of Washington, 122

Uribe, Alvaro, 92
Uruzgan, Afghanistan, 61, 101, 148

Vienna, Austria, 56
Vietnam War, 14, 162

Wafa, Assadullah, 123, 142
Walters, John, 125, 127, 135
Wankel, Doug, 79
war on terror, 19, 21, 23, 49, 59
Wardak, Abdul Rahim, 110
warlords, 22, 26, 28, 33, 49, 78, 103
Warren, Christopher, 31
weapons of mass destruction, 17

wheat, 34, 98–9, 143, 165, 166, 174,
  186
Wilson, Harold, 14
Wolfowitz, Paul, 17
Wood, William, 90, 128–9, 135,
  137–8, 140, 144
World War II, 9, 11, 14, 112

Yale Law School, 116
Yugoslavia, 15

Zabul, Afghanistan, 148
Zahir Shah, King of Afghanistan,
  26–7

EU representative:
Easy Access System Europe
Mustamäe tee 50, 10621 Tallinn, Estonia
Gpsr.requests@easproject.com

www.ingramcontent.com/pod-product-compliance
Lightning Source LLC
Chambersburg PA
CBHW051956270326
41929CB00015B/2675